D0960914

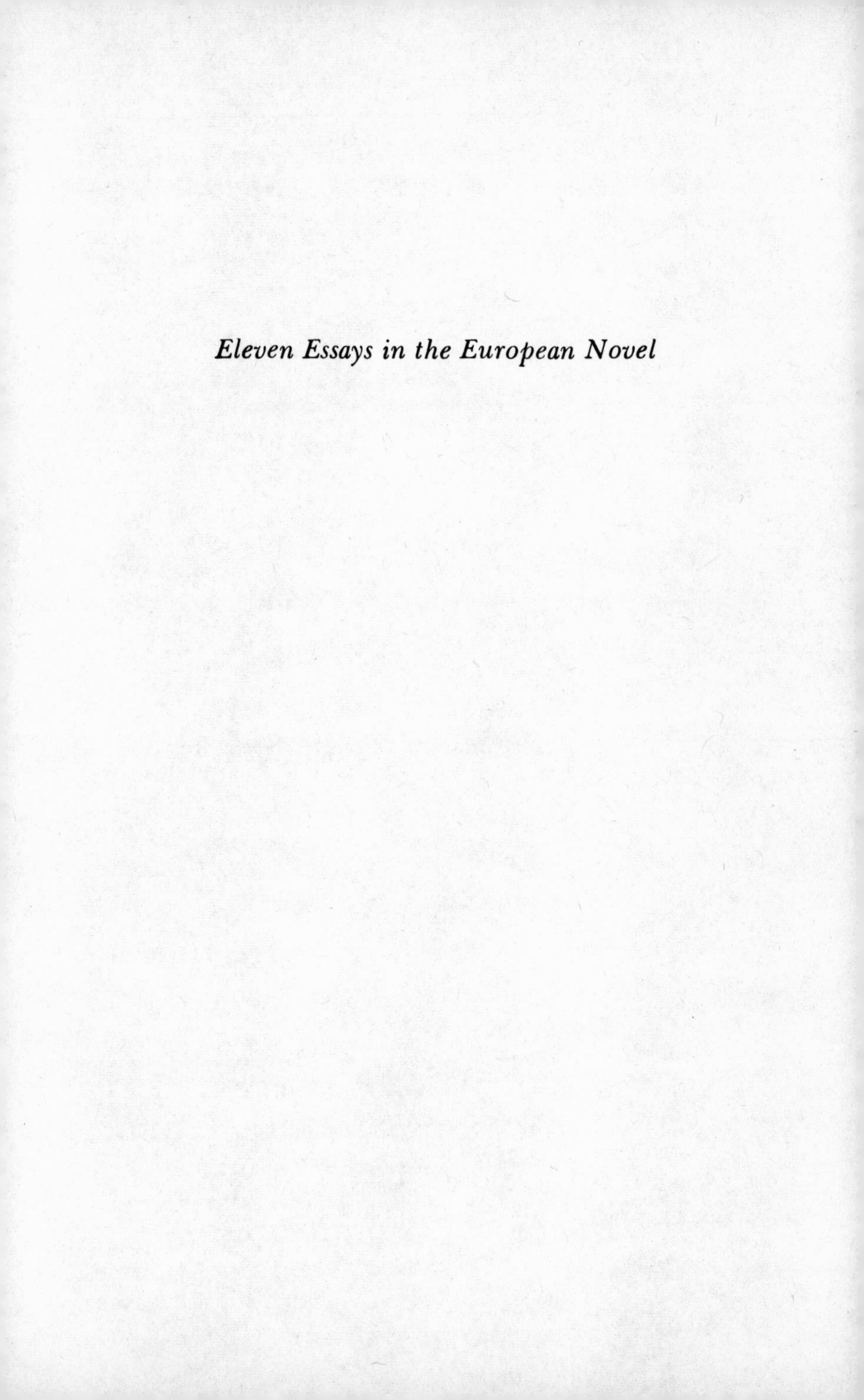

Eleven Essays in the European Novel

Eleven Essays in the European Novel

R. P. Blackmur

A Harbinger Book

HARCOURT, BRACE & WORLD, INC.
NEW YORK AND BURLINGAME

Essays gathered in this volume originally appeared in *The Kenyon Review, The Virginia Quarterly Review, The Hudson Review, Chimera,* and *Accent.*

LIBRARY OF CONGRESS CATALOG CARD NUMBER 64-19367

PRINTED IN THE UNITED STATES OF AMERICA

PREFATORY NOTE

The essays on the European novel here brought together were written during the last twenty years, the earliest, on *Crime and Punishment,* in 1943; the latest, the three on *The Brothers Karamazov,* were presented as Witherspoon Lectures at Princeton University in the spring of 1963. All but the last three—which are printed below for the first time—have previously appeared in the following magazines: *Chimera, Accent, The Virginia Quarterly Review, The Kenyon Review,* and *The Hudson Review:* to whose editors all grateful acknowledgments are due.

The essays must of course stand on their own feet or fall on their own faces, and if they lean on anything it must be on each other. But there are several things which it may be appropriate to say in their general neighborhood.

One thing is this. They form only a part of a good deal of work on the novel done during the same years and with much the same interests in mind. Some of this work has already appeared in one place or another, but much more exists in various stages of incompletion. The original scheme—a volume each on Dostoevsky, Joyce, and James, two volumes on the European novel, one on the English and one on the American novel—no longer seems feasible or perhaps desirable to complete. The present volume arranges fragments of an unfinished ruin, but there are more fragments I wish to heap up: something on Gide, Kafka, Broch, Proust, Balzac, and Stendhal; something more on Tolstoi and Joyce; something on Smollett, Jane Austen, George Eliot, and Conrad; and of course a small set of studies on James. Fragments cannot be rounded off, only shored up; and for that purpose I think of something on *Don Quixote* and something on that most lyric and exotic of all novels, *The Tale of Genji*. . . . The possible and inviting list could be much longer, but enough has been said to advertise the company the present essays keep and to suggest what three or four further volumes will I hope demonstrate: that the novel is indeed—and by no means so narrowly as James seems to have meant his words—"the most independent, most elastic, most prodigious of literary forms."

These words, learned by heart over forty years ago, lead me now to mention certain other notions which have come to infect and permanently to stain everything I have to say about the novel. To me these notions are clichés which refresh themselves with every use. They do not make a system of criticism; I do not feel I know enough to recognise a system; but they should fit into and animate any critical system that cared to adopt them—as for me they work back and forth upon each other. Here are my clichés.

One is from Croce where he says that poetry gives to feelings theoretic form. Theory is primarily a way of looking at things, especially a fruitful way; it need not be a world view. Form I take it here means the limits by which we determine the identity of a thing; the identification may be false or incomplete. Though Croce might have rejected the expansion, I should like to make his words read: The novel gives theoretic form to life—especially to the behavior that is our life in motion.

A good deal can be made out of this, but what it hints at or intimates about itself is almost enough here. It needs only the help of Ortega y Gasset when he says that the novel supplies us with new psychologies. Ortega is not thinking of the procession of professional psychologies in which our century has been so prolific but of the sort of thing we mean when we think of novels like *Liaisons Dangereuses, Great Expectations,* or *Fathers and Sons* as each supplying us with a new and distinctive psychology.

Nothing in the works of our imagination can be more distinctive than these psychologies and these theoretic forms. As society changes, or twists its old knowledge about, its writers—its artists—produce new theoretic forms which in turn require fresh psychologies; and sometimes a new psychology will seem to come from nowhere, or from the ear of Zeus, and be restless and frustrate unless it finds a theoretic form. Perhaps the novels of D. H. Lawrence are thus restless and frustrate; but not the novels of Camus. *The Rainbow* did not find what *The Plague* found. And so on. It may be there is no priority, only (in Hart Crane's phrase) "new thresholds, new anatomies."

If there is a priority it lies elsewhere; thus Aristotle, in a sentence from the *Poetics* (toward the end of Chapter 6: I use Else's version): "Well then, the plot is the foundation or as it were the soul of the tragic art, with character portrayal second." This cliché should begin to expand and to take on a relation to theoretic form and new psychologies, just so soon as the reader remembers that in Aristotle's Greek the word for "plot" is *mythos,* the word for "soul" is *psyche,* and the word for "character" is *ethos*—all words which reach into different territories from those touched by the English substitutes to which we are compelled. Let us say that with the Greek words we reach toward action and momentum and with the English words we do not. Speculation is endless; for me every good novel is a speculation—a theoretic form, a fresh psychology—a speculation in myth which reaches into the driving psyche: the psyche which endures and even outlives human behavior.

In Aristotle's rubric, it is right to put character (or *ethos*) in second place, but second only to plot, and to put it *before* thought and diction. But we are right, too, to put another cliché into the running. I first heard it when a boy as a Greek proverb: Character is fate. George Eliot quotes "Character is destiny" as a "questionable aphorism" from Novalis. In Heracleitus there is a fragment (number 69 in Wheelwright's edition, and it is that version which I quote) that reads: "A man's character is his guardian divinity." Again, as with Aristotle, I go further into the novel and into life if I transliterate rather than translate the Greek: A man's *ethos* is his *daimon*. In this form, the cliché "Character is fate" reassumes something of the force and scope that makes it true of every novel considered in these essays.

Let these phrases be regarded as early entries in a Commonplace Book on the Novel.

R. P. B.

1964

CONTENTS

Eleven Essays in the European Novel

PART ONE

FIVE MODES OF THE PSYCHE

The Dialectic of Incarnation: Tolstoi's ANNA KARENINA

If there is one notion which represents what Tolstoi is up to in his novels—emphatically in *Anna Karenina* and *War and Peace*—it is this. He exposes his created men and women to the "terrible ambiguity of an immediate experience" (Jung's phrase in his *Psychology and Religion*), and then, by the mimetic power of his imagination, expresses their reactions and responses to that experience. Some reactions are merely protective and make false responses; some reactions are so deep as to amount to a change in the phase of being and make honest responses. The reactions are mechanical or instinctive, the responses personal or spiritual. But both the reactions and the responses have to do with that force greater than ourselves, outside ourselves, and working on ourselves, which whether we call it God or Nature is the force of life, what is shaped or misshaped, construed or misconstrued, in the process of living. Both each individual life and also that life in fellowship which we call society are so to speak partial incarnations of that force; but neither is ever complete; thus the great human struggle, for the individual or for the society, is so to react and so to respond to "the terrible ambiguity of an immediate experience" as to approach the conditions of rebirth, the change of heart, or even the fresh start. Tragedy comes about from the failure to apprehend the character or the direction of that force, either by an exaggeration of the self alone or of the self in society. That is why in Tolstoi the peasants, the simple family people, and the good-natured wastrels furnish the background and the foils for the tragedy, for these move according to the momentum of things, and although they are by no means complete incarnations of the force behind the momentum are yet in an equal, rough relation to it. The others, the tragic figures, move rather, by their own mighty effort, in relation, reaction, response to that force, some with its momentum, some against it; some falsifying it in themselves, some falsifying it in society, but each a special incarnation of it; some cutting their losses; some consolidating their gains; some balancing, some teetering, in a permanent labor of rebirth. There is thus at work in the novels of Tolstoi a kind of dialectic of incarnation: the bodying forth in aesthetic form by contrasted human spirits of "the terrible ambiguity of an immediate experience" through their reactions and responses to it. It is this dialectic which gives buoyancy and sanity to Tolstoi's novels.

Let us see how this happens in *Anna Karenina*—how it happens not only in the name and tale of the heroine but also and in relation to the tale of Levin; and how these gain some of their significance through being told against the background of Stiva and Dolly Oblonsky's unhappy marriage. That unhappy marriage is the image of society in momentum, that momentum which only requires the right face to be put upon it to be tolerable, which is true neither for the illicit affair of Anna and Vronsky nor for the profoundly lawful affair of Levin and Kitty. Stiva and Dolly are too near the actual manner of things, are too wholly undifferentiated from the course of society and of individuals, ever to feel the need or the pang of rebirth. All they want is for things to be as they are. Stiva, as the old nurse tells him when Dolly has caught him in an affair with a governess, Stiva has only to do his part; and Dolly has only, now and always, to return to her part. Anna and Levin are very different. Each, in a separate and opposed way, can be satisfied with nothing less than a full incarnation, a rebirth into the force which at crisis they feel moves them. Anna craves to transmute what moves her from underneath—*all* that can be meant by libido, not sex alone—into personal, individual, independent love; she will be stronger than society because she is the strength of society, but only so in her death at the hands of society. Levin craves to transmute himself upwards, through society, into an individual example of the love of God; he, too, will be stronger than society because he finds the will of God enacted in the natural order of things of which society is a part, but he will only do so as long as God is with him in his life. What separates both Anna and Levin from the ruck of rebels is that they make their rebellions, and construct their idylls, through a direct confrontation and apprehension of immediate experience. There is nothing arbitrary about their intentions, only their decisions; there is nothing exclusive or obsessed about their perceptions, only their actions. They think and know in the same world as Stiva and Dolly, and indeed they had to or they could never have been in love with such eminently natural creatures as Vronsky and Kitty. They live in the going concern of society, and they are aside from it only to represent it the better.

This is the world, the society, which is for the most part understood through its manners; and that is how Tolstoi begins his novel, by showing his people through the motion of their manners, first those of Stiva and Dolly, then those of the others. By the end of the first Part of the novel, we know very well the manner of life of each person and could extend it to suit any further accident of life: we know the probable critical point in the temperament of each which rises or descends to some old or new form of action or inaction, and we know it by the kind of manners each exhibits and by how far into the being of each the manners seem to penetrate: into all that is on the surface of Stiva, into all there is anywhere for Dolly, into a layer of permanent irritation for Levin, into a layer of perpetual possibility for Anna, into the radiant sweep of things not yet her own for Kitty, and into the animal vitality of things for Vronsky (who is at the beginning, and always, less a man than a sensual force inhabiting a man).

For all this the comedy of Stiva's manners and Dolly's manners coming to terms with each other, not *they* but their manners, stands. Stiva deals with the ambiguities, Dolly with the intolerable things of marriage by manners. Stiva brings the huge pear of his own zest, but he can also weep. Dolly has a temper, but she can also weep. For both, tears are a kind of manners; and thus a reconciliation is effected. We see in this couple how it is that manners dictate the roles by which we escape acknowledging reality.

We begin with the same *kind* of manners Jane Austen mastered, the manners that pass for things otherwise only potentially present. But in Tolstoi we know at once that the manners are *of* something whose potency is pressing into the actual situation, something yet to be revealed in the words of the book, or at any rate to be carried into the open of our consciousness by them. Manners are a flowing stream; they are on the surface of what is swept along, hardly more by themselves but a wayward intimation of what is swept. In Jane Austen, even in *Emma,* the shape —the very water-shapes—of the stream of manners is itself pretty much the subject. In Tolstoi the stream will gradually take on the subject, will become united with it, as a brook takes on the brown of wood-earth and peat: as the Mississippi pushes its mud-color burden twenty miles to sea. Indeed the process begins, in *Anna Karenina,* in the first half-dozen pages, with the old nurse's remark to Stiva: Go, do your part. She tells us real things are at stake in this play of manners, things to be dealt with even the more because they are not acknowledged. And so it is with each personage as he turns up, except perhaps for Vronsky. There are hints of something pushing through.

For Dolly, there are the children, a noise in the hall and a clatter in the nursery, the *unattended* children; and they hint that Dolly's manners, temper and all, are only a part—of what? For Stiva, there is the moment of extreme aloofness after dinner in the restaurant, that aloofness among intimates for which he knew what to do: to make conversation with some *aide-de-camp,* or some actress, with someone not at the center but approaching the center; and so we are aware that the aloofness is from something. For Anna, there is, as an exercise in manners, her *first taking note* of her hypocrisy in dealing with her husband. For Kitty there are such things, still in the play of manners, as her recognition in Anna of something uncanny and her excitement at the utterance, not the substance, of Levin's declaration of love for her. Only for Vronsky there is nothing, as if his manners were so vital or his life so lacking that they were equal to his need.

But for Levin, the other half of Vronsky, there is enough to make up for all the rest. He is, in his unmannerliness, in his steady breach of the expected manner, an effort at declaring what the manners are about; but he is only one effort, one declaration, which can by no means minimize or defeat the others should they come to make their declarations. Levin's very breaches of manners are organized into manners themselves, as organized as the fools and the plain-spoken men in Shakespeare. He is a foil, a contrast, a light to Anna, Stiva, Karenin, Kitty, and Vronsky; and he is a successful foil by the accident of the condition of his temperament, by what he misses or ignores of what they all see. Stiva was right: Levin had no idea of girls as girls; he had no idea how good a fresh roll might smell and taste even after dinner—and indeed there is something vulgar in Levin when he sees a wife as a dinner, vulgar in the bad sense. But he is vulgar in the good sense when, thinking of Kitty, he tells Stiva it is not love but the force outside him which has taken possession of him. It is as if he had found a concrete parallel to the perception which had come to him in reading a sentence from Tyndall: "The connection between all the forces of nature is felt instinctively." Better still is his deep human illumination of the relativity of morals when under the impact of his rejection by Kitty in presumed favor of Vronsky, he comes to a new and compassionate judgment of that intellectual wastrel and revolutionary libertine his brother Nikolay. He thinks of him, and sees how the good force is corrupted. No doubt it is in this passage that we see through Levin's vision of his brother the death and life that are to come in the book. The shift from scorn to compassion, under the pressure of his own brooked love, seems a true act of imitation—of mimesis—which Aristotle tells us is a fundamental delight to man's mind, no matter whether the object of imitation is ugly or beautiful or monstrous.

But this is perhaps to get ahead of the story, when what we want is to become part of the momentum of the story to which the manners of the characters point. The instances of perception isolated above are all pretty mechanical; they do not yet occur organically, by the psychic drive of what has already been formed; they merely illustrate how the characters are being gotten hold of by the story: by the little or big things manners cannot quite either cover up or handle. Mainly, so far, it is a story told of how the people do cover up and do handle. We are on our most familiar living ground. For manners are the medium in which the struggle between the institutions of society and the needs of individuals is conducted. Viable dramatic manners exist so long as the struggle has not become too one-sided, so long as no total credit is given either to one side or the other. When in imagination or dogma the institutions are seen to triumph the manners become hollow, cold, and cruel. When the needs of the individual triumph the manners tend to disappear, so that life *together* becomes impossible. In either case we get a monstrous egoism, incapable either of choice or comparison, an exercise in moral suicide and sterile fancy.

No such case is reached in this novel. Far from breaking down in either direction, we find, even at the worst, at Anna's death or at Levin's access of life, everywhere but at the last retreat of Vronsky to a death in which he does not believe, that the great part of human behavior is viable in manners. It is through manners that the needs and possibilities of each person are seen in shifting conflict with the available or relevant institutions, including the twilight institutions—the illicit, amorphous institutions—which stand at the edges of the institutions of broad day. Stiva, Anna, and Vronsky depend on the twilight institutions of marriage and general social conduct which encroach on the edges of the broad day institutions upon which Dolly, Kitty, and Levin depend. Karenin, at Petersburg, belongs to something else again;

he has composed his dissatisfactions in a manner which contains its own rebelliousness: his jeering, desiccated conformity. But it is only the public aspect of the struggle which is between the broad day and the twilight. In actuality the struggle is conducted in the medium of manners between individuals trying from their different needs to shape institutions into some tolerable relation to their own partial apprehensions of reality. Here again it is Levin who has the first illumination; he knows there can be no victory and that there must be a balance. Himself a disbeliever in institutions, and therefore the more apprehensive of their force, he resents the maimed and maiming complaints of his brother Nicolay against the need of institutions: the forever need of make-shift. But best of all are the brother and sister Oblonsky, Stiva and Anna of the voided marriages: the one whose manners will last him forever, the other whose manners will be less and less good to her where they lead her, until at last she creates a fatal manner of her own. Stiva rises always into good nature. Anna is herself a form of nature. Both have something more than sincerity and both, because of the twilight of their actions, have something less than honesty. Think of Stiva at waking reaching for his dressing gown and finding, because he is not in his wife's bedroom, uncertainty instead. Think of Anna, away from home and because of that looking down the stairs at Vronsky and seeing possibility.

What Stiva finds, what Anna sees, is the momentum their manners had been about; and if we look at the gap between Part One and Part Two we see that the momentum is what carries us across the gap. Everybody has been left in an unfinished situation (Anna, Vronsky, Levin, the Oblonskys) or in a "finished" situation (Kitty) which must change. Thus there is both anticipation (uncertain but selected) and expectation (certain but unknown) but we cannot know which is which and cannot determine what is authentic until it has transpired. The business of the novel is how to find out and body forth what has already happened. We know only that for each of these people and for all of them together there must be more of the same thing, with the difference that they will know it better.

The emergence of this sort of knowledge depends on plot, but not upon the mechanical plot, not upon the plot of the "well-made" novel, or at least not primarily, but upon the organic, self-perpetuating, self-reproducing plot (reproducing whether by cycle, by scission, by parallel) which, as Aristotle says, is the soul of action. Surely it is not too much to say that the soul of action is momentum, and that, therefore, plot is the articulation of momentum. Only, in our stage of culture, we do not know ahead of time, we have only means of tentative guessing, what is the significance of plot conceived as the soul of action. We are not in the position of putting these people into relation with some received or religious or predicted concept of significance—as Sophocles, Vergil, Dante were. We are working the other way round: we have to find out in the process of the experience itself. We are about the great business of the novel, to create out of manners and action motive, and out of the conflict of the created motive with the momentum to find the significance: an image of the theoretic form of the soul.

To accomplish this art of psychology, this art of the psyche, this driving form and drifting form (as the stars drift) is perhaps the characteristic task of the novel in a society like that of the nineteenth century: a society without a fixed order of belief, without a fixed field of knowledge, without a fixed hierarchy; a society where experience must be explored for its significance as well as its content, and where experience may be created as well as referred. This is the society where all existing orders are held to be corruptions of basic order; or, to put it differently, where, in terms of the confronted and awakened imagination, the creation of order has itself become a great adventure. This is what Anna and Levin have, great personal adventures in the creation of order: an order is the desperate requirement each has for the experience each bodies forth.

Let us look at a few examples in the Second Part of the relation between manners and momentum and of the force under the momentum breaking through. There is the gradual spread of the scandal of Anna and Vronsky from rumor to declaration to conflagration. At first Anna *uses* the manners of the fashionable set to promote her relations with Vronsky, then she *breaches* manners to solidify them, and at last—with her husband, with society, with Vronsky—she throws manners away, and the force which has been there all along takes over although she does not as yet wholly know it. When asked at Betsy's party what she thinks of repairing the mistakes of love after marriage, she answers: " 'I think,' said Anna, playing with the glove she had taken off, 'I think . . . of so many men, so many minds, certainly so many hearts, so many kinds of love.' " After that party her husband, home to read, finds himself uneasy at the situation there tacitly (by manners) acknowledged between Anna and Vronsky. They have breached the formal role of the husband of a pretty wife, and he must speak to her in order to correct their estimate of the situation. As he thinks and walks the floor we see there is something more. When one set of manners impeaches another set—when the twilight assaults the broad day—an ambiguity appears. He who had always worked with reflections of life, and had shrunk away from life itself as something irrational and incomprehensible, now found himself "standing face to face with life." He had walked a bridge over the chasm of life and now the bridge was broken. Thus he is forced outside his official manners, is forced to think of Anna's *own* life for the first time. The plans he makes are all official, to communicate a firm decision and to exact obedience. But when Anna appears, glowing, a conflagration on a dark night, he found he was assaulting an impenetrable barrier and was reduced to begging. She had closed the door into herself, and he knew it would remain closed. As for Anna, his assault found her armored with an impenetrable falsehood and was strengthened, Tolstoi says, by an *unseen force.* His very speaking confirmed the new force and focussed it on Vronsky. In attempting to deceive him she makes the mistake of being natural, candid, light-hearted, qualities which in the circumstance are effects of the unseen force. In the new life between Karenin and Anna, Anna could lie awake feeling the brilliance of her own eyes, but Karenin found himself powerless because the spirit of evil and deceit which possessed her possessed him too. He could only implore and jeer.

When Anna and Vronsky perfect their new life in adultery they find they have murdered the first stage of their love. "Shame at their spiritual nakedness crushed her and infected him." Without the aid, rather the enmity, of decorum, manners, institutions, they cannot cope with the now visible force that binds *and* splits them. Being what they are—that is, being by Tolstoi condemned to full and direct experience—they cannot let the force pass. Vronsky tries to cover up with kisses. Anna tries, and puts off trying, to join together the shame, rapture, and horror of "stepping into a new life." She tries for and cannot find an order in thought. But in her dreams, when she was not protecting herself from her thoughts, she sees the hideous nakedness of her position. She dreams of two husbands, two Alexeys, two happinesses, and the dream weighed like a nightmare because it dramatized the impossibility of the only solution. As for Vronsky there is what happened when he went to see his mare, Frou Frou, the day before the race. The mare's excitement infected Vronsky. "He felt that his heart was throbbing, and that he, too, like the mare, longed to move, to bite; it was both dreadful and delicious." Swift never did this better; and Tolstoi does it without bitterness, though the scene is one which contains most of the occasions for human bitterness. What Vronsky wanted was Anna like the horse. But like the horse, Anna must be used in reckless pastime, or not at all. Take away the pastime, and the recklessness becomes uncontrollable and all the beautiful anarchy in the animal—all the unknown order under orders known—is lost. So, as with Anna, Vronsky failed to keep pace with Frou Frou and broke her back.

While Anna and Vronsky are bodying forth reality, Kitty is being cured of one reality by immersion in another. She is away, taking the waters. Tolstoi gives the tale of her cure lightly and ironically, but it is nevertheless accomplished by very hazardous means, and furnishes interesting analogies to what happened to Vronsky, Anna, Karenin, and in a way, also, to Levin who is immersing himself in the idyll of the simple life on his estate. Almost Kitty becomes a "pietist," a professional doer of good, a conspicuous instrument of false charity: a filler-up of the void of life with the "manners" of sincerity, virtue, and faith in the phase where life is left out. One hardly knows whether it is Mme. Stahl or Mlle. Varenka who better represents the negation of vitality. Both are unconscious charlatans of charity: the one for occupation, the other for duty. Kitty is taken in by both, and being a creature of vital impulse, herself tries the role of charlatan of charity from her heart. She has reached a moment of conversion, but not to recognition of life or God, rather to puerile substitutes for them, when she is rescued by the sick man Petrov's hysterical "love" for her combined with the return of her father full of health and humor and buoyancy. Petrov's "love" she recognizes, though she does not put it into words: "one of those things which one knows but which one can never speak of even to oneself so terrible and shameful would it be to be mistaken." Through her father, through the contagion of life he spreads, she sees Mme. Stahl's short legs and hears the feeble laughter of Varenka. And in the little crisis of these recognitions, she is converted *back* to life.

The figure of Varenka remains only as a threat, the threat of something the opposite of reality. This is the threat of public life, of life in public: the threat of turning the heart into an institution: the situation so desired by Karenin, in which one no longer feels what one ignores; when without conscious hypocrisy or deceit one ignores both the nature and the springs of human action, when all natural piety is transformed into the artifact of piety. There is no sympathy in it, much less mimesis, only empty histrionics: the vanities of spiritual ill-health mistaken for the pangs of vocation.

In all this Tolstoi never leaves us in the dark. It is only Kitty, the little Princess, who is led astray into thinking here is a career, or a new life, with these creatures who take no part in the momentum which sweeps them along. It takes only the lyric stagger of her "lover" Petrov, repeated to show it was doubly meant, a stagger for disease and a stagger for love, and the genuine momentum of her father the old Prince to pull her back into the stream. If we the readers remember in what language Tolstoi introduced Verenka we should ourselves never have been deceived. A creature without youth, nineteen *or* thirty, "she was like a fine flower, already past its bloom and without fragrance, though the petals were still unwithered." She is one of those who have nothing to suppress, no matter what the situation.

It may be, of course, that Tolstoi wrote all this to express his instinctive hatred of professional bad health: the bad health that keeps on living and makes of the open air a morass. These people also however make a parallel to the true purpose of the book: they cover up the encroaching reality of death much as Dolly and Karenin cover up what is for them the vanishing reality of life. The difference is that the sick and the charlatans succeed: they are equal to what they admit of their condition, and so take power over the living (nobody can so dominate a situation as the confirmed invalid); while Dolly and Karenin are never equal to their situation and still struggle with it, however pitifully or pretentiously, and lose power over others as over themselves with each successive act. The difference may be small from another perspective, but from Tolstoi's perspective it is radical. That is why the figure of Nikolay Levin passes, a small harsh whirlwind, across the scene: the very whirlwind of a man preparing and building into the reality of his death: tall, with stooping figure, huge hands, a coat too short for him, with black, simple, and yet terrible eyes: this figure shouting at the doctor and threatening him with his stick.

Tolstoi has many skills in the dialectic of incarnation. Here is one where the incarnation is of raw force itself, but it must be thought of in its setting. Consider how he surrounds the affair of Anna and Vronksy—the seduction, pregnancy and declaration—on the one side with the true idyll of Levin in the spring and on the other side the false idyll of Kitty at the watering place. It is across Vronsky and Anna that Kitty and Levin reach. At the very center lies Frou Frou, the mare, with her broken back, struggling up on her forelegs, then falling: all because Vronsky could not keep pace with her. Vronsky kicked her with his heel in the stomach. "She did not stir, but thrusting her nose into the ground, she simply stared at her master with her speaking eyes."

Vronsky's unpardonable act was no accident; neither was it done by intention. It was rather that, at a moment of high arbitrary human skill, at a moment of death-risk and momentary glory, the center of all eyes and the heart of an almost universal act of mimetic participation—at that moment something like fate broke the rhythm. Yet Vronsky was right: "for the first time in his life he knew the bitterest sort of misfortune, misfortune beyond remedy, and caused by his own fault." What is beyond remedy is beyond judgment: is its own justice; and if it is nevertheless caused by Vronsky's own fault, it is because the fault is universal. It is the fault that inheres in Kitty and Levin, in Dolly and Stiva, Anna and Vronsky alike: the fault of not keeping pace. This does not seem hard to understand in its general symbolic reach, that it may happen or that it may not that a breach of pace may be fatal. It is a harsher act of imagination to grasp the actuality of the absolute intimacy *and* the absolute inadequacy—the deliciousness *and* the dread—in human relationship; precisely what must be grasped if that phase has been reached.

But what is even more terrifying about Tolstoi's honesty—or let us say what is more astonishing about his genius—is that he could have broken the back of a mare in the midst of the crisis in the passion of Anna and Vronsky without either adding or diminishing *human* significance but rather deepening the reality. It is as if in this image he had gotten into the conditions of life from which the conditions we know of emerge: into conditions purer and conditions more intolerable: into an order which includes all human disorders.

These are affairs, as Tolstoi like Dante knew, of which the sane mind makes no report except in symbol, however they may remain thereafter the very growth of the mind. So it was with Vronsky. His friend Yashvin the rake understood it best, "overtook him with his cap, and led him home, and half an hour later

Vronsky had regained his self-possession." The death of Frou Frou had become a part of him, no longer separately recognized.

Like the death of Frou Frou, so it is with the passions that inhabit our heroes. The passion of the force will pass but not the force, and if the passion has not wrecked the hero (as it does Karenin) the force will be stronger after the passion has passed than before. That is why the notion of purification is attached to the passion of tragic action. Society, nature, and the individual in society and nature, have three common arrangements to take care of the situation when genuine passion has passed. There is the arrangement for outlets in the demi-monde or twilight world. There is the arrangement for the cultivation of passion for its own sake, which suits those afraid of being *otherwise* occupied. And there is the arrangement that when the passion passes those who have been joined in it will find themselves insuperably bound—unless a fresh passion of the force supervene. Both for Anna and for Levin, with their different aspirations, none of these arrangements is enough. Or rather, for Levin none of them will do at all, and for Anna they will all do in their turns. But both need the identification of force with love, the one outside society and nature, the other through society and nature. Anna needs to become herself standing for everybody, Levin needs to become everybody in order to find himself represented. That is why both Anna and Levin are subject to fearful jealousies. Their rebirth into new life is never complete and the identification of force with love is never complete. Thus the force remains free, capable of assuming all possible forms. That is why Anna dreads in Vronsky and Levin in Kitty the positive enactment of what is at constant potential in themselves. Their jealousy is that they crave each other's possibilities, and hence each is bound to muster out of the force that moves them a new burst of passion in the hope that this time the new birth will take place but in the hidden certainty that it will not.

Vronsky, even more than Anna, as their love becomes more of a scandal, is deprived of the social phases of "force" and is required to envisage it as if naked, and an enemy. The worm of ambition in him which had been covered in the first stages of love is now uncovered by the scandal of love. He understands perfectly what his friend the successful general means when he says, "Women are the chief stumbling-block in a man's career. It's hard to love a woman and do anything." He understands but he answers softly that the general has never loved, and he understands even better when the general returns it, "We make an immense thing of love, but they are always *terre à terre*." It is what he understands, and keeps out of sight, that gives him a hard expression when Anna tells him she is pregnant. He is thinking of all that is lost, and of the duel that must come. Anna does not understand that and gives up all hope that his love will be enough for her, though in the same breath of her mind she tells him that it will be. She sees he has already been thinking and will not tell her all he thought. She is, she tells him, proud, proud, proud—but she cannot say what she is proud of; and Vronsky if he had spoken must have said the same thing. They get at so differently what lies between them that they wholly misunderstand each other, but never for a second do they fail to grasp the force that compels the misunderstanding.

As for what happens to Karenin there is no better image than the lawyer whom he consults about a divorce: he plucks four moths out of the air, as if he were the law engorging the individual. Unlike Anna and Vronsky, who are deprived of them, Karenin is more and more taken over by the brutality of the social phases of "force." He makes one final effort to reverse himself—as do Anna and Vronsky—when Anna, in childbirth, thinks herself dying. Then all three reverse and renounce their roles, and do so in deep analogy to Levin and Kitty at the true death of Levin's brother Nikolay where they gain great access to their true roles. It is the image of death—the attractive and repulsive force of death—which takes over each of them. There is something in the rhythm of death which for Vronsky, Anna, and Karenin elicits a supreme failing effort to keep pace, as there is for Levin in his brother's death. For each, it is as far as they can go in their opposed directions.

Indeed it is Anna's literally incomplete death-scene which is the death in which rebirth takes place. She makes a histrionic mimesis of death because of the two women within her. Thinking, in her last spasm of social guilt, to kill one, actually she kills the other. No, not by thinking does she do this, unless it is something outside the mind that thinks. Rather she, the whole of her, takes advantage of the vision of death to find out what can be seen through it. Her mistake is only initial. The rebirth is accompanied by an exorcism, which she sees and feels but which, so great is the force of the world, she does not at once recognize for what it is. She has become single; it seems to be by renunciation; actually it is by an access of devotion—for she is not a woman gifted with renunciation, and her first practice of it shows as irritation and inability, as something to overcome and something to perfect. Had Vronsky not come, had he not rushed in, and stroked her cropped hair, calling her a pretty boy, she might never have found out in actuality what her new singleness was. Instead of positive desperation she would have ended in self-contemptuous despair. There would have been nothing to break down, only the collapse of a dry shell. As it is, she begins at once, against the world-and-his-wife and contemptuous of both, the long course of building her own desperation, the positive desperation of her own cause, to the point where her own strength but not that of her cause should be exhausted.

That is the nature of her tragedy, that her own strength cannot be equal to her cause. The independence of the individual is never equal to the cause of independence. And the flaw is as it should be, both in her and in the nature of things, and not at all less guilty for that (or if you like, less innocent): a flaw in any case, a human need, which as it finds its mode of action and creates its motive becomes less and less the kind of flaw that asks for the forgiveness of understanding and is more and more revealed as a single, eminent aspect of the general nature of things which brings the mind to compassion.

How otherwise—how if it is not this train that has been set going—can we look at the irony of the pure, lawful, and successful love affair of Levin and Kitty as anything but cheap and puerile "moralism"?—that is, not irony at all. Levin in new life, Levin on wings, has also singled his life, has made an act of devotion, to which he will necessarily turn out inadequate, not so much because of inadequate strength but because the cause itself (in the form of his original impulse) will desert him. The very, brutal force of the world and his wife which will bring ruin to Anna and Vronsky because they contest it, is the force Levin leans on—his cause—and it is a force hardly less reliable taken as a cause than as the enemy. No institution and no individual may ever be more than a partial incarnation of the underlying or superior force; nor can any set of individuals and institutions taken together. It is only Stiva or the peasant with the pretty daughter-in-law whom Levin had seen pitching hay who can use or abuse this force indifferently: with the kind of faith that makes no enquiries and would not know a vision if it saw one. For Stiva, there is always a way out, not death. For the peasant girl—she is herself a way out, and death is a matter not yet experienced. These are the creatures not subject to individual rebirth, they are the nearest thing to permanence: momentum or recurrence.

But the shoe of Anna's rebirth pinches sharpest, under the impact of symbolic death, on Karenin and Vronsky: the one with his head in the hollow of Anna's elbow, the other with his face in his hands: the one suffering total and permanent spiritual change, the other suffering total humiliation followed by recovery through violence: the one inwardly transcending his society, the other rejecting his society and both to be ever afterwards victimized by it—though one, Karenin, is put in contempt by society, and the other, Vronsky, is made a hero so to speak outside society. Karenin can never get back into society and is in a misunderstood position above it. Vronsky can never leave society behind him: it goes with him: he is a kind of pet public outcast. They have passed, by humiliation and self-contempt, through their relations to Anna's symbolic death, to the roles most nearly opposite to those in which we first saw them.

That is, to each of them comes a deep reversal of role through a direct, but miscomprehended, experience of the force of life in the phase of sex under the image of an incomplete death. We shall see the deaths completed diversely. Meanwhile we see Anna, Vronsky, Karenin, and Levin tied in the hard knot of individual goodness, and each, in that goodness, in a different relation to the manners and momentum of society. I mean, by goodness, that each has been reborn into a man or woman for once, and at last, proper to his or her own nature. Each has *virtu,* and to the point of excess, but—such is the power of Tolstoi's imagination—without loss of humanity. Each, seen beside the self, is more the self than ever. Levin, seen in society, is no more representative of it than the other three, who are seen against it.

It is for this goodness that they pay the cost. The good, said Aristotle, is that which all things aim at, and when an aim has been taken everything flies that way—whether the target was indeed the good or not. We see Levin in doubt and delight about everything, desiring not to desire, as we see Vronsky equally in doubt, but so full of *ennui* that he desires desire. We see that Anna's problem is to maintain the state of crisis in love, to be always a young girl in love, and that Vronsky's problem is to find substitutes, caprices of action, to prevent *ennui* from absorbing crisis. In Vronksy's house all were guests, in Levin's all were part of the household; and so on. Tolstoi gives us hundreds of comparisons and analogies of the two honeymoons. But perhaps the most instructive is the comparison of Veslovsky at Levin's and at Vronsky's. This young man with unseemly eyes, fat thighs, and hand-kissing habits was very much a gentleman of the bedchamber: altogether in place at Vronsky's, very much a part of the general pretense at occupation. Vronsky ignores in him what had genuinely put Levin in a rage, and Anna was amused at him where Kitty was ashamed. Kitty and Levin made a fight for life within the fold, Anna and Vronsky fight in abuse of the fold; and a little in the background Dolly surrenders to life within a broken fold.

Each of them is inadequate to him or herself as a solitary actor; and perhaps this is nowhere shown so clearly as in the image of Dolly making her solitary visit to Anna sitting in the coach, afraid to look in her glass, daydreaming herself a perfect paramour. Again we see it in Dolly in her darned gown listening with aversion and distrust to Anna talk of birth-control. She knows suddenly that in the very numbers of her children is her safety: not in perspective, future or past, but in numbers, in everyday life. Dolly is the monitor of all that is living: she has paid the cost of goodness without ever having had it, and in so very deep a way that no fresh start—neither rebellion nor new effort along old lines—could ever get it for her. She is neither good nor evil; neither hopeless nor desperate. She believes in high principles, and that they must not be forgotten, but in every act of her being she knows the necessity, if she is to survive, of the alternate assertion and abuse of these principles. The compassionate gesture of her visit to Anna is symbolic of all this; and it is the kind of peak of meaningfulness she can reach at any time, with no need for crisis. So we begin to see what she is doing in this novel: she is to be recognized, not understood. But we should never have believed her, or in her, had we seen her in such a moment at the beginning; nor would she have believed in herself. She would have been a bad Varenka, a hypocrite unendurable. It was right that she had to be brought round by Anna, just as it is right now that her presence should remind Anna of all the life she was smothering. But best of all is to think of Dolly with the road dust in the creases about her eyes, imagining at the end of her daydream of illicit love, what the expresson on Stiva's face would be, when, like Anna to Karenin, she flaunted her infidelity in his face.

This image of Dolly may have come to Tolstoi as an afterthought, as a debt to his novel he had not known he was incurring and which he had therefore all the more obligation to pay. He had thought of Rachel, but not of Leah. But with the other image in this part of the book—the death of Nikolay—it is the other way round. This is the death that lived in Tolstoi all his life, for which he made three great images of which this is the first and greatest—the others are "Ivan Ilyitch" and *The Living Corpse*. Death is the inevitable thing from which there is no freedom by recognition but only by enactment. Where Anna (as Dolly saw) has learned a new gesture, to half close her eyes on what is threatening her and cannot be dealt with, Tolstoi himself has to force a steady gaze on death physical, spiritual, and dramatic (poetic, dialectic, rhetorical). He has to mime death. He has to show in fact that death, as well as good, is what all things aim at; that death is the moving *and* the fixed background of life. He knows and must show that it is a commonplace truth and illusion that men die well. The whole commonplace is there in the physical—the terribly physical—death of Nikolay: and in the longing for death that surrounds it.

This death—the most innocent and most mature in all fiction—though it has nothing to do directly with the plot is yet a center of attractive force presiding over its whole course. Everything else is drawn to it, across a gap. It is this attractive force that begins to complete the actions of each of our persons, those actions which were focussed in the partial deaths endured by Anna and Levin in the middle portion of the book, and which were initiated by the death of Frou Frou at the first crisis in the action: it is the solitary and menacing incarnation of all these. And it should be well noted that in this death everything is as near the physical as possible without affront to the spiritual and the dramatic. The turbulence is all of something watched by Kitty or felt by Levin. It is death as raw force, a concrete, focal, particular epiphany of the raw force of death. It is the after part of every forethought.

Surely that is what is somehow in Levin's mind when, in making his one call on Anna in her Coventry, he sees her face as stone and more beautiful than ever, the very Medusa-face of life (Henry James's phrase) to which for a moment he succumbs. Altogether these nine or ten pages of Levin's vision of Anna are a high example of what may be meant in the novel by full drama. As in the modern stage drama, a great deal depends on what has gone before, now summarized and brought to a fresh and conclusive action against a background which may and will come forward when the action is done: when the violent inner light of conflagration in Anna is changed to the lightning that momentarily obscures the stars for Levin. That is what the dramatic action is for, to pull the whole background forward. It is the background in which they are all implicated, and in which the action is a series of parallels and a series of analogies which show all our principal persons in deeply but narrowly different responses to the same force: each lawful, each valid, complementing each other like ice and water, or night and day, converging like slush or twilight, like midnight and noon. Each is brought to a clarity, of which the meaning is seen, not alone in relation to the other persons, but also with respect to the sweep of things: the sweep which moves with the strange intimate noise which Shakespeare calls the endless jar of right and wrong in which justice resides. It is against this that Anna's face was stone and more beautiful than ever.

There is a nakedness in this sort of experience for Anna which ends in death, and an unarmored defencelessness for Levin which begins in birth. It leaves both of them without the protection or clothes of the intellect. And there is a harshness in the compassion required of total response to each—the compassion of peace with a sword—which is possible only to a saint or a great artist. Such response touches what is under our behavior, and what comes into our behavior, which whether we shun it or salute it, remakes, while the contact lasts, our sense of relation with ordinary life. We cannot live at crisis, at the turning point, but must make out of it either a birth or a death in the face of ordinary life. This is what happens to morality in art. It is an image of passing one way or the other; which may explain what Eliot had in mind when he observed that as morals are only a preliminary concern to the saint so they are only a secondary concern to the artist. That is the condition, between the preliminary and the secondary, of harsh compassion that made Tolstoi reject his novels, including this one, along with Shakespeare. He rejected the uncopeable truth, because he wanted to remake the world piecemeal in terms of morality as a central authority. In the novels he wanted only the mimesis of morality as a central experience, both in the world and in the crisis of individuals who were somehow, because of the crisis, removed from it.

The novels wanted to show the tacit, potential crisis which gave the ordinary world meaning, and which in turn put individuals to the test. It is in contest and concert with the ordinary world that crisis is reached and given worth; and it is into the ordinary world that things break through and are bodied forth, visibly in crisis, actually all along. The last two parts of *Anna Karenina* put into parallel and analogy such recognitions as these. Under pressure of the action even the parallels seem to become analogies, to be in proportional relation to each other: as in the stream of consciousness—the articulate hysteria—in which Anna's last hours are recorded, which is both parallel and analogous to Levin's final conversion in company with the beetle under the dusty shade of the poplars at noon.

For a major parallel which is also analogy, let us look at the whole structure in the next to last part of the book. We begin with Kitty's delayed confinement and from it see Levin moved through Moscow's "society," intellect, and club life, to reach that other form of delayed or arrested vitality which is Anna, and in which he is for a moment absorbed. Then through quarrel and jealousy we are moved sharply to the scream of birth for Kitty and the plunge to death for Anna: the birth which for Anna meant death not herself, which to Kitty meant new life not herself, and which to Levin were one and the same. Between the two sets of movements there is a chapter in which an independent evil spirit grew up in Anna because there was a delay in her affairs, just as there was an independent new life in Kitty in the delay of *her* affairs. The one ends in senseless rage, the other in senseless joy. In either case it is the uncopeable power not themselves which moves them, and to each it shows with the terrible ambiguity of an immediate experience.

Surely it is not providential that before returning to Anna and her death, Tolstoi carries us to Petersburg, the city of government and decorum and manners, and gives us, so we may make our own irony, images of what happens when people insist on coping with their own troubles in terms of the unilluminated ordinary world. We see all this in Stiva pursuing his double errand, to get himself a better job and to get Anna her divorce. To get the job he has to descend into humiliation. To prevent himself from giving the divorce, Karenin, with Lidia aiding, has to descend to a false appeal to a false force pretending to govern a false society: he descends to the clairvoyance of a charlatan, to an "induced" change of heart. By betrayal of his own traditions, Stiva gets his job; so does Karenin refuse the divorce. Anna is not a matter of genuine consideration. In this analogy, Tolstoi presents all that is left, in these people, of the true force: he sees that Stiva and Karenin have become all manners and no men.

Nor is it providential, it is the very essence of the prepared drama, that we return from Stiva in Petersburg to find Anna in Moscow, herself clutching at manners—in the form of quarrels, jealousies, formal emotions—in the one place where manners cannot act but can only cover up ugly action—the place where people are outside society, but where, since so little else is left except the raw emotion of the self, appearances must be kept up. It is their manners, failing, that keep Anna and Vronsky from joining their emotions. They neither do their part nor keep pace. It is when her manners wholly fail that Anna brims over, sees herself clear, and comes on that unintermediated force which makes her suffer, and it is in desperate pursuit of some manners into which she can deliver that suffering that she finds her death: precisely as she thought she had done so long ago in her false death. Her tragedy is that she has destroyed too much of the medium, too many of the possibilities, of actual life, to leave life tolerable, and she has done this partly by dissociating manners from the actual world and partly by losing her sense of the sweep of things. Thus her last turning point, her last effort at incarnation, was death.

With no less of the force in him that drove Anna, Levin turned the other way. He too had been at the point of death and for months at a time, but through the death of his brother and the delivery of his wife found himself alive instead. It could have been the other way; Levin and Anna were aimed equally at life or at death. Human life cannot stand the intensity of Anna, but works toward it; human life requires the diminution of intensity into faith and of faith into momentum which is Levin. The one is very near the other. Only Anna's face was stone and more beautiful than ever. Yet it is in the likeness not the difference that the genuineness and the dialectic of Tolstoi's incarnation lies.

The Jew in Search of a Son: Joyce's ULYSSES

Reading over Richard Kain's book on *Ulysses, Fabulous Voyager,* reading also Harry Levin's *James Joyce,* and remembering Gilbert, Gorman, the Wordbook, and the rest: the whole clutter of exegesis, adulation, and diatribe (e.g., the 1935 essay by P. E. More); reading all this sends the mind astretch on far questions that have to do with the relation of the individual to his society in our time. How far has literature become inaccessible to its natural audience? How far has the natural audience (let us say for convenience the sum of those who go about the job of reading) itself lost the tools of access? Is it inevitable that the field of reference of the most responsible authors of our time should be largely unavailable to the most responsive existing audiences? Is it unavoidable that the area of conviction and belief that lies between such authors and such audiences should seem rather an area of the indifferent or the provisional? Is it necessary that the guidebook to the puzzle should replace the criticism of literature? How is it that the vice of scholarship should replace the *élan* of reading?

The instinctive answers to all these questions are on what, until recently at any rate, would have been called the unfavorable side, and on what should still be so called. Hence the mind's recoil. The guidebook to the puzzle *is* necessary, for most readers, as a preliminary approach; it serves to create a substitute for what the author used or ought to have used in writing and for what the reader ought to have brought with him in his reading. But it is not Joyce alone; Mann, Proust, Gide, Yeats, Kafka, all also require the guidebook approach and the puzzle for quarry; so would Bernard Shaw if anybody took him seriously, for the burden of his work and the relation of it to contemporary society are just as inaccessible—just as much of a culture-puzzle—as the theology in *The Trial*. Yet these are the masterpieces of our time, and it may be that if our relations with them do not gain in fullbloodedness—if we cannot meet them with *élan*—they will come to be called the last European masterpieces, and it will be the qualities that made them masterpieces that also made them unavailable for full relation to most readers. It is not that the continuing enterprise of Europe is dead, but that we are not very conscious of it because we are in the middle of one of the jumps—metamorphoses, like that between Augustus and Augustine—by which it moves. The Augustinian jump took eight centuries to recover consciousness; no doubt we move faster, certainly we feel the motion to the point of vertigo, which is, socially, the characteristic feeling of an interregnum, of motion through a gap, what the old religionists call the fall into the abyss or a doomed experiment towards a secular world. Whatever the outcome, it will remain interesting to know what the jump was from and what it was that was metamorphosed; it was exactly the springboard that moved us and our present propulsive energy; and our masterpieces, being reactions willy-nilly to their time cannot help telling us, and beyond rather than merely within their intent. It is indeed their function; and it is to make use of that function that makes the best reason for getting into full relation with a given masterpiece: we can see what operations it performs upon its society. The *Ulysses* of James Joyce is a wonderfully promising example to tackle in that way.

This essay is then in some sense a use of the work of Levin and Kain; it rests upon them in that it expects its readers to be at least as familiar with "Ulysses" as they make possible; and it pillages their ideas with the privilege of a crusader. But essentially it is a supplement to Levin and Kain, written from a point of view which Levin only adumbrates and which Kain is not apparently concerned with: the point of view that there is a gap between *Ulysses* and its author, between the author and us, and between the book and us, which is much the same gap, and which is a gap that can be crossed—which, since we are in it, is a gap that must be crossed. Levin, if I understand him correctly, does not think the gap can be crossed, believing it inherent in modern society. Kain's book does not come on the gap; it sets up an easy activity and sheds a good deal of unfocussed light which might well get many people to read and be moved by their reading. He no doubt means more than he was able to write down, but he makes no visible effort to cross the gap between what is in *Ulysses* and what is in the minds of contemporary readers. Yet—unless I am wrong—the gap is there; and not to deal with it is not to catch the momentum of the book, and so not to catch one version of the momentum of the society of which it is an expressive part.

But let us see how what we have been calling the gap turns up in the arts. It is the kind of gap familiar to everybody in the life of action. Like the gap between heart beats, between the words of a message, or between the votes cast and the candidate elected, it is the distance between idea and reality which must always be crossed if work is to be done; public and private life both depend on crossing it. Yet what lies between is what actually goes on. The life of action cannot afford direct familiarity with it, but cannot lose relevance to it except at great peril. With the arts it is the other way round. The arts take no action and do not seek directly to change the world; their domain is precisely the actual experience of what goes on between the idea and the reality; but they must nevertheless, if they are to escape the condition of total flux or total chaos, hold some implicit allegiance to the idea as intent and to the reality as aspiration. When the imaginations devoted to the life of action—religion, ethics, philosophy, politics—break down or become inadequate or distrust themselves, there is a double consequence in the arts. They become either abstract or too much in the flux, and they find themselves taking on as part of actual experience—like an injured heart, a halting breath, an hysterical speech—the breakdown, inadequacy, and distrust. In T. S. Eliot's phrase, you get an incredible public world and an intolerable private world. The arts can deal with the quality, the actuality, of such a world only with difficulty and intermittently, and so to speak by falling back upon their own momentum. Because there is too much for the artist to do and too little for the audience to bring, there is a failure of relation between the artist and his art and between the art and its audience; and the gaps widen. It would seem that Joyce wrote *Ulysses* during the first stages of what was then thought to be only a partial breakdown but has since so far progressed that many do not know that a different state had existed. In a sense, the breakdown was itself Joyce's theme as it was Mann's theme in *The Magic Mountain,* Proust's in *Remembrance of Things Past,* and W. B. Yeats' in the poems of the twenties with their images of annihilation and annunciation, the Tower, Byzantium, and the Phases of the Moon. It was the pressure of the breakdown to become itself the theme of work that led all these authors to take on obligations towards expressing the actual experience of the *concepts* of religion and philosophy and ethics and politics (often against their wills) and that led their audiences (perhaps against their wills, too, or at least willy-nilly) to find that these concepts had aesthetic, frivolous, or personal values only. These were obligations and consequences which the literature of Western Christianity had never before shown.

Taking *Ulysses* as a characteristic example of the novel into which the breakdown has forced itself as theme, we see at once how the artist has on the one hand been compelled to take a series of arbitrary aesthetic, technical, and intellectual measures to get his work moving and has on the other hand been required, in order to fill out these measures, to present an inordinate mass of detail. He is arbitrary because what would formerly have been his authorities have become part of his subject-matter, and he is omnivorous of detail because without his authorities he has no principles of economy. This vast craving for the actual—this tendency to develop total recall—in modern authors has something to do with the loss of authority in the forms of the ideal; just as the addiction to the abstract in modern art (unlike that in Byzantine art) has something to do with the weakening of the relation between the ideal and the actual. In either case, where the movement ought to be towards mastery, whether by bulk or line, it is in fact towards impotence—saved, when it is saved, by the dramatic verisimilitude of the impotence, its acceptance or its repudiation.

In *Ulysses,* there is both repudiation, by Stephen, and acceptance, by Bloom; and also, by Molly, a gesture of surpassing indifference. The repudiation is arbitrary; the acceptance direct and detailed; the gesture of indifference immediate and lyric. The repudiation accents, the acceptance expatiates, the remains of a Christian frame; the lyric gesture is from a prior source to any frame, not so much integral to the work of the book as capable of integration in any frame, past or to come. That is why Stephen blasphemes, why Bloom mediates and compromises and why Molly pulls up the sheet and sniffs of herself,—like a pure force, more lost, and more recoverable than either of the men. Stephen knows what he repudiates; Bloom does not know what he accepts but only that he must do so with relish and anguish and good will; Molly affirms the continuum which has nothing to do with repudiation or acceptance but includes them both without discrimination.

These rôles of repudiation and acceptance become dramatically more intelligible and gain greatly in force if we emphasize and even exaggerate the degree to which the whole Graeco-Christian (and in this case Irish as well) tradition has in its breakdown—its partial survival as ideal, its increasing decrepitude in action—become the right theme for the exile, the outsider, the artist, the wanderer. *Ulysses* is in this sense an aesthetic version of the Graeco-Christian-Irish concert. But it is not the official concert, not the concert which pretends the world is like that in the reality to which we ought to conform. Joyce's concert is at the double level of the ideal and the actual, in which what has happened to the ideal in actual experience is expressed, in terms of both, by the imposition of arbitrary aesthetic orders. No more orderly book of fiction was ever written, and no book in which the principles of order, unless taken aesthetically, seemed so frivolous or impotent. Dante is casual in comparison, for Dante tried to put things in order only within reason and tradition, whereas Joyce went ahead anyway, presenting a kind of nihilism of unreasonable order. He had an overmastering predilection for order and a cultivated knowledge of many kinds of order, and their heresies, within the Graeco-Christian tradition, catholic, classic, historical, and aesthetic, but he had to treat them all, in fact, as if they were aesthetic, images or stresses rather than summaries or concepts of the actual. Thus the waywardness or high jinks in the book is order pushed, the chaos is order mixed, the disgust is order humiliated, the exile is order desiderated or invoked. Thus, too, the overt orders of the book—homeric, organic, stylistic—make obstacles, provoke challenges, not all of which are overcome; and also serve to get around (by forcing overflows, damming power) such psycho-ethical matters as motive in character, meaning in action, and purpose in sequence.

Precisely because Joyce could not assent to the official version of his Dublin-classical-Christianity, he was all the more condemned to the damnation of imposed orders. Imposed order—forced order—always mutilates what is ordered and tends to aridify it. Not the observation of Stephen or of Bloom (or Molly) is imposed order, but the conceptions of those characters under the observation and the aesthetic frames in which the book chooses to see them: e.g., the parodies of English prose style in the hospital scene, the theory of hallucination in the bawdy house, or the dialectic in the homecoming scene. Perhaps all art is imposed order, but it ought to be the order called for by the substance in terms of the governing concepts of those imaginations which are not aesthetic. These Joyce's experience of his society did not provide; his only providence was the gratuitous one of the whole undistributed flux of sensation and possibility; and into this, every order he chose to use poured willy-nilly. Neither parody of old orders nor that substitute for order, research-naturalism, could restrain the flow of the parade into the mob. Perhaps that is why he distrusted—or at any rate never for long used—either of the "great" modes of traditional prose literature, the full narrative or the full drama. Joyce had none of that conviction which is the inward sense of outward mastery; and those who feel the lack of that sort of conviction tend to truncate their merely outward skills: truncate, mutilate, and mock. In such a predicament it is almost the normal solution to choose, instead of full statement in narrative or drama, some dessicated dialectic and try to make it pass for fresh because it was chosen. Such trials are self-laceration, as the monastic impulse, denied access to its own insight in the body's life, becomes ascetic fury. So it happens in some artists; as in ordinary people similarly deprived you get hair-splitting *in extremis* despite the major issue of love or security, where the *categories* of relation are argued as if they were reality itself.

The character of Stephen Dedalus is a good example. Joyce was right in changing the title of his first novel from *Stephen Hero* to *Portrait of the Artist as a Young Man*. It is not Stephen that is heroic, only his rôle, his category; his substance is agonized. Stephen was, as Mulligan said, an "impossible person." He had great need (but in his impossibleness had to deny it) for Bloom, who is the ideal-actual of the possible—an unrealizable Christ. Stephen is damned; it is hard to know *with what* he could be forgiven, nothing in himself, nothing in us. We know Bloom is not damned precisely because—by his ideals or by our own or by none at all—there is no point at which he would not be forgiven. There is a goodness in him which is the sign of his privation: he is the living penance of his sins. Cyril Connolly quotes Baudelaire as saying that the man who will not assent to the conditions of life is damned. Assent is very difficult when undertaken, as Stephen can only undertake it, independently and intellectually; trying, he can only abort his intellect and his freedom. Bloom does not so much as try the hard game of assent; he doesn't have to; he is the other thing, the one thing the imagination in Joyce's predicament can handle, he is himself a way of expressing what the conditions of life are. Stephen does try—and maximizes his arrogance (his sense of the difficulties) to the point of sentimentality. Seeing the sentimentality more in others than in himself, he sends Buck Mulligan the telegram in the words of Meredith: "The sentimentalist is he who would enjoy without incurring the immense debtorship for a thing done." Foster Damon long ago argued (in his "The Odyssey in Dublin") that Stephen is, in Blake's sense, Satan; satanic pride is always sentimental: hence the temptation of it. In the weak, pride becomes destructive; in the strong, humble. Joyce *chose* to show Stephen weak *in* his pride, which is what made him "impossible" in the eyes of others. So, but on the contrary, Joyce chose to show Bloom strong *in* his pride and humble; which is why to others he seems weak, sat-on, contemptible, and humiliated. Stephen and Bloom are not so much complementary as equivalent, but their equivalence is seen as a polarity: the polarity of the mature artist who would yet cling to the desperate vanity of his adolescence. Levin thinks that the polarity in Joyce was the polarity between the modern city and the artist, but he would be nearer right if he capitalized the City. The City of Plato or St. Augustine or St. Thomas is where Banquets are, and it is that City which to Joyce has become full of monsters who have taken away the food for all who are like Stephen too weak in their pride to struggle. To him Bloom was such a monster, and yet at the same time, for the wink of a drunken eye, Bloom was also the Christus or another—perhaps the man in the brown macintosh; that is to say, for Stephen, Bloom is the city against which he struggled as an individual, the City which was the only energy he could draw on outside his own pride, and the nameless sign of the thing to come. Bloom is what has actually happened to Christianity; Stephen is what has happened to those who refuse or are unable to accept Bloom. Joyce created both out of his own nature.

Instead of the polarity of the ideal and the actual, there was for Joyce the polarity of the City and the individual, as there is for the next generation the polarity of the giant Urbs (the city as agglomeration) and the individual. The point of distinction is that Stephen could still feel, what the next man of his type cannot feel except with difficulty, a heretic and a blasphemer. Stephen Dedalus, on the model of the first martyr in his given name, and on the archetype of artificer in his surname, could still feel his losses. He had the horrible actual hallucination of unreality in his central situation, which is the fate of those who transpose the summary conceptual forces of the intellectual to the immediate values of the aesthetic imagination. He not only felt his losses; he included them; he was their monument.

That is the portrait of the artist that shows in the first three chapters of *Ulysses:* in brief, the young man to whom "Etiquette is etiquette. He kills his mother but he can't wear grey trousers." The mother is his own mother, mother Rome, mother Ireland, and mother of us all, the Greek sea; Stephen kills access to all his sources, but because they are with him in feeling, cannot accept the consequences of his act: the immense debtorship for a thing done. Buck Mulligan, the plump prelate and patron whose gold teeth-points remind Stephen of St Chrysostom the golden-mouthed, makes mock of the Mass with shaving bowl, combining the introit and the elevation of the host, and proceeding with the miracle of the transubstantiation whistles for help and gets two back. His lather bowl is crossed with mirror and razor. But he is also Malachi Mulligan, in which guise he is the Greek Mercury signalling with his mirror and also that Malachi which means the messenger of God's Covenant, and his message may be found at the end of the book of Malachi, traditionally the last book of the Old Testament. Whether Joyce had the passage in mind is immaterial; it becomes an animating presence in the book once it is seen in the context: "Behold, I will send you Elijah the prophet before the coming of the great and dreadful day of the Lord: and he shall turn the hearts of the fathers to the children, and the hearts of the children to their fathers, lest I come and smite the earth with a curse." Whether we think of Stephen's private situation, his situation in parallel to the Odyssey, or his situation with regard to what we have been calling the breakdown of the Christian world, the passage has illuminating force; and a force which is only incremented when we reflect on what the breakfast eaten by Stephen and Malachi (together with the alien Haines) may mean in its Christian background. They eat butter and honey. In the service for the Annunciation of the Virgin Mary there is used a passage from Isaiah (vii, 14–15) which reads as follows. "Behold, a virgin shall conceive, and shall call his name Immanuel. Butter and honey shall he eat, that he may know to refuse the evil, and choose the good." Perhaps these are aesthetic echoes; but perhaps they are also epiphanies; at any rate they are followed by the manifestation of the old woman with the milk who is Ireland and a "messenger from the secret morning," and by the manifestation of that theory of *Hamlet* where that prince is the ghost of his own father, by a misunderstanding of which Stephen becomes both Hamlet and Japhet in search of a father. (In Genesis Japhet covered his father's nakedness and was blessed.) To all this Mulligan makes an antiphony with the ballad of the Joking Jesus, Stephen, in the seriousness of his unbelief, responds by saying that he is a servant of two masters, Britain and Rome, "and a third there is who wants me for odd jobs," and by thinking of the heresiarchs, Photius, Arius, Valentine, and Sabellius, all of whom found everything at stake, as Stephen does, in the father-son relation. (In Stephen, it should be noted, it is a heresy to a different orthodoxy; the relation of doctrine to emotion has reversed its direction: it is the doctrine, taken as actual feeling, that now leads to the emotion.) Lastly, unanswered and uncommented, Haines the Britisher says that the national problem just now is to keep his country from falling into the hands of the German Jews; not so much an epiphany as the promise of one to come of the Jew as the specifically Christian problem.

It is exactly the epiphany made clearest in the second chapter in which Stephen Telemachus Satan does his job of teaching history without perspective and collects his pay from Nestor Deasy the outlander and refuses his advice. But first the chapter goes on where the first chapter began. The victory of Pyrrhus at Asculum, which is the victory that destroys, like that of Stephen over his mother: another victory like that and we are done for, leads into the crack about a pier being a disappointed bridge. Stephen's mind remains partly in the cost of victory while it takes up, with the boys, the reading of *Lycidas;* both the history of "history" and the history of his own mind. Thus there is a parallel between "Sunk though he be beneath the watery floor" and his memory of his own mind at Paris in the library, where there was "in my mind's darkness a sloth of the underworld, reluctant, shy of brightness, shifting her dragon scaly folds"; and "Through the dear might of him that walked the waves" is parallel to: "Here also over these craven hearts his shadow lies and on the scoffer's heart and on mine. It lies upon their eager faces who offered him a coin of the tribute. To Caesar what is Caesar's, to God what is God's. A long look from dark eyes, a riddling sentence to be woven and woven on the church's looms." Then, closing the class, he puts his thoughts together with the riddle about the fox burying his grandmother under a holly bush and keeps that mystery in mind while he is standing over poor Cyril Sargeant the weakling who had been kept alive against all reason by "the only true thing in life"—the love of his mother, *amor matris.* Inserted in his feelings about the boy are two sentences of different rhythm: "His mother's prostrate body the fiery Columbanus in holy zeal bestrode" which combines Stephen and his own mother and reference to St. Columbanus who started the struggle in the sixth century of Celtic Christianity to win northern Europe from mother Rome; and, the second sentence, about the riddle: "A poor soul gone to heaven: and on a heath beneath winking stars a fox, red reek of rapine in his fur, with merciless bright eyes scraped in the earth, listened, scraped up the earth, listened, scraped and scraped." Then, a little further down the page, Cyril's algebra reminds him of Averroes and Moses Maimonides: "dark men in mien and movement, flashing in their mocking mirrors the obscure soul of the world, a darkness shining in brightness which brightness could not comprehend." There he reverses John i: "And the light shineth in darkness; and the darkness comprehended it not"; but whether to mock or to affirm or as a free movement of the mind is not certain. Then, looking down at the boy, Stephen comes his nearest to accepting the conditions of life, and does so with a tenderness which transcends all his intransigence:

> Like him was I, these sloping shoulders, this gracelessness. My childhood bends beside me. Too far for me to lay a hand there once or lightly. Mine is far and his secret as our eyes. Secrets, silent, stony sit in the dark palaces of both our hearts: secrets weary of their tyranny: tyrants waiting to be dethroned.

But these reflections and their induced images were also for Stephen—and apparently for Joyce—a reflection of the course or cycle of history, the succession of the Lion and the Fox; and with this double force in his mind he goes in to collect his pay from Mr. Deasy. This Nestor is a man of good sense and dangerous platitudes, of another persuasion to Stephen, requiring different scapegoats. He has conventional prejudices and good will and public spirit; he keeps the world going; he is the brightness of money which cannot comprehend the darkness which shines. He is one of the conditions of life which must be accepted, but which Stephen cannot accept. He has pictures of winning horses on his walls; he has a tray of Stuart coins, which are apostles preaching to the Gentiles world without end; he has a stone mortar full of shells, including a scallop which is the pilgrim's shell, for a museum; and for use he has a savings box for small coins. He speaks of Iago's advice to put money in the purse; of England's creed: I paid my way, I owe nothing; of the Jewish merchants as the death of England, and of the Jews in general as having sinned against the light; of the hoof and mouth disease; of woman who brought sin and downfall to the world of man. These are his platitudes and these the dangers he threatens.

To him Stephen answers aloud: I fear these big words which make us so unhappy; Who has not sinned against the light? A merchant is one who buys cheap and sells dear, Jew or Gentile, is he not? History is a nightmare from which I am trying to awake. God is a shout in the street. But he agrees to get a letter about the hoof-and-mouth disease into the papers.

So much aloud. To himself says that he can break the bond of bargain and money; considers that it was, not the Jews, but the harlot's cry from street to street that ruined England; sees images of the gold-skinned men on the Paris Bourse with their unoffending gestures; asks, what if the nightmare of history should give him a back kick? and remarks that Mulligan will call him a new name, the bullockbefriending bard.

Thus Maimonides and Averroes have their successors. The "Jew" has been raised by Haines, Deasy (both, for Stephen, aliens themselves), and by Stephen himself; if it is not yet an epiphany, it is a preparation and a prophecy. Mr. Deasy is money and sunlight and humor; he has "always struggled for the right"; and at the last we see of him, after explaining that the Irish have never persecuted the Jews because they never let them in, "On his wise shoulders through the checkerwork of leaves the sun flung spangles, dancing coins." It is because of such men that the Jew becomes everywhere Everyman the outsider, and in each of us, in the exiled part, sits a Jew: the darkness which the brightness does not comprehend: the emphatic problem of what has happened to Christianity.

In the third chapter, Stephen's last to himself but one, he makes morose delectations along the sea's edge, trampling wild sea-money under his feet, and lets all things change in his imagination by the protean will of the sea until all reach death in the sea, with the sea not the mother but the vampire. It is the self struggling with the self to find out the self devours the self through each form that it takes. In the midst of these metamorphoses lie images and identifications with Jonathan Swift and Joachim Abbas. Swift is seen as himself a Houyhnhnm, his mane foaming in the moon; then, remembering Dryden's letter to Swift: Cousin, you will never be a poet, Stephen addresses himself: Cousin Stephen, you will never be a saint—not even on this Isle of saints. Joachim Abbas, a prototype of St Francis, was the polar opposite of Swift, and had been read by Stephen in the library of Swift's cathedral. His "fading prophecies," as Stephen calls them, had as their focus the prophecy of a Third Testament, coming in the sequence of the Trinity, which should be the testament of the Church Spiritual. Stephen joins Joachim and Swift together. "Abbas father, furious dean, what offence laid fire to their brains?" Then he joins himself to them: *"Descende, calve, ut ne nimium decalveris* [translated later by Stephen as: "Down, baldynoddle, or we'll wool your wool"]. A garland of grey hair on his comminated head see him me clambering down to the foot pace (*descende*), clutching a monstrance, basiliskeyed." This is his history, the rôle he cannot play, the epiphany he cannot make. That is why, later in the day, finding at a bookstall a charm to win a woman's love by the most blessed abbot Peter Salanka, he finds it as good as "mumbling Joachim's." Nevertheless he hides the book when his sister Dilly comes up behind him. The seriousness of his unbelief rests on a desperate hope. It is what makes him a "person" as well as "an impossible person." And his hope is to make an epiphany of the darkness shining in brightness: which would indeed be a third testament, and a remaking of the Christian world.

It is that darkness, exactly, which shines in Bloom. Bloom is that darkness projected—in Stephen's scholastic language, godpossibled as actual; and he has in him all the momentum of that darkness which Stephen could only invoke: Bloom is the wanderer, the movement and enterprise in man, the only thing immortal in society which persists from form to form. He is Everyman in exile, the exile in every man. A transigent man, easy, warm, thinking, he makes up in little acts of imagination for frustrations not of his making. What in Stephen were morose delectations, in Bloom are transcendent escapes. He is Virag—Bloom—a Flower—a thing of weather, and actually assents to the conditions of life. He does not sell his soul, but his soul is what Stephen conceived the soul to be, the form of forms. Where Stephen goes East to the Fathers of the Church, the heresiarchs, Eve, and Buddha in terms of Spain, Averroes, Moses Maimonides coming out to the sea which is both all-mothering and old Father Ocean, Bloom goes East for warmth and oranges and ease in terms of Spain, Moorish eyes, and Moses Montefiore coming out on the dead sea that could bear no more. Bloom is the Jew: "Grey horror seared his flesh. . . . Cold oils slid along his veins, chilling his blood: age crusting him with a salt cloak"; and he shows, in Yeats' line, all "the changing sorrows of his pilgrim face." He passes through many image-experiences cognate or parallel to those of Stephen but at a less intense level (not, however, less deep) and very much less rebelliously. Bloom accepts the world and keeps his soul. He does not wish to remake or destroy the world, only to take better advantage of it; and he regrets some of the points where he had been frustrated without at all feeling the likelihood that he could ever be wholly frustrated. He is not annoyed to find his thoughts straying to small pleasures; he is rather delighted that the pleasures should be there. Thus, too, he is anxious to understand how things move, where they go, and how people accommodate themselves to things by means of ideas. When he goes into church during service, the versions he gives of IHS and INRI (I have sinned or suffered; Iron nails ran in) are, to him, mediums not of belittlement but of accommodation. Yet there is more truth in him than that: as the things turn to symbols they become larger themselves, the flower becomes flowers, the service is indeed the Eucharist, and the bath he projects is indeed creativeness. If the technique of the chapter in which these images occur is correctly called narcissism, then narcissism is another name for one aspect of fundamental human momentum. Bloom is indeed bloom: he is the exemplar of Stephen's best phrases to Deasy—about the distrust of big words, the nightmare of history, the shout in the street. His soul walks with him, form of forms.

But he has his characteristic burdens; and in the Hades chapter we learn what burdens lie on his back, what creatures leap on him in the dark of noon, the elements of death or devastation others build for him. We learn what both humility and humiliation mean to him. For this is the chapter of the divination of the dead, both those before us and those not yet, in both love and anguish, in nature and dread. Bloom is to all the mourners not one of them, but an outsider; the livest man there, he is identified by accident with the man in the brown macintosh, the incubus of death; he is the Jew, with no son, and with a father who killed himself: the man to be used, and blamed, on whom, because of his inner universal kinship (what makes him alien), must be forced the rôle of butt and scapegoat. Even the dead die out, says Bloom to himself, and the rat eats all. Yet it is Bloom's kneecaps that hurt him from kneeling; it is he the outsider that brings honor and dignity to this human death, and not the faithful who have brought only their shivering selves. It is only the outsider who can see how the actual still lies between the idea and the reality.

Having run over lightly the two batches of three chapters each which introduce Stephen and Bloom, let us sample the chapter in the newspaper office where the two converge, but pass each other, unknowing. This is a chapter of the fresh start. Bloom is at his business. Stephen is about to be at his business. Aeolus' anger is vented on Bloom as Odysseus the Jew; it reduces to irascibility of the "kindly" or amusing sort when it billows over Stephen. Yet Stephen—trying to be more of a man than he is—is more disappointed than Bloom who is content to be taken for less of a man than *he* is. No doubt Bloom gets the blurb to go along with the ad, which is his object in the story. No doubt, too, Stephen plays his hereditary part of wit and card well enough to confirm the position entailed; but Stephen feels a little that he is cheating. It is not his real part, and he has to be a hypocrite to himself to play it at all. Hence he overtells his fantasy of the two biddies, the plums, and the one-handled adulterer; and, telling, gives a loud laugh. It is in this sense that the chapter is enthymemic (Joyce's term for its technique): there is a suppressed premise to the syllogism for both Bloom and Stephen. Each has something on his mind that cannot be shown. Each is putting up an argument on an argument concealed. Thus everything in the chapter gives voice rhetorically—for persuasion and effect and high jinks; for oratory—where truth is assumed, unknown, or hidden, never said, except unawares, no-man to no-ears. Because the wind blows where it will (winds of doctrine, too) and is gusty and in its pressure disproportionate to the purposes and needs of those blown, both our heroes are victims of "undeserved" frustrations. There is a kind of aching doldrums air of the Pisgah sight of Palestine (an image either a joke or a symbol as you will), not only for the two old biddies but for Stephen who is telling their story. As for Bloom, he does not now complete the business of his ad, collect the debt owed him by Lenehan, nor meet Stephen (that old artist Bloom's less than conscious wish), though in time he may come to do so. So, too, Stephen makes less than his intended effect. Nobody says all he means or means all he says; yet everybody—and everything—gives voice; and all the ruses of persuasion—all the substitutes for expression—are resorted to. Glibness is to cover the thing not said; more is recognized than can be affirmed; Dante and Augustine are cited but not spoken. What a beautiful picture, aside from the novel about Stephen and Bloom, of the beginnings of the Christian breakdown.

The novelistic purposes of the chapter are different but related; they have to do with seeing what Stephen and Bloom are like when the wind ruffles them. Stephen winces, bridles, blushes, and is wooed. Bloom is perturbed but goes on his way; for Bloom underlies all this and is the thing expressed—just as Stephen, when he becomes truly articulate in his own pride of rhetoric (in Circe), will transcend and transgress the thing in the effort to express it. Stephen has somehow to become Bloom, or see the need of it; but Bloom has no need to become anybody, not though the world fall on him. It is Bloom who is Odysseus the everlasting hero of the quotidian: truly protean. Stephen, as his name suggests, can only make a martyr of himself without glorifying his cause: unless he can show, and it is his curse that he cannot show, the darkness shining in the light which the light cannot comprehend.

It is at this point, it seems to me, that we ought to see how the true polarity in *Ulysses* is in Joyce himself. Bloom is exactly as autobiographical as Stephen, and the place to see the equivalence between them is in the last three chapters of the book, Eumaeus, Ithaca, and Penelope, which we may think of as two postscripts followed by an underthought. In the first of these chapters everybody is worn out. Effort is only possible on the basis of repetition at the level of cliché: of idiom once fresh. The metamorphoses of Circe have come to an end with the identification of Stephen as Christ, *secundum carnem,* according to the flesh. There is death-distance—abstraction—between, say, Bloom and Blazes Boylan. Stephen and Bloom are on common ground, but talk at cross-purposes, which Gilbert suggested was perhaps "the secret of true atonement." In the second chapter we have the complement to the cliché, what we like to believe to be the inevitable or mathematic forms of the analytic and statistical intellect. But there is present neither catechist nor catechumen. Bloom and Stephen are there and are accidental objects of the *form* of catechism. Here, in the two chapters, is the futility after action: futility nailed down by our regular tools of cliché and intellect. How else do we put Circe and the Sirens out of sight?

But there is a difference of position between them. Stephen belongs to the formalism that destroys; Bloom retires to the formalism that gets us across gaps. Stephen is *non serviam,* Bloom *secundum carnem.* Stephen is the detestable blasphemy the world creates, always inadequate to his own intent. Bloom is the repository and resource that makes creation possible. With neither intellect nor passion, but "a little good will all round," he is the object of their concern. He is the thing blasphemed; he is what happens to intellect and passion. As Odysseus passed through his whole journey essentially untouched, but yet took into him the charge of his every experience, so Bloom "feels" or "is" everything at his own level without any loss or deformation or denial of sensibility. He is the man infatuated with life; hence he needs a son, who must be, not Stephen who is only the sought son, but himself the child in womb, Darkinbad the Brightdaylor.

These two postscriptive chapters send us back into the body of the book which they formalize in cliché and catechism, the exhausting material out of which inexhaustible symbol can be made. Of this the proof is Penelope, which is not a postscript or appendix, but the symbolic declaration of all that has gone before so far as it can be resumed by Molly Bloom. She it is who waited, and she who was waited for, a kind of underthought or other thought underlying even Bloom. She comes after the theological inquisition, after the summa, all fire inside, an act of grace. Molly is necessary to any culture but not as its foundation; she is rather the basic building material: the problem that first *and* last must be controlled.

Here Joyce lays out the material. Molly sees, excuses, cultivates herself to herself. She casts neither light nor darkness: she is the self before it understands itself. She is a mixture, not of intellect and will, but of cunning and good will. She echoes thoughts and is her self: is willfully (like the pure idiot) herself. She does not mistake aspiration, she ignores it: she is desire. Hence she pleads her youth is perennial, and hence she anticipates a future infatuation as again giving her something to think about all day. In her cunning she suspects Bloom of whoring; in her good will (reversed, and rightly) she realizes Bloom has sent Milly into the country so as not to expose her to the Boylan contamination. Being ignorant of aspiration, she misunderstands Bloom as "cold" where he is frustrated. She is one of those who accept themselves first, and to that extent accepts others. Bloom is the opposite: he accepts others and then himself. Thus Bloom sees Molly humiliating him and is not touched, and Molly sees herself humiliating Bloom as a necessary occupation. Bloom clings to Molly in admiration of her powers and in service; Molly clings to Bloom because he has been these sixteen years in her posesssion as an acquired part of herself. Bloom, seen in her context, is the man loving the world he assents to. Molly is of the unloving underworld: the *demimonde sensuel.* She is ploughed, penetrated, seeded like the earth in spring and heaves Yes to what happens to herself, Yes to variation and repetition, gestation and parturition. Yes Yes, Yes to Yes. She bears: Bloom is being born. She is the object of rites, the answerer. He is the maker of rites, the questioner. Her many lovers bring her nothing; who knows what they take away?—Nothing, so long as the procession does not stop. She is there to be embraced and adorned, but always (her cult deceives her) newly. Thus she believes that Bloom is responsible for her adulteries. But it is her fertility, her earthly incontinence, which leads her on to enact the experience of which Bloom had been the instigating type. So, in her monologue, she judges, *is herself,* the periodicity to which all the phantoms of love and intellect are condemned. She is the "coarsened" or verbalized mystery to which men return as they came from it.

If these notes suggest a single picture, surely it is the picture of Joyce, working out the polarities of his nature in terms of the breakdown of the Christian world as he actually experienced it in his youth. What survives even the blasphemy of thwarted faith is the double figure of Stephen the inalienable individual and Bloom the inalienable Jew; survives, for Joyce, with so acute a sense of loss and inadequacy, that he had to turn to Molly—the mystery itself coarsened but still lyric—in the end. The actuality was all that the honesty of the artist could give. It is up to the "other" imaginations—not the artistic, not the critical—to redeem that faith; to resume it, rather, on some new impulse of the old energy, with the realization that what was called the Church, like what was called the Crown, were temporary and temporal, were almost merely expedient, forms of the energy of man itself.

But if contemporary readers can no longer see the Christian-Greek picture—if there is no access or turning to it, or none except as ancestral utopia; then there is all the more reason why we should educate ourselves to assume such a picture for Joyce at the conceptual level, assume it for our own reading at the aesthetic level, and, most important, assume at the actual level whatever it is that corresponds to it in the experience of Stephen and Bloom and Molly and whomever, and so passing through the actual experience come on the impulses, the forward stress or trope as Santayana would call it, with enough faith for feeling and enough mind for thought. It is by the deliberate cultivation of such assumptions that we can find a means of crossing the gap between the actual society in which we live and the ideals—the dogmas of vital purpose—to which the expressions of that actual society formerly bore direct relation.

What we come on will be what for us is living in the tradition; which, as it once created the symbols which became the Christian world, will no doubt create the symbols which will become whatever it is that will follow Christianity. Many of the symbols will be the same, though they may seem to have opposed forms, or seem formless and only the story of the experience itself, as there was once only the story of Christ's life. Such a possibility seems to have been a part of Bloom's actual experience during his day in Dublin (as it was the experience most impossible for Stephen); the experience is actual both as he is aware of it himself, and in the projections of Joyce's own nature which did not so much enter into Bloom as surround him in penumbra. Bloom the Jew is the most living part of the Christian world, and he is therefore the inalienable problem of what has happened to Christianity. The Jew is in search of a son. Thus the quotation from the book of Malachi which was the impetus of this essay seems even more fitting at its close.

"Behold, I will send you Elijah the prophet before the coming of the great and dreadful day of the Lord; and he shall turn the heart of the fathers to the children, and the heart of the children to their fathers, lest I come and smite the earth with a curse."

Beauty Out of Place: Flaubert's MADAME BOVARY

Whatever *Madame Bovary* may be in the history of the development of the European Novel, or of French sensibility, or of Flaubert's genius, it has as the author says in his dedication "an unexpected authority" of its own. Into that authority, not so much unexpected as beyond expectations, these remarks propose to enquire. It is a novel which is the shape of a life which is the shape of a woman which is the shape of a desire. It is one of those structures of the imagination where we can count on sexual force to fill up all the hollow places, and it is such a structure seen in one of those situations where we may expect the force to be taken as a sentiment and where, at critical junctures, the sentiment will be taken for a force. Somewhere among these shapes, structures, and situations the theme finds itself. Everything goes towards the theme, and "all" the theme does is to pull everything together. It is that pulling together which is the theme. Depending on whether we think of the book as an object in art or of the uses to which we put the book we include the theme by calling it Emma Bovary or Bovarysme. It is either the history of Emma so reaching for a passion that the act of reaching was itself a passion; or it is the moving, receptive symbol of the tendency, the need, the drive in each of us so to overreach ourselves that we hang on for dear life—so to speak in order to live at all—to the image of what is other than we are. The passion of the reach becomes the compassion of the symbol. To put it again, it is the history of one of the great ways by which we accommodate our inner or our true selves to the bruise and press of society. It is nothing so simple as escape. It is something Dmitri Karamazov had in mind when he said that the immense mass of mankind could find beauty only in Sodom. It is also the history of that kind of damnation which comes when we are unable to accept the conditions of life; a damnation in which the indifferent rejoice; but a damnation which to those conscious of the beauty that is actually being damned becomes tragedy: the tragedy of long perspective.

The imagination which Flaubert *could not help* bringing to his history (the very perspective of his personal vision) is what transforms the mere beauty and the mere human damnation into tragedy. Perhaps the sentiment of some such power in Flaubert was what made Henry James record of him in an early notebook that he was "tender, manly, deeply corrupted, but uncorrupting." This is a way of getting at the objective imagination—what Flaubert is generally assumed to have had. When it *is* imagination, there is nothing so personal, nothing so capable of receiving the personal, as objective expression. Being objective it is created, it comes into existence. Its very objectiveness both keeps out some of the illusions that go with our predilections of personality and liberates into our expression a great deal of our actual experience for which our predilections had no form. It liberates images: all the things that being their own meaning gather meaning unto themselves. Who can tell what an image will be up to next? Who can tell what will happen, once an image gets going under the level at which we have convictions and careers yet illuminating both, telling us what convictions are made of and what careers come up against? Here piety comes in through the window-breaking glass.

This is the process of the objective imagination, so-called. It comes into existence and drags being after it; as to our vision the sun does when we watch its light. In *Madame Bovary* we see the process as we observe the changes from malice, contempt, obduracy of perception in the early frames of the book to the later frames for passion, assent, and the dramatization of perception. We see the story instigated, see it get under way, then see it take over: with all Flaubert's predilections and predeterminations gone by the board. If what you call your convictions are tied to your predilections, you had better not risk the mode of the objective imagination; you will either be dishonest or transform your convictions (or transvalue them) unless you lose them altogether. And this will happen whether you think so or not. Your images will get ahead of your intentions. As you did not know what they were till you found them, so you cannot know what they will do to what you did know; nor can you know—or complain of—what others will find in them or bring to them. All this is why the objective mode tends to the dramatic.

Drama is the normal medium for the objective mode. Not every age dares have drama. Yet nothing man makes lives so long; even the oldest drama demands of us our freshest life. In the nineteenth century the novel of Flaubert, Dostoevsky, and Tolstoi took on the risk of drama and was forced into objective imagination. Each of them created differently from his predilections, his received convictions; each undermined his own edifice; each fell on his own reality. Flaubert no less than the others, for in his novels like theirs, the things he wished to repudiate or transform persisted and surpassed themselves. Indeed, in Flaubert's case it is precisely what he wished to anathematize, to exorcize, that became dominant in Emma: she gave it reality and anguish; it gave her what life she felt she had; and it destroyed her in as real and consuming a death as art comes to. I mean *The Temptation of St. Anthony* and *Salammbo,* all that Flaubert tried to force out of himself when he wrote his images of Emma. I mean romanticism, the nostalgia for the unknown, and the identification of these with the illicit: the desire for the illicit as the available equivalent for salvation. It is these which are made actual in the novel, and it is their actuality which gives it "unexpected authority."

This is one way to explain the authority of the novel—and of other arts: it drags up the illicit as the very birthright of the law. The more lawful the society, as we say the more *bourgeois* the society, the more universal is the temptation to the illicit *per se,* and the stronger the impulse to identify it if not with life itself at least with the beauty of life. This is Dmitri's Sodom. Neither the rhetorician nor the sentimentalist see this; as Yeats says, the one would deceive his neighbor, the other would deceive himself, that the temptation to the illicit is some sort of slip, or backsliding, or excess; the artist sees the vision of reality.

There is of course a nonsense in all this view of the novel. The man is never all artist, the artist all art, or the art—whatever the art—anywhere near all expressed in its own terms. Further, even at the time of composition, the artist is neither possessed of enough tools, nor is the audience possessed of those the artist does have. There must always be a great deal imputed by the artist and a great deal taken for granted by both artist and audience. Most conventions in art must be *presumed* to work; only a limited number can be actually attended to. All we have safely, in the novel, are point of view, accent, emphasis, level, pitch; plus all the invoked powers and skills that have to do with telling a story, arranging plot, the use of images and symbols, and what happens to all these when used dramatically; plus, finally, all the accumulated reality, both live and dead, in language and the habits of language. It is with all this in mind, the skills known and the skills taken for granted, that we struggle to get at the life in a novel and what happens to it there.

With this in mind we can say that art shows the human cost of society or if we want to be arrogant about it we can say that art shows the criminality of society from the point of view of every individual within it. It was for this reason that *Madame Bovary* was condemned by the state. The state is never in a position to understand anything of itself but its own precariousness, and is set free by the individuals within the state who see through it, not with it: those who wish, like the novel, to conceive the crime of the state not merely as damnable but as tragic: a tragedy theoretically afflicting ourselves.

It is "ourselves" who surround the book like the arms of a parenthesis. When we understand that, we understand who the "we" is in the first sentence. "We were in class when the headmaster came in, followed by a 'new fellow,' not wearing the school uniform, and a school servant carrying a large desk." The French is better and the differences begin our criticism in clarity. "Nous étions à l'étude quand le Proviseur entra, suivi d'un *nouveau* habillé en bourgeois."

It is we who feel the rhythm, at its inception, and who are ourselves afterwards the vehicle of the rhythm—in whom it happens; whom it modifies—and we remain so till the last sentences of the book, where there is a return, not to *nous,* or *on,* but to a perpetual third person (what happens to "we") in the continuing or historical present: Il vient de recevoir la croix d'honneur. The *new one all bourgeois*—le nouveau habillé en bourgeois—has come and gone, a victim of all that is in authority, harassed and demolished by public opinion, while Homais, without right but by conformity, has a terrific practice:—un clientèle d'enfer; l'autorité le ménage et l'opinion publique le protège. Il vient de recevoir la croix d'honneur.

And what is in this rhythm that we feel? Bovary is the permanent *nouveau* at the lowest level in which action can take place or upon whom action can be directed; he is man as no-man; he is the gibberish of his own name: *Charbovari.* Look at what happens when he says his name. His fate is announced, and the conditions of his fate.

> A hubbub broke out, rose in crescendo with bursts of shrill voices (they yelled, barked, stamped, repeated 'Charbovari! Charbovari!') then died away into single notes, growing quieter only with great difficulty, and now and then suddenly recommencing along the line

of a form whence rose here and there, like a damp cracker going off, a stifled bomb.

Immediately there is the aborted interposition of the God—the *Quos Ego*—and the *nouveau* habillé en bourgeois is required to conjugate *ridiculus sum* twenty times. The pity and the fear are in the rhetoric, the epithets, the images. His cap has a "dumb ugliness [which] has depths of expression, like an imbecile's face." It is a cap, it is Charles; it is also the book so far as it represents Flaubert's intention to record what he would repudiate. But it is not only the cap. Old Madame Bovary bored her husband "with a thousand servilities." Again young Charles does his work like a mill horse, eyes bandaged, round and round. He is bought a practice and procured a wife, aged forty-five, dry as a bone, with as many pimples as the spring has buds, who asks of him "a dose of medicine and a little more love—quelque sirop pour sa santé et un peu plus d'amour." Whatever he is Charles gains nothing from natural advantages: it will all be fundamental; as in the depths—*profondeurs*—of an imbecile.

This is Charles Bovary in theoretical form, already all before us, together with his circumstance and his relations to society, and crushed in advance with an ambiguous judgment, sketched in a few pages. We see in it ahead of time his absolute fidelity to Emma. In his small way he is capable of heroism on her behalf, not by any possible admission of hers, but in relation to her, and also in *fact*. It will be the major fact of his life that within himself he will be heroic in his relations to Emma. His heroism is classic: he suffers both unmerited misfortunes and those which are like to happen to ourselves. It is the heroism of the dumb upon which the heroism of the rash depends. Charles, Charbovari, the *nouveau,* is the centre of heroic possibility within the law upon which the illicit, the anarchic heroism of Emma draws strength. *Ridiculus sum* will indeed be copied twenty times; and her brown eyes, her eyes *bleus foncés,* her ever-changing eyes, will regard it as the ordinary thing. It is always those who break the law that regard the law, and the adherence to it, as the ordinary thing: both to be taken in stride and as ultimately reliable.

This is Flaubert's *caractère* of Charles; done with verve as well as malice, there is gusto in the expression. This unpromising young man is rendered as if in hexameters; except for the hexameters he is blank. It is the character of a butt, an unconscious fraud, one of those substitutes for the real thing, a functionary seen from the outside about whom anecdotes are told but who are seldom supposed to feel what happens to them. In private life such people are assumed to be drags, hindrances, foils, to the feelings of others. We deal with them with verbal malice in order to separate them from ourselves. They exist to support our hidden cruelty; and we are always inventing them as Flaubert made a *caractère* out of Charles. There is a sense in which the whole novel is the imposition of *caractère* upon the drama. This was how Flaubert protected himself from his own romanticism, or if not that was how he controlled his romanticism. As for the whole novel, so for Charles. With regard to him the drama is chiefly anecdotal—select, focal, and characteristic. That may be why we tend to take Charles less seriously than we do Emma; his hypocrisy even, we are told, is naive; his possibilities are pursued only to attach him to Emma.

It is Emma who is allowed to dramatize herself: in the terrible bitter seriousness of the dinner table of her first loss of illusion; in the sweet sweep and growth and action of her beauty; in the extraordinary apparitions of her body in relation to light, whether sunlight through a window or sitting in boredom reddening the tongs before the fire, or in the dining room at the inn at Yonville, or, again, in the uniting of her body with her surroundings (also at Yonville) where her new house greets her—"the cold of the plaster fell about her shoulders like damp linen." It could have been Charles of whom this last perception was made. Here he was in a new town, again the nouveau habillé en bourgeois and again Charbovari and no-man. But it is not Charles, it is Emma, and we know in this trope what she does not know except in her potency: in the menace her warmth is in itself. We know, as she knows, that it is the inauguration of a new phase in her life, this fourth time she had slept in a strange place. We know that she is wrong in reflecting that "since the portion of her life lived had been bad, no doubt that which remained to be lived would be better." Our different knowledge is with us because of Charles and his *caractère*.

Emma's body sweeps us through Charles right into her arms, where we, unlike him, are put into the position to see what is going on in her heart. But it is through Charles. The aimless hope which replaces the aimless regret at his wife's death finds its target and redoubles itself, in the affair of the glass of curaçao which sealed him to her. They are alone in her father's kitchen on a hot afternoon. After discussion, she

> reached down two small glasses, filled one to the brim, poured scarcely anything into the other, and after having clinked glasses, carried hers to her mouth. As it was almost empty she bent back to drink, her head thrown back, her lips pouting, her neck on the strain. She laughed at getting none of it, while with the tip of her tongue passing between her small teeth she licked drop by drop the bottom of her glass.

Charles does not see all that we see: neither the beauty of the light in the kitchen nor the fatality of society gathering up its forces to marry off Emma and to repair Charles's widowerhood. Charles sees the tip of her tongue in the cordial glass, and for him that tongue is all he knows of the whole conspiracy of society with its grace and its brute force to maintain its institutions. The image is worth looking into; it is a vivid apprehension of the forces not its own which society uses and truncates; it symbolizes the cost of society to the individual; it confirms Charles's initiation into the mystery he began to seek at four in the morning on his first trip to Emma's father's farm when "the warm smell of poultices mingled in his brain with the fresh odor of dew—la verte odeur de la rosée." The image tells us that so long as society can count on the tongue in the glass—the force of sex—it cares nothing for any other considerations, or who wins what casual battle on the way. The tongue in the glass and the dark eyes, whether brown, black or blue, are always available; here they brought together and articulated in action social purposes. Charles wanted a wife to go on with, to take up the slack; he got also a new experience as if it were he and not Emma who had been virgin—for Emma showed no change. Emma had wanted a husband as a new beginning, as something additional, as a realization of the unknown. Charles got the experience; Emma got only the husband. It was no reason of *hers* by which she had married him. Charles was ready to chew his cud; she had not yet eaten, and by marriage her desires were more than ever unsatisfied. Her hunger showed the more clearly as she began to play fragmentary parts of the role of the body in society. What she wanted was to have come true in life the meanings of those revolutionary words, felicity, passion, rapture (*ivresse*) which had seemed so beautiful in books. Like Julien Sorel in *The Red and the Black* she took books seriously, but to help her to a career against society, not in it. Though both Julien and Emma were terrible idealists, Julien practiced hypocrisy and Emma submitted to an invasion of it.

The first part of the novel, at least after the marriage of Emma and Charles, is concerned to dramatize the admixture of illusion and hypocrisy to the pure aspirations of Emma in the sweeping beauty of her body. We see built—around the ball at Vaubyessard, Emma's one visit to the great world—a detailed local disillusionment accompanied by the growth of a dominant illusion. Gradually we acquire a working knowledge of what this does to Emma: her tantrums, contrarieties, torpors; her hysterias, drabnesses, and persisting beauties. We understand why it is that she says "I have read everything" and why she "sat there making the tongs red-hot, or looked at the rain falling." We also know the full sentiments that go with the bonfire of the wedding bouquet —the black butterflies up the chimney. We know it is not her fortune—good or bad—to invent resources but only the craving for them. We also see how the great illusion of life to come is part of her revolt against society, and how it shows as a force working outside herself. Her "vapors" persuade Charles to give up his successful practice at Tostes and go to Yonville, into the unknown—as if a new routine might provide Emma the force to work out her illusion into reality. It is only Emma who cannot know that it would have made no difference. She is a woman; she is a force of nature; she is never abstract—only abstracted;

she is the prodigal daughter. All she knows of herself is that she must have been someone else, some other place, some other time; but here, now, herself, just the same. This is what those of us without prodigality and beauty feel as ennui, and stay put.

The other thing to say is that in the first part of his novel Flaubert has surrounded a possibility (whatever Emma Bovary is; and we do not yet know) with anecdote, comment, scenes and images, and has submitted the whole to the temptations of languages and images. This is the animus of the *mot juste.*

II

In the second part of the novel the sequence begins to discover a direction, an infatuation of motion, which required the *mot juste* to keep it in order and give it critique. The direction is sometimes called Bovarysme. Webster says this means: domination by a romantic conception of the self, but this is an English or American sentimental version of what the word ought to define. Bovarysme is an habitual, an infatuated practice of regarding, not the self, but the world as other than it is; it is an attempt to find in the world what is not there. This is not an unworthy effort as is plain if we look not only at Emma but also at Charles. Charles's vision of the world and of Emma and his conduct toward both—his loyalty, trust, love, tenderness, industry—are all locked up in an attempt which is also a need for an infatuated version of what ought to be. His security in that vision depends on what is "lawful" turning out to be right and not only right but effective. Emma's security depends not on rebellion against the lawful, nor on denial of law, but on her capacity for taking advantage of the lawful at another level than Charles—precisely the level of the illicit—the wrongdoing which the law prescribes by definition. She creates herself in the very imperfections laid out by law and found in literature and art as images of passion and the infatuation of passion. Charles is nothing without the law, Emma nothing except outside the law.

Bovarysme has to do with what is not prudential and also with what ought to be prudential. In this book we have Lheureux the money lender taking advantage of the one, and Rodolphe the seducer taking advantage of the other. If either scoundrel had been lacking the other would have done little damage. Together, and in the presence of those who are not scoundrels but men of good will like Homais at his best, they bring her her tragedy. Between these scoundrels and good men society carries itself along; and both sets understand how much it is life itself that is contorted and expressed in Bovarysme. Bovarysme is *what* it is to be *habillé en bourgeois,* Charles low, Emma high. Here is Emma: it is just after she has been seduced by Rodolphe:

> Then she recalled the heroines of the books she had read, and the lyric legion of these adulterous women began to sing in her memory with the voice of sisters that charmed her. She became herself, as it were, an actual part of these imaginings, and realized the love-dream of her youth as she saw herself in this type of amorous women whom she had so envied. Besides, Emma felt a satisfaction of revenge. Had she not suffered enough? But now she triumphed, and the love so long pent up burst forth in full joyous bubblings. She tasted it without remorse, without anxiety, without trouble.

There is beauty in Emma, which suffuses this passage, and without which it would have no force, and this beauty is more important than the Bovarysme which is one aspect of its medium or than the *mot juste* which is another aspect. As we look back we see that this beauty was always there and that it has the force we like to find in beauty out of place—in the gift of nature not used and therefore craving abuse. It is half the obsessive drag of the beautiful woman as sex, half the formulary pattern of Cinderella: as if the gift of nature had in it inevitably the seed either of triumph or tragedy or oppression, or destruction by debauch—mire, mutilation, botch. Though we always expect the mire, no matter how deep it is we always see in it the lost triumph or the missed tragedy. That is why Emma gets mud on her shoes going to her assignation at La Hutchette; it is her aspiration that is soiled.

Emma shows her aspiration in her enthusiasm (her capacity to renew illusions), in her disillusionment (her refusal to accept her lot), and in her ennui (her writhing incapacity to sit still). But it is her beauty that aspires; and which, aspiring, fastens on unlucky objects for gratification. If she were not given, and shown, as beautiful, we would not give her credit except as a mere fact nor give the "illicit" credit except as sordid. Without her beauty we could not wish these things to happen to the selves we would create. Not goodness, not wisdom, not practical need—only beauty is a law to itself and turns the illicit into the "necessity that knows no law." At least we like to think so; it is a measure of our Bovarysme; it makes an idol of our merely imaginary nostalgia for the unknown; and it gives us means of believing that the universally available and stale illicit will be *this time* a fresh creation.

How does this come about, this fresh creation?—By the shake of the kaleidoscope, by looking at the stale fragments through or with the emphases of a change of scene; by the shift from Tostes, about which we never knew very much, to Yonville about which we at once learn a great deal and from the life pattern of which we are never for long separated. It is a new place which yet has been going for a long time—so long it is run down and the land is worn out. Emma is cut away from her past so that it can work on her like an outside force, and also so that *her* force can take a fresh start and go to work on others. It is a repetition, in a new form, of what happened to her at her father's farm when Charles arrived. There are new barriers to break down—those of a more complete, and more completely bourgeois society, the society in which she has a "place" through her husband and her child. The barriers are challenges and require responses earned by that whole past—real and dreamed—of which she is the ripe product. But some of the barriers are within herself, so that there is internal struggle; and some of the response is in the ambience of the book, in the extruded sensibility of the author ("Emma is myself"), and with this she cannot even struggle. Taken all together, then, Emma is not so much ripe to act as ripe to be plucked—of all those treasures which we see attached to her (though they are common treasures) because of her beauty, of figure and face and availability.

The little clerk Léon sees at once this availability; his puberty tells him; what he does not see is that it is available for him. He only perfects his assault on her virtue—her hypocrisy—without having overcome his own. He does not enjoy what actually he has won. Thus when he leaves for the great world, embraced by Homais, his hand shaken by Emma, he leaves with his image in Emma's imagination the nostalgia of the created unknown, the habitually cultivated day dream in which every kind of human energy enters the phase of ennui: when all our time is spent in *bearing* our burdens. Ennui is the ignoble form in which we exercise our instincts for martyrdom: in which we cannot sit still but are aimless in motion, looking for motive.

So looking, Emma has made the habits of her virtue an instrument of access to the illicit: she is already in Rodolphe's arms when she sees him in the dooryard. Rodolphe enjoys her without having to win her, and therefore without having to corrupt her or force her or trick her. Léon has done all his spade-work for him: all that reading and mooning, all that tacit intimacy, with none of those barriers of the actual which stop intimacy at the edge of understanding. Only the riding habit, the ride in the forest, and the *green pool* where they stopped, were necessary. Thus she got from Rodolphe only half of what he had to give, and thus she made a profound mistake as to his role. She got nothing of his corrupting power, which might have saved her, and she failed to see that in his eyes the most important thing about her was that she had and must continue to have a husband. Rodolphe played his hand with great skill and for nominal stakes. Emma played with only instinctive skill and for what seemed to her the highest possible stakes. I have a lover, says she to her mirror, seeing a new face there.

In the net we may say that Rodolphe got more than he bargained for, and that Emma got only a first chance to exercise her powers. It begins to be plain that it is her fate to overreach herself: that is what her beauty does to her. Each seeing this in a different way, each draws back, not in a mutual but in a separate action. He repels her seriousness: he is unwilling to assume the burden of love. She is tempted—by the resumption of her old life in a letter from her father and also by the rancorous dissatisfaction she feels in Rodolphe—to take up deliberately the martyrdom of wife and mother. But Rodolphe is not yet either bored with Emma or afraid of her. Emma can still vent herself upon or through him, and so far as husband and child go her virtue can now express itself only in the velleity of sacrifice. When beauty ventures into the illicit with the aid of mere corruption this is the sort of predicament to be expected. We feel a conventional sympathy for Rodolphe; we do not know yet what to feel, compassion or terror, for Emma.

We do not know because Flaubert has arranged it so. There is all that business of the "continual seduction," and there is all that other business of the highfaluting language—the ambience in which both Emma's direct sensibility and her romancings are made to glow. Again there is all the malicious characterization of person and place. And again there is the stroke of compassion in Emma's father's letter of general blessing on all the Bovaries dusted with ashes from the old hearth. Lastly, there is all the extraordinary visualized detail which stands for we do not know what unformulable identifications of Emma's body, in all its parts and movements, with the story.

And of the ambience, how much of it is black or dark or stormy, or how much towards evening, candle-light, lamplight. This darkness rises to use whenever Emma is alone, or struggling, or bored, and often when she is with Rodolphe. Consider her abortive struggle with the curé to realize her sinfulness, which is after the Angelus, in shadows, with one light, a night-light, shining in the church. After the curé, distracted in his own darkness, recognizes nothing, she strikes her child. These are the stresses, in and of the whole novel, which surround and inform with their gloomy uncertainty and threatening possibility the fate of Emma.

No doubt at any given point some other detail would have done as well, but not *after* the particular detail has been given. There is a disparity between the theme and the story, between the underblows and the plot, between both and Flaubert's own animus. The area governed by the stresses is so intensely agitated—enacted—that anything would have done for representation, and, once done, have seemed inevitable at that point. The inevitable grows through a series of choices, the field of choice narrows, there is a rising wind of momentum, and the story assumes relation to the theme beyond any possible original intention. Here we touch on the quick both of *Madame Bovary* and of Flaubert the author. There is something wayward and accidental as well as "inevitable" about all but the greatest masterpieces; for in all but the greatest the intellect of the author and also the created nature of the author are unequal to the themes the process of his work developed for him. So with Flaubert; he lacked conceptual honesty, of the matured or completed intellect; and he had instead to depend on the chaotic and contrived will of preserved adolescence. He had like Emma a succession of second puberties. He was one of those men capable of maturity only in terms of those institutions to which they profess adherence. His only institution was that of the novel; which was in his day and is no doubt in ours, an institution insufficient to act like maturity. But he therefore lets in a vast amount of actuality (for he is a very common type, and the type the literary artist often follows) without knowing it or exactly intending it. He had too little the false strength of impertinent convictions to keep his theme—the permanent adolescent; the prodigal daughter—from discovering itself and bringing judgment upon its own instance.

That is where we are now, almost exactly midpoint in the book. Flaubert has prepared his case, has delivered it. With the affair of the club-foot Madame Bovary takes over; hereafter the author is only one of the obstacles she has to overcome in running her course and finding her fate. Her own ambience is henceforth as good as anything Flaubert could provide. More important, it is stronger than anything Flaubert could bring against it. There is the cordial glass, there is the body by firelight, there are the scarves flicked by Lheureux on the table, and there is the blue veil tumbling over her, under her man's hat, tumbling over her *amazon,* in the twilight forest, in the fire of the horizontal sun.

III

It is indeed a case of second puberty, of preserved, of maintained adolescence—this ambience of Emma. There is much to be said for it; especially when we look at the hardening of surface—the capacity for mere polish—the gradual achievement of imperviousness—the induration of prejudice—the decay of the senses—which we are expected to regard as the visage of maturity, when it is only the visage of those who have a capacity for *dealing*. There is also *this* to be said: Emma remains accessible to experience, to invasion, destruction, hysteria, to desire; she has within her the extreme possibility for metamorphosis, an absolute change in her whole system of relations. As the moth has once in its lifetime a total metamorphosis, usually the last one, for the sole purpose of procreation, Emma has the chance of change for sex and death; she has in her an energy for change which presses till satisfied—but presses within the frame of a constructed society, and so has to deceive itself in order to survive, to transform its objects in order to act.

She has all the energy of beauty out of place with which to transform the illicit, the prodigal, the nostalgic from the low price, narrow motives, and contemptible manners in which she finds them: the maximum against which the adolescent can compete. Emma's energy is of the highest price: the high price of beauty out of place raised still higher by hysteria. Beauty out of place will always be marred; its efforts at self-assertion and self-protection must always be excessive, since it must create its object as well as its response to it, and when the object fails comes hysteria: the disease or disorder which is the convulsive effort of the womb that cannot create. Love must indeed in such persons be habit-hysteria; it cannot be anything else, since it persists in being, not a quality of experience, but experience itself.

That is why we think that it is to lovers above all that things happen; not that it is true, but that we know that to the heightened, crippled consciousness that goes with being in love experience is keener and makes a deeper mark; besides which there is the experience that hysteria adds.

Emma is one of these women to whom things happen; but she is also the normal woman, the bourgeois wife of the bourgeois functionary in the small town—like everybody she tends to sink into the pattern, the cycle; to be part of the social institution whose function it is to bridge or absorb happenings, suffering or enjoying them only at a low degree, *as a matter of course,* vicious or virtuous indiscriminately. All her energies, even her hysteria, are accidental elements of her Bovarysme: her life other than she is. She herself is a combination. Thinking of both we achieve the sense of her identity, her motive, her fate. It is the art of the novel to show this migration of being, and it is the special craft of Flaubert to reach a special sense of identity through the progressively intensive balance of the normal and of Bovarysme. Rodolphe, let us say, would have been meaningless without the clubfoot; Lheureaux would have been meaningless without Léon's return; there was no nostalgia without sordidness, no sordidness without hysteria. All are used to situate, to give extension to, Emma and our sense of what she is. Extension, in this sense, is only another word for verisimilitude; as intension is a name for what it is that seems true.

We get an excellent example of this at the beginning of the club-foot chapter where Homais, by propagating the operation, provides Emma with a chance to transform her velleity into a desire to sacrifice herself and her love affair for Charles and their daughter. Charles might become *successful,* even famous, if the operation on poor Hyppolyte should succeed, and all the more successful since it would involve her giving up Rodolphe if she were to enjoy the success. She has reached the point, says Flaubert, where she "wished to lean on something more solid than love." She distrusted the very hysteria she could not acknowledge. Emma's love was not enough because it was only her own, she could not forever create its object as well as its motive; and at its then stage of banality she could transform its insufficience in her wish for Charles's success, for a part in the going concern of society.

The operation was as a matter of course a failure: success was even less in Charles's line than in Emma's. It was Homais' idea, and he had chosen a poor instrument to work on an irrelevant object. Hyppolyte's club-foot was doing very well, had acquired by hard work "moral qualities of patience and energy." It—or he —was open only to selfish motives, motives of reform, motives of possibility. Of these the best were the selfish motives of Charles. Homais was the reformer. Emma saw the possibility of success for her own sake. When failure is total she rejects Charles completely; it is her life that is ruined, his ruin merely *fidgets* her. "She repented of her past virtue as of a crime, and what still remained of it crumbled away beneath the furious blows of her pride. She revelled in all the evil ironies of triumphant adultery." And her love for Rodolphe becomes at this time a convulsive creation of her hysteria, and at the same moment destroys in Rodolphe all that had been actual in his feeling for her. He is now the creation of her passion; she is now the creature of his lust. She involves herself to the limit; he extricates himself. She steals to buy him gifts and begins her social destruction. He coolly promotes the immediate possibilities. Meanwhile, like the chorus that knows the truth, little Justin attaches his adoration to her, admiring her underwear and cleaning the mud of her assignations from her boots: reading secretly of *Conjugal Love*.

Flaubert expresses the situation in two paragraphs, in the first of which he generalizes both Rodolphe and Emma, and in the second makes as near as possible a concrete image of Emma as a force in herself. He arrests the momentum in the book so that we may feel its pressing hand.

> Emma was like all his mistresses; and the charm of novelty, gradually falling away like a garment, laid bare the eternal monotony of passion, that has always the same forms and the same language. He did not distinguish, this man of so much experience, the difference of sentiment beneath the sameness of expression. Because lips libertine and venal had murmured such words to him, he believed but little in the candor of hers; exaggerated speeches hiding mediocre affections must be discounted; as if the fulness of the soul did not sometimes overflow in the emptiest of metaphors, since no one can ever give the exact measure of his needs, nor of his conceptions, nor of his sorrows; and since human speech is like a cracked tin kettle, on which we hammer out tunes to make bears dance when we long to move the stars.

The other paragraph comes at the moment when Emma believes, wrongly, that Rodolphe will elope with her:

> Never had Madame been so beautiful as at that period; she had that indefinable beauty that results from joy, from enthusiasm, from success, and that is only the harmony of temperament with circumstances. Her desires, her sorrows, her experience of pleasure, and her ever-young illusions, that had, as soil and rain and winds and the sun make flowers grow, gradually developed her, and she at length blossomed forth in all the plenitude of her nature. Her eyes seemed chiselled expressly for her long amorous looks in which her pupil disappeared, while a strong inspiration expanded her delicate nostrils and raised the fleshy corner of her lips, shaded in the light by a little black down. One would have thought that an artist expert in corruptions had arranged the curls upon her neck; they fell in a thick mass, negligently, and with the changing chances of adultery, that unbound them every day. Her voice now took more mellow inflections; her figure also; something subtle and penetrating escaped from the folds of her gown and from the line of her foot. Charles, as when they were first married, thought her delicious and irresistible.

Charles, not Rodolphe. This is the success of beauty out of place, and it is the triumphe of Bovarysme. Here we see how although the bears do dance, still the stars move. It is Emma's success that the world can take away, and her tragedy is that it cannot take away her beauty also. Her beauty is the name we give to what in Emma is deeply corrupted but what even in death is itself uncorrupting: it is the vital, rising, buoyant quality of her response to life.

When Rodolphe jilts her and runs off to fresh fields, Emma fails at suicide and ends her period of manic hysteria and lapses into what was called forty-three days of brain fever. There she cultivates a depressive hysteria, and among other things summons M. Bournisien to give her communion for the dying. The result was different from what convention requires, though Emma observed the convention externally with what looked like excessive piety. In the created reality, her "illusions ever-young" took another form, or entered another phase. She used religion (the occult force which works on us from outside) as she had used sex (the force, only secondarily occult, which works on us from within). She turned to religion as to another form of adultery, another form of the illicit: another means of creating a self other than the intolerable self of the "normal" world. She is reported by Flaubert with straight-forward irony as doing what is usually done with cant in religion or sentiment in sex: making escape from reality.

> When she knelt on her Gothic prie-Dieu, she addressed to the Lord the same suave words that she had murmured formerly to her lover in the outpouring of adultery. It was to make faith come; but no delights descended from the heavens, and she arose with tired limbs and with a vague feeling of a gigantic dupery.

But her corruption in religion is no more full than her corruption in sex. Her sincerity, her capacity for candor, is unimpaired. So far, her corruption is something that at most others put to corrupt use.

The reality of her corruption only begins when Charles takes her to hear Lagardy in *Lucia:* the reading of her youth in a new form. It is in the Opera—that remote-near conventional art in which no emotion is ever left frustrate but all are fulfilled in multiple forms—that she learns that high happiness "was a lie invented for the despair of all desire. She now knew the smallness of the passions art exaggerated." But she learns this in a way and with a result singularly her own: through the attractions of Lagardy's "admirable charlatan nature." It is Bovarysme in reverse: her momentary illumination into the illusion of desire somehow makes the contrary *choice* possible. Rejecting the singer-actor's part, she chooses the actor instead—chooses the charlatan role of being an actor. Surely he has incalculable love to spill. It might have been hers. It was the charlatan in her nature that made the choice. Hence she could turn from the thought of Lagardy instantly to the person of Léon when he appears holding out his hand like a gentleman. She sees at once that Léon is now capable of playing a part, and that to play a part is now the one thing left for herself. It is what is left for life. Where her great attractive force has been the candor in her that could be corrupted, it is now the image-idol she can raise out of herself that has itself the power to corrupt. But it is not a reversal of roles; she is not to play Rodolphe; it is rather an extension of her own role from the true to the corrupt. It is thus that we undress Emma Bovary, not with the anticipations of Rodolphe.

Consider in this light a sentence on Léon in Paris. "As for excesses, he had always abstained from them, as much because he lacked heart for them as refinement." This is the prod to action —to "ruin" or to tragedy, depending on what we know—which lies in the fear of not being excessive; for in excess we envisage the redemption or the grandeur of what is otherwise folly or vice. We are all, we think, capable of our own excesses. Léon is not one of us—he has only the resolution of the poltroon who stops at nothing; the resolution of those who are without courage. Emma has now to discover her courage.

IV

Léon among the grisettes did not lose all his desire for Emma: she remained his superior image. The capacity for creating reality is not infinite, and in Léon it is more limited than in Emma. He has *encore* the image of Emma, like a closet-ghost or a night-thought recurrent but not continuous in apparition. Thus her actual return to his life has a force beyond the immediate. So with Emma; she puts into Léon a degree of being which is not his but hers. She has therefore to force response to become attack, temptation to become corruption, suppleness to become agony, submission to become excruciation. Yet the vitality of her shamelessness is what remains in it of shame. Her behavior is excessive, hysterical, habitual. She has held nothing back except what she could not give: that irreducible part of herself which does the giving because it needs it to make life supportable. Emma cannot become libertine like Rodolphe precisely because she cannot deliberately hold anything back. Rodolphe pays his bills with money and boredom and pomade, using almost nothing of himself. Emma uses money and boredom and luxury but only that she pay more fully with herself. With her, the limit is the optimum. Léon can be for us nothing more than a receptacle into which Emma pours her created self. As Emma who thought to find herself in him discovers, as a reservoir he is nothing. He acts upon Emma less as an individual than as the focus in which her passion combats the forces of society and is beaten. He represents that compromiser who forces the candid to compromise against their vital will to the point where it cannot be redeemed —when it must needs both become corrupt and die.

Emma is one who cannot leave things alone, full of the creative spirit of adolescence. Lacking training she depends on instinct, which beyond a point always works badly because it must work in unfamiliar circumstances. Instinct never created either society or character. That is why she is done for. There is no possibility, after Léon, of a fresh start; it is her starting power that has been used up. It has been converted downwards—toward entropy—and has reached the phase of immediate unavailability. She has only ruses, not plans; convulsions, not motives. She is all haggard, all wild and waste, inside; if she lived, soon all hag.

Let us say that she is unwilling, in Baudelaire's phrase, to assent to the conditions of life and is therefore damned. Emma's aspirations, like her beauty, were out of place. As she sank down, when they failed her, damnation came up all round her. She is inside herself a haggard witch, and in these her last days the visage begins to emerge.

There is an image of this witch, in three parts, of which the first is the strongest—is almost a fresh start. It is when, about to be sold out and with the bailiff in the attic, she rushes to Rouen, first to brokers and lastly to Léon, to find money. Léon makes an hour's trial while she waits at the Hôtel de Boulogne; waits, and drinks water. Léon has no success. Emma suggests that he steal the money from his office. "And she looked at him," Flaubert continues. "An infernal boldness looked out from her burning eyes, and their lids drew close together with a lascivious and encouraging look, so that the young man felt himself growing weak beneath the mute will of this woman who was urging him to a crime. Then he was afraid, and to avoid any explanation, he smote his forehead, crying–" And he tells her some transparent lie.

We might hear, as an echo above this scene, Laforgue's lines: *Allez! Steriles ritournelles! La vie est vraie, et criminelle!* This hellish boldness which shows between narrowed lids–so that the eyes half lose their focus–as lascivious and inviting, as tempting the flesh and giving heart, would have come out into the open, a thing between and binding them, would have reached *éclaircissement,* a hellish *clair de lune,* if Léon had not put her off, not for the moment, but permanently, by the exorcism of his lie.

If we had been writing about Léon here we would have felt a great release of will, perhaps something amounting, within his capabilities, to a conversion of the upwards kind. But it is Emma we deal with: Emma trying, as she is faced now with the whole of her life, trying to convert the sum of its forces into the single force that is hers. She wants to make crime possible by making it sexual. She sees–she represents–the sexual nature of crime, by the simple act of personal identification. Léon feels the force; he knows that if he allowed her to bring it into full light he would have to accept the crime of theft as he had accepted the crime of adultery: as an angelic act, lascivious only because illicit. For Emma, they are already the same; her thefts have been only phases of her adulteries. When he rejects one he rejects the other; he rejects *her*. That is why, when he presses her hand in Adieu, it is lifeless. The angel is a witch. A witch shall not live, was a prudential law of Moses long before it became a sexual orgy for Christians. There are no such true partners in crime as in witchcraft.

The second part of the image of this witch turns up when Emma makes her last effort at a fresh start; harder for her than the attempt with Léon, and all the more hopeless; the effort to get money out of Rodolphe. "Emma went on with dainty little nods, more coaxing than an amorous cat." She tries to seduce him not for love but to adulterate her ruin. When she fails, she loses all her own force.

The third part of the image is when she seduces young Justin to let her into the glory-hole where the arsenic is kept—little Justin who has made of her, and of her service, a sweet fetish which he loves undividedly whether called on or not. Speaking first in "a low voice, a sweet, melting voice, 'I want it; give it to me,'" she then confronts this young boy with what is left of herself. She is quite beyond estimation of the evil of her act. Her total candor has been replaced—reversed—with a total *black* candor. She "seized the blue jar, tore out the cork, plunged in her hand and withdrawing it full of a white powder, she began eating it."

Emma dies forthwith. She does not make a death for herself; she has been doing that all along, and her energy is used up. Night was falling, crows were flying about. *"La nuit tombait, des corbeilles volaient."* It is left for Charles, who has the unbounded energy of his magnanimity, to make something as big as he can out of her death: as indeed, by being the clearest measure against which it has been seen, he had made something of her life: botching it because he had tried something beyond the means of his intelligence, like the club-foot: but disinterested, magnanimous, bearing all burdens—bearing most, and best, of all, the burden that she had been unable to bear his love—or anybody's love. Charles loved someone who would not accept him; to him the platitudes of marriage remained perpetually fresh statements. She loved her love, and found all reality either lies or platitude. He had not enough force to win reality; she had too much to accept what offered, too little to make it over. Charles was right in his last recorded speech—to Rodolphe, on the occasion when he understood what Emma had made of him—"It is the fault of fatality."

It is a defect in fortune, a weakness in chance, a sickness in circumstance: the tongue in the cordial glass, the prodigal who never went away, the beauty out of place; the compulsion of the illicit, the convulsion of hysteria, the haggard within. It is the momentum of all this that carries the corruption of Emma beyond the grave into Charles. He had to re-create society at the moment when he was removing himself from it. "He put cosmetics on his moustache, and, like her, signed notes of hand." He died with her saved hair in his hand; he was her meaning without her force. He was himself, dead in his arbor with the sun coming through the vine leaves, much as he had last seen her. "The watering on the satin gown shimmered white as moonlight. Emma was lost beneath it; and it seemed to him that, spreading beyond her own self, she blended confusedly with everything around her—the silence, the night, the passing wind, the damp odors rising from the ground." And at the end so Charles himself; much as he had been when we first saw him in the schoolroom with the cap, which he lost, "one of those poor things, in fine, whose dumb ugliness has depths of expression, like an imbecile's face." It is right that the life of Charles should enclose the life of Emma, and that it should be so recorded. He measures the fault of fatality.

We keep him in mind and must return to him, almost, but not quite at the end. At the very end it is Homais who receives the Legion of Honor, and among his services so rewarded was that he had got the blind beggar of Rouen put permanently out of sight, not long after the death of Emma to whose death he had sung. The beggar was first introduced, with his song of a young girl in love who loses her petticoat, as a monstrous image to crown Emma's honeymoon period with Léon. His empty eyesockets and song of love were to Emma a whirlwind in an abyss. Hivert, the driver of the coach to and from Rouen, feels his weight on behind and lashes him with his whip. The apparition is directly following the scene in which Emma seems to Léon an angel, and Léon to Emma a child. Consider his next apparition. It is when things are all up with Léon, she has just been nearly run down by that Vicomte whose image at the ball first set her dreams to attempt actuality. There at the coach—L'Hirondelle, The Swallow—is Homais with his bag of Gothic bread, and there also is the blind beggar. "I cannot understand why the authorities tolerate such culpable industries," says Homais, tells him to diet, invites him to Yonville for a poultice, gives him a sou, and asks change. Hivert tells him to sing, which he does. Emma throws him a five-franc note. "It was all her fortune. It seemed to her very fine thus to throw it away." Then, as Emma is in the midst of prayer and her own death-rattle, there is the beggar's voice outside, and this time we hear all his song. "The blind man" she cries, and they are her last words. "And Emma began to laugh, an atrocious, frantic, despairing laugh, thinking she saw the hideous face of the poor wretch that stood out against the eternal night like a menace."

The structure is too cunning, the apparitions too apt, for this image to have been presented out of hand. The beggar and Homais between them represent all that has not otherwise been presented of the fault of fatality, and they must be felt together to be felt justly. Homais is all "respectable" society means; the blind beggar is the outcast, the cost of respectable society; neither can exist without the other, as neither is *necessary* without the other. Emma—that beauty out of place—found the one a bore and the other a horror and made of herself a vain image of glory in between. There she found Rodolphe who made her his mistress out of habit, Léon whom she made her mistress out of hysteria, Lheureux, to whom hysteria opened the door, who used up all her little social good, and Charles whom she could not use at all except basely, and whose magnanimity was so intolerable that she killed herself rather than submit to it. She could not do what Eliot thought poetry must do: to see beneath both the ugly and the beautiful—to see the boredom, and the horror, and the glory.

But the book can so see, and does. It is in the images of moonlight and witchcraft. It is also in the apparition of the good man, Dr. Larivière. Maugham in his essay on *Madame Bovary* asks idly why there is one good man in the book. Is it not clear? It is the apparition of a god to whom all these things are acceptable, and against whose image all the story of Emma Bovary gathers meaning, implication, and horizon. It is out of such material—out of the story of such beauty out of place—out of such hysterias and abortions, otherwise construed, that men like Larivière, and also the vital sentiments we attach to them, are created. It is like the morning star Dr. Williams addresses in his poem: Shine alone in the sunrise, towards which you lend no part. Good Good, said the doctor, as he sees Emma is to die. Good Good. She shines alone.

The Lord of Small Counterpositions: Mann's THE MAGIC MOUNTAIN

Prophecy, like revolution, is a convulsive or expressive reaction to what has already taken place, whether in the heart, in the actual world, or in a confusion of both. The truth of prophecy is therefore a matter of feeling or inspiration. Prophets rage in religion and politics; in the arts, prophets dramatize the conditions, the feelings, which underlie the rage. The rage of the priest comes about because he has to look ahead to salvation, and that of the politician because he has to look ahead to action, and neither priest nor politician can confront the terrible cost of salvation and action without the protective aid and personal momentum of rage. It is exactly those who must deal directly with the actual world who cannot stand it plain; they have to rely more upon inspiration than upon feeling, or they could not play the prophet's role at all. As George Herbert's poem has Christ ask of Judas:

> Canst thou find hell about my lips? and misse
> Of life, just at the gates of life and blisse?

Christ was more than a prophet, though he began in prophecy. The artist is always less than a prophet, though one of the high values that may be placed upon his work is that of prophecy. He does not look ahead to salvation or action; rather he dramatizes what is saved or lost, what acts or fails to act. He looks at the actual world with only a secondary regard to the terrible cost it exacts in religion and politics. Since he is not compelled to deal directly with that world, he can afford a plain vision of it with only the protection of his form. He relies upon his feeling, and, rather than needing inspiration himself, inspires others. In that inspiration which he creates, not that to which he pretends, is his power of prophecy; he prophesies, by giving form to his feeling of it, what we actually are.

It may be of course that he pretends more. Of all forms of purity the least possible is that a man shall be purely an artist, and that is especially so in an age like our own when we make so much more use of our artists than in ages just past; when, in fact, we pretend that our chief access to reality is in the aesthetic experience of it: that is to say, in experience without responsibility. In such an age the temptation is great for the artist to pretend to the roles in which his audience casts him and to become the culture-hero to whom all things are possible. Perhaps temptation is the wrong word, it may be a contagious disease, of which the artist is only the alternate host, and for which he cannot be held responsible. At any rate, the masterpieces of our time gradually reveal themselves, by the uses to which we are forced to put them, as philosophies, religions, politics—and as the therapies and prophecies of these. This seems to have happened only partly in the sense that the arts have tried to take over the *functions* of these modes of the mind; it has happened much more in the sense that the *experience* of these modes of the mind has become the most pressing part of the subject-matter of the arts. It is not the artist's fault if his audience insists on confusing function and experience by the special arrogance of ignorance and the special vanity of uncommittedness in relation to existing society. The point is, our masterpieces are therapy and prophecy, though they cure nothing present and envisage nothing future. They see and state. And of course, with the formal advantages that go with the arts, they state better than they see.

These considerations ought to apply to almost any devoted reading that we do; it is almost an accident that they are meant here to apply to a re-reading of Thomas Mann's *The Magic Mountain*. It is less of an accident because these considerations have become natural *as a result of* the character of that book, together with its sequels. When first read, in the early twenties, one looked at it backwards through the war of 1914; now one looks at it through the second lens of the second war, and the double lens shows it in greater magnitude—so great, it looms the more the more it recedes. And this greater magnitude depends precisely upon that power of prophecy which comes to the artist who dramatises the actual thought—thought in all its senses—of his own time. It is this aspect of *The Magic Mountain* we here examine.

The artist of this kind shows us where we are ahead of ourselves; shows us with what in ourselves we have not yet consciously caught up; shows us, in short, as at the verge of a new shift, a new metamorphosis, of the old omniform which is our mind. It is ourselves—creatures, as we think, of the mid-twentieth century—whom we see in this legend of the *haut-bourgeois* at the climax of the nineteenth century; and we see all the clearer because the mechanisms and predilections are nineteenth-century, and we know how to discount them. It is not the nineteenth-century mind which Mann shows, but what had happened to it.

He shows it, of course, by a special twist; by the idiom of his sensibility; by establishing confines for his vision, outside which he will not look unless the pressure of his sensibility forces him to do so. It is the special twist body and soul take when they do not know where to lie. It is the idiom of an infected sensibility, with a polarity each extreme of which spreads like a stain into the other. The confines he sets for his vision are those of seemly obscurantism, which become, under pressure, the looming confines of the anonymous and the communal. This sequence is not a trick of the mind, it is a mode of operation common enough everywhere the bourgeois mind survives in its old honesty. It is a mind bent on protecting its certainty from its own restlessness and random anarchic promptings: hence the seemly obscurantism becomes unseemly, a demagogy of the soul addressing the soul, with a following tendency towards the intemperate, whether in discipline or the breach of discipline. But if the mind is honest in some dark corner it finds it cannot abide on its own practice; its obscurantism becomes indeed unseemly—the protection of something intolerably smothering; and the anonymous and communal, if the pressure of honesty is great enough, break through and set the mind again upon its task of making full assent to the conditions of life with will and choice, with reason and imagination. The story of Hans Castorp is told according to this sequence; but what happens to him is not that he takes up the mind's task, but that his example (the confines in which he is envisaged) shows us, the readers, that the task is there but cannot be taken up, at least not by the kind of man this young engineer stands for in any society he can comprehend. In the actuality of Hans Castorp's predicament is Mann's prophecy: where it works we have a feeling that reality itself is mired in the predicament; where it fails is where the terms of the predicament seem to have mired, not reality, but some human idiopathic horror of it.

That horror of reality—that cultivation of hallucination and fantasy—is what revulses us in the book, and one would like to believe it merely some way-station on a route we need not travel; yet it seems also the positive, ever-tempting escape of suicidal shame. The rate and scope of prophetic power in the arts vary. It may be that we have left behind Mann's vision without, yet, the power of seeing how we have done it or where we are. Mann's vision is gloomy: of an illness so uncopeable that it must somehow be identified with life: the vision of a society composed at every articulate point, of outsiders to that society. The gravity of our disorder seems plain in the fact that we do not think the heroism of the outsider or of the artist unnatural, but in the right course of things. Thus we resort to private force as if it were evangelical; to private absolutisms as if they were magnanimous; to panaceas as if they were specific. This is our own form of the suicidal shame which overcame the world of the magic mountain, and which Hans Castorp, though he could not handle it, could in the end see straight, see through, and reject. It was not his disease after all, this shame of the surface convulsion—of the Blue Peter and the Silent Sister—but a deep parallel to it, at the very bottom of the anonymous and the communal.

It is because we can recognize that this is so—so of Hans Castorp; so of us—and because we can use Mann's novel about Hans Castorp as also about us, and therefore as both an instance and a part of the act of recognition—it is because of these things that we may yet escape the stop-short predicament of Hans Castorp. To recognize, to say, is almost everything in the life of the mind. What we say, what we master in the saying, is our creation; and what we create is necessarily what we are. We create, in the end, only what we potentially are. Creation is discovery.

It is in the arts above all that creation is discovery. Every form of the imagination belongs to the heuristic mode of the mind. Better, the heuristic mode belongs to the polymorph of the imagination. Better still—and here is where the adventures of Hans Castorp come in—the use of the imagination prevents us from the seemly obscurantism of thinking we already know what we are, and what others are, by compelling us to find out, in the instance, as an exemplum, and by an act of recognition. That is what we do symbolically in the arts, and that is what, by the symbols they make, the arts do in us. And there is this blessed difference between our relation to the arts and to other modes of the mind: the heuristic imagination is always a renewable act and can never pretend to be complete. America must always be rediscovered, because *this* America was never discovered before, though of course, as we like to reassure ourselves in the dark, it was always there.

It was always there; and, as always, it must be found when not being looked for; it must be a true discovery and yet must seem an accident; otherwise one would reject it in advance as being either incredible or intolerable. *It was always there,* and whatever it was, it was what the settled forms of knowledge either excluded or converted into an institutional mystery. Only the charlatan and the quack got at it as a regular thing. Only in dreams did it invade the ordinary nineteenth-century individual. Therefore, if the spirit was quickened or agitated enough—restless enough without force, dubious enough without reference to conviction—one turned to the charlatan and the quack, to the unseemly, the illicit, the shameful, the equivocal, one turned and thought the turning a part of the process of rebirth; for so to turn was to come on the missing half of reality, *to what was always there all along.* One thinks of the French symbolists, of the less energetic hedonists, of art for art, of pure poetry: one thinks of the biography of the artist from 1800 to 1900, of the biography as a kind of standard for subject-matter, and how what was at first appropriate to the biography finally came to be the subject-matter itself: the artist against society. It remained for the artists of the twentieth century to show, on the model of the bohemian artist, the ordinary man against society: man devouring himself in the effort to renew himself, to come on the thing, still alive, *that was always there.*

Mann's *The Magic Mountain* is a legend of how such an ordinary man tapped the resources within him of charlatanry and the equivocal, and came, by the growth of his sensibility, upon what it was that made charlatanry possible and the equivocal inevitable as the mode and the result of experience. Where the artist takes hold of his material expressively and molds as much of it as his form will take, the ordinary man is taken hold of by the material as far as he can be reached. The chief conceptual form of Mann's novel is the relation between Hans Castorp and his experience, and the relation is predicated more or less equally by the simplicity of Hans at an intellectual level and by the equivocalness of the experience at the level at which it is felt. The relation, then, is the stress between the simple and the equivocal; and the progressive epiphanies of that stress constitute the movement of the book. Everything that works towards these epiphanies—and everything that can be *converted* from a less to a more available phase—adds value to the conceptual form. Everything that works against—everything that hides or obviates—these epiphanies detracts from the value. Everything merely intellectual, for example, must either be converted into, or deeply allied with, the sensibility. Hans must never lose his naivety, no matter how high a value is assigned to it. On the other hand, as the experience represented takes up more and more of the intellectual burden of the modern mind, it must always be brought back to that equivocal status in which it had appeared in the first place in the mind's history.

This is, of course, one way of getting at the problem of remaking culture, and it is interesting to note that society should have gotten into such a situation that a novelist would tackle the job from a point of view so near the amorphous, so anxious for metamorphosis, certain only of the polymorphic: as if culture were again embryonic, but with a prospect, not of original birth in sin or imperfection, but of rebirth in disease and shame. As readers, we need keep the problem of remaking culture only in the background, precisely as Mann may have kept it only for future consideration. The conceptual form of the stress between the simple and the equivocal, especially when exhibited in terms of a pattern of rebirth, is an extraordinarily powerful instrument with which to compose a novel. As a form it cannot help putting into relation what it takes hold of, and it has the great advantage that it works as well no matter in which direction the stress is set up. In Mann's story of Joseph, it is the hero himself who is equivocal, and his experience one simple blow after another. In the story of Hans Castorp the direction is opposite. But in both stories the conceptual form is identical and bears the fullest possible burdens of the experience of culture as it actually is: what *occupies* the relation between the hero and his world.

The weight of culture and its reformation is imponderable and ever-pressing. Let us take it here only as a novelist's subject. Let us see how Mann went about making his subject malleable, keeping it plastic, letting happen to it what must, under the force of his strict conceptual form. It is the form—such is the seriousness of the novelist—that stands for the weight of the culture, stands for it with a kind of ascetic abandon. The novelist plays it for all it is worth, but binds himself not to exceed that worth.

Therefore he takes precautions. He makes his hero not only simple but ordinary, and he makes the experience of his hero not only equivocal but also an extension of ordinary experience—the little expected, but always astonishing and puzzling extension from a particular health to its corresponding disease. The words are all familiar, but the accents come in new places; there is either more emptiness or more thickness between the syllables. The more one knows what is going on, the more one is disconcerted; precisely because it is the familiar that has been converted into the strange, and never—here is where the asceticism comes in —the strange that has become familiar.

The sequence in which Mann leads his readers to receive these impressions, constitutes another precaution. Hans is felt as ordinary before he is discovered as simple, but the experience is emphasized as equivocal before it is discovered as familiar. Only the achieved simplicity can cope with the familiar. Had Mann reversed his sequence—had he led from the simple to the ordinary, the familiar to the equivocal—the relation between them would have existed, but only at a minimum stress, like a ghost at high noon, and been immediate prey to the nearest intellectual formularization. That is why, as a further precaution, Hans does not come to us with much useable intellectual furniture; the lack of it not only prevents him from substituting formula for response, it also hinders the reader from doing so. It is the sensibility stands between, for Hans, and for ourselves.

There are more precautions, but we do not need to examine them. Let us touch rather on some of the forces Mann risks letting loose on Hans without precaution just to see what they will do. As Mann is far from an economical writer there are a great many of these forces that cluster about Hans; if he is not furnished with ideas he is furnished with a multiplicity of attributes, and the meaning of many of them is not fixed but floating.

Thinking of all these attributes together, one concludes that Hans is representative but not himself the thing—perhaps not even a part of the thing—he represents, though touched by it. He is bourgeois, but he is haut-bourgeois, that is to say, the lever but not the substance of the characteristic phase human power took in the nineteenth century. He is the conservator of something no longer there to conserve; rather like the eighteenth-century gentleman in nineteenth-century England or America. He belongs to that aristocracy which, unless it has individual talent or predatory ability, is without function beyond the preservation of ritual against a better time. Mann puts it that he is mediocre, but in an honourable sense. He is a man disinclined to active life or any function of it. Trained as an engineer, he can feel no calling in it, and cannot open his great textbook on steamships. But he puts a good face on it; he will appear active, and will live with what good face can go without a good heart. He is something of an artist, but only in the sentimental sense where talent is not an issue; he neither takes nor gives authority in his relations to the arts, but bemuses them to his own less than conscious purposes. He takes care about eating and drinking and smoking his Maria Mancinis, about his clothes and all creature-comforts, and about music of the kind that heightens or obviates creature-comforts. He has even a kind of taste in all the arts that protect and occupy his indolent repose. In short, he is representative rather than conscious of the weaknesses of the age he feels so little a part of. He is his own foil; he shows off clearest against himself. Yet in some sense he could see that there was no positive reason why he should exert himself; he seemed to know that incentive and motive must come from outside—and the outside gave no sign. Hence, in Mann's view, he is not quite mediocre. He is therefore a possible victim of a spiritual and physical palsy of doubt and discontent in a world which gave no answer to ultimate questions. The ritual of his being craved a little the substance of conviction. He could not, like the extraordinary man, conquer an alien world by "moral remoteness and single-mindedness" or "exceptionally robust vitality." But in his mediocrity, he might, under the right circumstances, find out what things are; and in that possibility lies his honour. We see at once that he is one of those young men who are to be occupied with a search without entirely knowing that he has undertaken it. It will be more as if the search had undertaken him. He will respond more with his sensibility than his mind, yet his mind will shift with his sensibility, a kind of permanent reserve accommodation ready at no matter what destination. But it is the sensibility, not the mind, we see shift as he moves from the role of life's delicate child, who can practice only seemly obscurantism, to the role his mistress assigns him of *joli bourgeois à la petite tache humide,* in which he finds he can sink into obscurity itself, thence to his third role, where he re-emerges as life's delicate child but at an infinitely higher rate of value.

When he comes, this pretty bourgeois, to the magic mountain, it is partly to visit a sick cousin, and partly to give himself a change of air, a vacation, an interlude, before taking up the serious business of life. Thus the trip combines duty with license; it is a legitimate extravagance of spirit—a confession that life rests on something other than its settled forms, an avowal that there must be an occasional respite from virtue to make it regularly tolerable. The bourgeois, by inventing the idea of vacations, made only one in the long series of devices men have made to maintain themselves in an intolerable society; and his further step is to have made the vacations themselves intolerable. Hans Castorp's experience on the magic mountain follows the pattern of vacations, with the difference that it lasted longer than expected and discovered new modes of the intolerable.

The difference is because he takes his vacation among men and women of all races of Europe, all young, all in the service of death, and all fevered. The youth counts more than the death, and the fever counts more than either. Fever is that shifting standard by which things are never right. In fever, though the old things happen, they do not happen at the same rate, in the same relation, nor with the same result. In fever even the most ordinary things are equivocal. The magic mountain is inhabited by the youth of Europe at fever-pitch, and serves as a kind of excess paradigm—a prophecy in darkness—for William James' speculation that if you raised the body temperature a degree you would change the human race. The fever is the sickness that accompanies the change—the *process* of a shift in phase; when the fever goes, stable phase will have been reached, the phase either of a new thing or of death, there is no telling which. Fever alters, fever cleans, and it burns up what it cleans; fever is like spirit in Santayana's phrase, it chills the flesh and is itself on fire.

At first, so to speak, Hans is feverish but does not have fever. He has feelings of extravagant joy, of reckless sweetness; he sees the advantages of shame over honor, and he has, rather feverishly, the characteristic need of the bourgeois for the illicit when the law has gone (as, up here, it has gone) bad: the illicit is a restorative and it shows as the blessedness of the seductive. The push for the unseemly replaces the practice of seemly obscurantism. When he identifies his interest in Clavdia Chauchat with an unseemly boyhood experience his interest turns to infatuation with her reckless flabbiness and diseased flesh, and he produces, as the act of communion, a genuine fever in himself. Thereat, the two doctors make him one of them; the chief doctor assures him he has a talent for illness, and the other—that lover of disease to whom disease is love—shakes him warmly by the hand. It is a conquest.

It all goes back to that special characterization of Hans as mediocre: a product of an age he is discontented with; without moral remoteness or unusual vigor; without effective education either of past ages or of his own; a lover of death (that is of a stability not vital) and of his own ease. What should he want more than to prolong a holiday which has trapped him with both its actuality and its ceremony: compared to which his previous life and its ceremonies were only laid on. Now that he had the fever he had the sense of reality. Yet this mountain only showed the life below with the palsy to which it was by nature prone, and with its shame a little nearer the surface. Here everything was infected with itself. Ideals, intents, motives which had become pretenses of themselves were the first to suffer change to their true phase. Disorder, confusion, disease had become the immediate order of nature.

But if the story of how Hans developed a fever goes back to his mediocrity, it also goes forward—or inward—to something else. If the disease is seen straight for what it must be—Hans' moist spot *cannot* be tubercular, as his soul *cannot* be bourgeois—if his novitiate is truly passed through, it will be because there is a magnetism under the magic of the mountain, some attractive or propulsive force, something which when recognized as well as felt will seem a principle of order, clarity, health. Whatever it is, it will be whatever has made all this disturbance take place by the mere rise of a degree of temperature. At the moment when Hans has affirmed the rise—a little over a quarter of the way through the book—the disturbance is convulsive, a war of the equivocal which has not yet forced upon Hans' mediocrity the increment of simplicity but which has rather only immersed him in the half-awareness of elated abandonment. Nothing has moved towards clarity, let alone order and health; the magnetism is still magic, the force still seductiveness, the principle still contradiction. In Joachim Ziemssen, Hans' sick cousin, there is one remnant of the old world, the soldier's avowal of glory in death, but this Hans does not share. In Behrens, the medical director, there is the uncertainty and the humor of the question whether the disease comes to the mountain or the mountain makes the disease. In Krokowski, the psychiatrist, there is half a charlatan, but the other half is force, of darkness in light: of disease as what shines in the light. In Settembrini, the humanist, there is half-pretence and wayward emotion in the masquerade of order—the organ-grinder's order in the shape of a dancing monkey—but the other half is the force of aspiring rational will. In Madame Chauchat there is a tainted place—the taint of a cat always half in heat—but she is also what is tainted, or at least the sentiment of it: the vitality of the other thing, possibly shameful but in essence the very thing Settembrini would dignify if he had in reality the power he strove so feverishly to represent. To all these, Hans abandons himself with triumphant laughter and dreadful anticipation, and builds a double infatuation: with Clavdia Chauchat—sex as disease; and with death—life as a sickness, an infection, of matter; each in its most voluptuary form. That is what happens to the bourgeois who has conjured, or found, in himself, and thereby in his world, a rise of a degree or two of temperature: a passion for the moribund.

Only scorn—that earliest form of criticism—can momentarily pull him back. When Madame Chauchat scorns his hysterical advances, his temperature drops to normal; when she accepts him in manner it rises; when she accepts him in full—on carnival night when the Thou holds sway—he goes into delirious rhapsody of the shameless and the sacred. But it is only scorn of sex and death that has this reactive power. The scorn of Settembrini the humanist, the furious rebel of reason, only drives him on, a kind of unconscious devil's advocacy of further abandonment. Hans may be, as Settembrini calls him, life's delicate child; he is also more European than Settembrini thinks. Europe is not all Mediterranean, neither all reason nor all latinity. Nor was latin reason ever enough. It had always to be founded on something not itself, and commonly discovered that by itself it made life unbearable. The world was not yet ready for the atheism of reason, no more for Settembrini than for Hans; both served forces of an occult character, and Hans knew this better than Settembrini, for he had little protection—only the power of engorgement—against the primitive things which continually assaulted him. On the other hand he did not know enough to use Settembrini in fullness—for his dream of history and the noble lies by which the fragments of life are put together; he knew only enough to quote him and misuse him—which is what the bourgeois has chiefly done with the classical tradition. Settembrini was right, with the rightness of tragic insight that takes up the impossible role of evangelist and teacher; Hans Castorp was life's delicate child, and it was up to him to teach Hans the mature form of the European tradition: not what brought it to life but what permitted it to survive, what kept it alive, plastic, possible, plausible, prophetic.

But just as Settembrini did not have the effective scorn of Clavdia Chauchat, so he did not himself represent the whole of what he wished to teach; there was not enough in him to make a true simple. He needed the help of his rhetorical enemy the absolute will. This we get at once in the sickened, corrosively ugly, puny, and fashionably dressed figure of the Jewish Jesuit Naphta. The two argue, and in a peculiar sense complete each other, by confusing themselves. Hans, listening, takes up the attitude in which—in this Circe's palace—he had drawn pigs, and decides that Naphta is not a true Jesuit but a *joli jésuite* with a *petite tache humide*. Time passes, Joachim goes, Hans, alone, stays forever, and continues listening to argument after argument between the rational humanist position and the super-rational absolutist position. The one sees life philanthropically, the other sees life as a disease; they push into each other, and bind, like the dovetail joints of a box, until their friction is maximum. It makes little difference where the arguments take off, the result is the same. The crucial argument, for example, starts over capital punishment, and ends up with the will behaving like reason, and reason asserting itself wilfully. The argument has reached the merging point where nobody knows who is devout and who free-thinking. Mann's imagination is right. Surely the rational humanist is devout. Surely the Jesuit who will sacrifice everything to blessedness is a free-thinker. Surely he who would build a tolerable universe is devout and praises God. Surely he who insists on an intolerable universe at any cost is a free-thinker and blasphemes God with the degraded remnants of his faith.

It is a real question—the kind that forces such ordinary souls as Hans to simplicity as the only response to the equivocal—the question which is the greater temptation: to insist exclusively on that which is possible to know, or to insist wholly on the force of that which it is impossible to know. Each temptation leads to reckless omnicompetence and disaster; which is why each not only consents to, but invites the intervention of the terror. Perhaps the temptation *is* the invocation of terror, the one in the form of the eagle treading the dove, the other in the form of invoking the devil as incentive to God; the one by Revolution, the other by Inquisition. Here is the terrible dilemma, in Eliot's phrase, of the incredible public world and the intolerable private world: the dilemma of the impossible choice between doing good even though evil come, and doing deliberate evil in the hope that after the destruction good may have a chance to supervene. Either choice is heresy, one the heresy that goodness leads to blessedness, the other the heresy that good may be force.

Mann did not invent this dilemma. To the ordinary mind everywhere, but especially to the mediocre mind of the disinherited bourgeois who has any sense of simplicity at all, it is the central form of the struggle between the tolerable world and the intolerable world as ideals for action. It is the struggle between the fool of virtue and the ascetic libertine. The pity is that there is no escaping action, and the curse is that action cannot escape the infection of thought. In this argument which sprang from a difference about capital punishment, we see how thought becomes action and how action takes resource in thought. The more otherworldly the source of power, the more the power seems to withdraw itself, the more the devil is uncovered and the more the power takes the all-touching, all-penetrating form of the terror. Total security would be total terror: the savage absolutism of the advantage of mankind seen in kingdom come, or the savage absolutism of rational truth as moral law: absolute spirit or absolute man.

Hans makes his spiritual exercises listening to all this. He has not mind enough to know how *little* mind is in Settembrini's reason or how *much* there is in Naphta's absolutism; how little the one, how much the other created in his own image. Naturally, therefore, when he tries to choose between the "all-consuming all-equalizing chaos, that ascetic-libertine state" and "the 'critical subjective' where empty bombast and a bourgeois strictness of morals contradicted each other," he tends towards Naphta's "morally chaotic All." All Clavdia Chauchat represented: abandon, adventure, sin, shame, elation: all this tended that way. Hans understood very well the *petite tache humide* of extreme submission and even better the palsy in his neck and chin. Thus he took his spiritual exercises. Life's delicate child stretched his sensibility in terms of the Operationes Spirituales of the diseased Jesuit.

But he is not done stretching, and each further stretch is either in parallel or developmental response to this spiritual exercise. Here we will limit ourselves to the dream in the snow and the adventure of Peeperkorn, for in these two we have at the maximum the relation between the simple and the equivocal which is the conceptual form of the book, and have also the maximum reach of this novel as prophecy, both in relation to the polarity of Settembrini and Naphta. The chapter called Snow is a dream—part waking, part sleeping, part hallucinated, and part reawakened—in five parts. The first is Hans' innocent impulse to try the lion's maw, the sea's depth, the desert place, the winter wildness of the snow: by submitting consciously to nature he might find out the rank and stature of *Homo Dei*. In the second part, his heart struggles alone in the icy void, and he escapes his impulse by finding himself back at the hayhut where he had started, deliberately lost. In the third part, as he forces himself to wander on, ethics and religion, the will of the mind and the narcosis of the body, struggle to possess him. So begins the danger state in which abasement is the right action: he thinks of death in formal splendor, of Naphta's knout of discipline, and—while there intrudes a hallucination of Settembrini with a horn and a handorgan—of Clavdia Chauchat. Hands pull him to lie down in the snow. But he stands—there must be no coying with the bride of the storm—letting only his head droop. At once he is below, on the plains, their fragrant abundance, birdsong and rainbows, the climate of the living. Here, with the unbearable purity of an Italian tenor's voice, begins the fourth part of the dream. Spread before him is the pastoral of Mediterranean metempsychosis, full of sweetness and light and ceremony and maternity. Hans feels an unscrupulous outsider till he follows the gaze of a lovely boy within a temple. There two hags dismember and devour a child—life's delicate child—and he wakes, wrapped in the cold whispered brawling of their curse upon him, lying in the snow. The fresh strength of withdrawal from fatal sleep gives him, in the fifth part, the power of waking vision. He knows that it has been the great soul dreaming in him the anonymous and communal dream of human hope and its cost.

In this dream is the paradigm for Hans' conversion; it is also the point where Mann pushed his prophecy beyond the discovery of the actual into the revelation (that is, the pushed vision) of the real; and it should be noted that both for paradigm and prophecy Mann sticks to the conceptual form of the stress between the simple and the equivocal. In his dream Hans reaches that simplicity which absorbs the equivocal. It is, for him, the great man's dream, and while it still presses on his mind he not only knows the task of the mind but feels, in his healthy exhilaration, potent to perform his part in it. It is as if the fever had dropped and the future had *come again* upon the anterior state of what it always was. For the moment Hans is both morally remote and exceptionally robust, and he has that sense of conclusion that goes with necessary action. He has known reason and recklessness, all of man—flesh, blood, disease, death—and knows the name for all: the human being, the delicate child of life. He knows that behind enlightened man lies the blood sacrifice; and he knows that this is better than either the pennypipe of reason or the *guazzobuglio* of God and the Devil. He sees that if man can keep a little clear in the head and keep pious in the heart, then disease, health, spirit, nature are not themselves problems. "The recklessness of death is in life, it would not be life without it—and in the centre is the position of the *Homo Dei,* between recklessness and reason, as his state is between mystic community and windy individualism. . . . Man is the lord of counterpositions, they can only be through him, and thus he is more aristocratic than they. More so than death, too aristocratic for death—that is the freedom of the mind. More aristocratic than life, too aristocratic for life, and that is the piety of the heart." So for the access of moral remoteness. With the new exceptionally robust vitality he sees one more thing: that love and death do not couple, but that love is opposed to death. "From love and sweetness alone come form and civilization—but always in recognition of blood sacrifice. . . . I will keep faith with death in my heart, yet well remember that faith with death and the dead is evil, is hostile to humankind, so soon as we give it power over thought and action. *For the sake of goodness and love, man shall let death have no sovereignty over his thoughts."*

Hans thinks that he will know all this forever. But this great man's dream cannot last in this middling young man, at least not as a force, only as a change in the beat of his heart, and as the sense of a mystery lost, held as a memory of rapture and as an incentive to gallantry. Though the dream had faded and the thought was no longer clear after dinner that night, it was with that memory and that incentive (that remoteness and that vitality) that he could see his dead cousin's face smile in its warrior's beard and could meet in full faith the extra-human vitality (without remoteness) of Mynheer Peeperkorn. Before both this life in death and this supererogation of life, Hans was himself a little lord of great counterpositions, owing and giving allegiance that shifted, but always the allegiance of self.

Almost he loses that allegiance when he is confronted with Peeperkorn. Peeperkorn wears a clerical waistcoat and checkered tails; he is Naphta and Settembrini together, without the emphasis of either, and with a tremendous blurred personality lodged in gin, wine, coffee extra-strong; in a voice of high moment but without matter or sequence but with a speaking gesture that made good what he did not say. He might be the lord of counterpositions, but he is more likely a torrent, the thing in man like a mountain, a waterfall, or the sea. Nobody like Peeperkorn can last very long in our lives nor can such men often last out their own lives. The pitch is too hard to keep and we are mostly unequal to the demanded effort of its example. Yet it is the pitch of life as force, force as fever—the pitch of the life force—of the going-on-ness without some pressure of which, some shifting stage of which, we should all stop; but it is a force converted too far beyond the human phase—even though it is what humans are made of. So converted, it is destructive force; in serving it we are destroyed by it if we do not protect ourselves from it, just as Peeperkorn, when love and alcohol fail him, destroys himself. Surely that is what is meant when his death is called abdication: he is the king of all those parts of ourselves we cannot be and live. Yet, as we are human, we yearn to serve his force even more than we dread his apparition. We seek what we must shun, as Melville said of Shakespeare; and we organize what we shun in order to go on seeking it. In armies we organize it as discipline and in religion as ritual, though we know that the act of war is beyond any discipline and that the act of religion is beyond any ritual. In the lesser creations of ordinary life we think we purge such apparitions, by toadying, by indifference, by ridicule, by thought—but if we stop thinking we feel the force within us.

That is what happened to Hans when confronted with Mynheer Peeperkorn. When he stops toadying and stops thinking he feels Mynheer Peeperkorn within him. That Clavdia Chauchat has returned to the mountain as Peeperkorn's mistress—attached to him because of his feeling for her and the anguish of that feeling—does nothing to bring about Hans' discovery of full feeling, but her presence makes a true contrast to that discovery. As she had become Thou to him on the night of the carnival of fever, so she is no longer so after the moment in the new carnival of feeling when Peeperkorn and Hans become—precisely in their struggle over her—blood brothers, become Thou to each other, and the reign of Thou holds full sway. Hans learns that Peeperkorn is human too; more human than anybody: the all-too-human we cannot be is human too: human on the grand scale, that scale which has the long perspective we call tragic when we do not call it love, but which taken out of scale, taken close, is holocaust. But here are Peeperkorn's own words, when he reprehends Hans for glibness over their relations to Clavdia. They are drinking wine by twilight, the old man abed, Hans at his side. "Feeling, you understand, is the masculine force that rouses life. Life slumbers. It needs to be roused, to be awakened to a drunken marriage with divine feeling. For feeling, young man, is godlike. Man is godlike, in that he feels. He is the feeling of God. God created him in order to feel through him. Man is nothing but the organ through which God consummates his marriage with roused and intoxicated life. If man fails in feeling, it is the surrender of his masculinity, a cosmic catastrophe, an irreconcilable horror." It is on this basis that the Thou holds sway between them. Yet, as they separate in the dark, Hans imagines Settembrini coming in suddenly and turning on the light, to let reason and convention reign. In the dark, alone, feeling becomes that wholly human, wholly intolerable creation: that thing out of the womb we call hysteria. Perhaps that is why, in the next chapter, after raising his voice, half man of sorrows and half sybaritic rogue, to harangue the waterfall ("that long catastrophe of foam and fury") he kills himself that night. It is not possible to convert nature into one's own hysteria, and if you try life becomes intolerable.

No matter. Such a push of hysteria is possible of actual experience at any time—it is the terrible temptation in the exercise of human powers of creation, and to feel it is to come on the quick of our disease, our ultimate giddiness. After his exposure to this temptation, Hans falls successively under the spells of the Great God Dumps, Music as the means of self-re-creation, Traffic with the questionable morass of the subhuman or unclean traffic with one's own nature, the General Contagion of rancor and hysteria ending in Naphta's suicide in the duel where Settembrini fires in the air, and lastly the spell of the coming war and Settembrini's death. Then Hans goes down into battle and vanishes. Living or dead, says Mann, his prospects are poor. Yet he had known in the Spirit what in the flesh he could scarcely have done: in moments—out of death and the rebellion of the flesh—a dream of love: that is to say the Reign of Thou over all the counterpositions of the human spirit. Mann addresses Hans, in closing, with the Thou of love and allegiance. Hans was indeed a small Lord.

Thinking of all this we see that Mann is indeed the innerly twinned child of Dostoevsky and Nietzsche. He springs from the human depths and also from those depths which are all-too-human. He understands the Apollonian and the Dionysiac, also the Inquisitor and the Galloping Troika (Dostoevsky's image of Russia, an image which Clavdia Chauchat had on her cigarette case): four precarious roles all resting on a surface which convulses, through the anonymous and communal, with its own appropriate terror, its underlying moral chaos and orgiastic freedom. He knows that terror intervenes because we forget it is there, a part of ourselves, into which we slip with dismay; but he knows too, that we can recast ourselves, if we will, if we remember and do not deny what lies under us, without the intervention of terror. But since it is not done, since terror does come, it is his business to prophesy what ought to have been remembered. He shows us therefore upon what violence, and at what extremities, the Thou comes to hold sway: by carnival, within the presence of personality, at death, and at war: in each case in response to a breakthrough.

In the simple, but mutually reversed, dualism of Naphta and Settembrini—that is, in the stress of Hans' relations to it—it is not so much their confusion that is shown, as that the conditions they have to meet are shown breaking through. The part of the mind that makes choice has still the old choice to make: namely, choice of the method of protection and control. The moist spots in each are in their attempts to replace the conditions of existence with themselves. The difference between them is that where Settembrini seems to ignore the abyss of feeling within him, Naphta, seeming to know it, does no more than create a false abyss of his own. In the structures of the mind there can be no sharper difference. Yet the current temptation will always be to take Naphta's invention of the private abyss as a real solution, needing no transformation, never seeing how relatively easy it is to make up for Settembrini's deliberate failure of vision as a mere oversight.

As a clarifying example, consider how Naphta could do nothing with Clavdia Chauchat, no matter how far you pushed him; yet Settembrini could, with but the restoration of his original insights (those in Hans' dream), do anything with her: her abyss is the real one: she is the force of it, as she tells Hans, which is why Hans changes his Thou from her to Peeperkorn. Both rest upon Clavdia as the sacred condition of life. As it is, both Peeperkorn and Hans feel Settembrini's prejudice against Clavdia somehow justified, as in her own way Clavdia does too. He is not "hu-man," she says, but she knows he understands the human, in her as well as elsewhere. It is Settembrini alone among all these diseased and defective figures who comes to his end as a part of human life, not by disappearance or self-destruction; and it is only by thinking of Settembrini that we understand the tragic failure of Peeperkorn's hysteria of the human: to remake the conditions of life in his own image. It is only Settembrini who suggests that man can still be lord of counterpositions.

What are they—these counterpositions? Do we not come at them in this novel which hints at reality by showing the actuality of all those conditions of life which it is the constant task of our waking moments to accommodate, expiate, and refresh? They are the golden eagle overhead, the anonymous and communal within ourselves. They are the actual of what one already knows, the reality that was always there.

Parody and Critique: Mann's DOCTOR FAUSTUS

In this country, at this time, our way of looking at our culture makes it difficult for us to look at a work of literary art which announces itself in its title, in the motto on its title page, and in the attributes of its hero as in intention a great work dealing with a very great man. We do not take to great men unless they be criminal or popular or fashionable or dead in some other way; we resent claims to maximum attention and maximum response—we like our great men to do our work for us, and we like to take up their greatness on the side, without noticing it, and without pain. The attitude is prudent, avoids risks and avoids snobbery but it leaves us at a loss before Thomas Mann's *Dr. Faustus,* the Life of the German Composer Adrian Leverkühn as told by a friend—and the sense of being at a loss is all the more acute when we see that the rest of the title-page is covered by nine lines of Dante's Italian taken from the opening of the second Canto of the Inferno where Dante pauses to take his first breath in the unutterable human hell in which he found himself. Because I have now read this work three times, and have been moved variously and incongruously each time, it seems not only necessary but a good thing to risk both mistaken judgment and possibly snobbery—it seems good and necessary to take this work in its asserted role and attempt to frame the maximum response which maximum attention can initially yield to this image of greatness in our time. I have no fear I am alone in this attempt; I know of others, though they do not crowd; but first of all I have as friend and companion him who tells and meditates upon the life of this modern Faust, I mean of course the Catholic humanist, Serenus Zeitblom, that serene flower of the hellish time, and it is because of him, and so much of faith as we share—we are both humanist though not both Catholic—that I understand how to begin.

I begin with the humanist's natural questions. I ask, in order to remind myself, what the name Dr. Faustus on a modern work might mean; and I ask what Dante's Italian is doing there under the title. What have a devil myth and an invocation of the Greek Muses got to do with contemporary bourgeois humanism? (We are still bourgeois, for the time being, if we are humanists at all.) Why should a work purportedly written by a humanist go so far back for its title and its motto—so far back that in each case it touches upon forces recognized, if at all, as prior to the human? Is it the predicament of the humanist that in order to combat the inhumanities of his own day he must get succor in remote forces that must seem at least as menacing as they are propitious? Or is it rather that he feels he must refresh in himself the stream of daemonic inspiration, of hidden and inexplicable strength, in order to combat not his enemies but his own weaknesses? I think both. But let us examine into title and motto for their own sakes.

What or who is Faustus? A medieval legend, an Elizabethan incantation, a German epic, a French opera, an attribute of the arrogance of the modern or experimental man; but in all cases combining the two traditions that inhabit us from our past and trouble us as to our future, the two traditions of light and darkness. There is on the one side the tradition of reason and revelation and inspiration, and on the other side the tradition of the daemonic, the chthonic, and the magical. Somehow in the image of Faustus the two traditions are combined; the things of darkness work into the broad day; and the combining agent is the devil, who offers us the pride of mastery of both traditions. All images of Faustus have to do with the mastery of absolute knowledge followed by the loss of it altogether. The devil tempts us by offering us knowledge of the truth about ourselves which, without the power of his temptation, we should not have the strength to bear; the knowledge refused to Adam in Paradise. How should we put it? It is a temptation to the absolute possession both in knowledge and of the substance of knowledge, so that we might know both our inspiration and what keeps us going: the knowledge both of what we love and of what we shun to think we are. The glorious and the sensual—neither of them "reasonable"—are in this image reconciled with the humiliating and the ascetic—which are not reasonable either. Faustus woos the Muses with the aid of the devil, the divine with the daemonic. Goethe was correcting nothing in the old legend when in the Second Part of his epic the marriage of Faustus and Helen serves for the reconciliation of the Greek and Christian worlds; he only developed the human necessity that was there to be declared, and to be created if it was not there. And it is on such an insight that Thomas Mann brings out his Faustian image; but because of his particular moment in time—our moment when so much has been taken away—he cannot proceed where Goethe left off; he has to begin behind Goethe in Dante, and he has to try to go further back still, not only into the old legend, but also into its roots in that country of the mind which is neither Christian nor Greek, to the country, in Mann's own phrase, of the naked human voice.

To do all this you have to be a little solemn and dedicated, but you have also to be passionate and exact. You have to believe and you have to wrestle with your belief in the flesh of the actual world around you. You have to be a humanist, not of the renaissance but of the bourgeois world—the bourgeois in that rebellion against both reason and flesh which constitutes his vitality; you have to be the bourgeois humanist seeking to rediscover, now that his order is failing, what all that turbulence was which he had put in order. You have to see, like James Joyce in *Ulysses,* the darkness that is in the light as well as the darkness that is all about us. You must look into two kinds of chaos, the mere disorder and the original black. Othello, you will remember, saw both kinds at once when looking after Desdemona in anguish of self-impalement he cried out:

> Excellent wretch! Perdition catch my soul,
> But I do love thee! and when I love thee not,
> Chaos is come again.

In short you have to deal with the devil in order to reach the daemonic, and as a humanist you will remember that, without the human, the daemonic is the diabolic. The daemon is the indwelling power, or spirit, or genius in things, whether for good or evil; the daemon represents the basic conditions of human life; the devil is their corruption, the temptation of finding means of not accepting those conditions. Thus the devil in our psychology is a way-station to the demon, providing by rebellion and denial and parody, the incentive of remorse to go further. Look in the dictionary: Diabolose is the slanderer, the calumniator, in Greek; in Hebrew, the tempter and spiritual enemy of mankind—offering other than human conditions. One form of Christian tragedy is in the confusion of the two, the merging of that which slanders with that which tempts; Greek and Satanic pride here touch; and it is that confusion, that equivocalness, which inhabits the Dr. Faustus of Thomas Mann. So it is that in the first chapter of that work, we find Serenus Zeitblom, the Catholic humanist and son of the Muses, meditating the life of his friend the great musician Adrian Leverkühn, and finding that that life forces him, by its God-inflicted genius struggling with the corrupt Faustian bargain, into the further meditation of the daemonic: in his friend's life and, above all, in his friend's music, both of which he loved with tenderness and terror. There is the whole theme of the work announced at once in terms of its title.

Now let us look at the motto or epigraph from Dante which appears under the title. The motto is an appeal to the Muses, to high Genius, to Memory, and the appeal is that of Dante, that rebel of reason and liberty against the hardening of order into violence; an appeal made between the middle age and the renaissance, between the beating of light and the spread over Europe of the odor of death. The passage is worth looking at, in itself and for Dante, and also because it is quoted to set going a Faustian work by this last product of the northern renaissance and baroque reformation; a human type so much more *aware* of the under-barbarism than the Mediterranean world has ever been. It is we northerners, always, who understand the *ground of appeal* to the resources of the Latin and Catholic spirit; we need them more. I do not say this was so for Dante's time; certainly not for Augustine's; but it is so for us. We know what is corrupted, what corrupts, and how the relation may become tolerable: we know what we must acknowledge although we do not wish to acknowledge it: the terms of an everlasting and vital predicament; and it is characteristic of our age that the acknowledgment should be attempted in works of art. And so, in the similar age of the fourteenth century, it was with Dante.

> Lo giorno se n'andava, e l'aer bruno
> toglieva gli animai, che sono in terra,
> dalle fatiche loro; ed io sol uno
>
> m'apparechiava a sostener la guerra
> si del cammino, e si della pietate,
> che ritrarrà la mente, che non erra.
>
> O Muse, o alto ingegno, or m'aiutate!
> O mente, che scrivesti ciò ch'io vidi,
> qui si parrà la tua nobilitate.

(The day was going off, and the brown air taking the animals that are on earth from their toil; and I, one alone, was working myself up to bear the war both of the journey, and of the pity, which memory that errs not shall relate [retrace]. O Muses, O high Genius, now help us! O memory, that has inscribed what I saw, here will be shown thy nobleness.)

Half the Graeco-Christian world is here, and very nearly all that remains of it: what is human and invocably human. The twilight is there, and the task: the journey from birth to death, and also the pity of the journey seen in itself; and so the war between the pity and the journey and the war in each. Then Memory, whose daughters are the Muses, is invoked as the image of the truth—the truth of the tradition and the truth of the actual experience; memory as the high or presiding genius of man —not man himself but his nobleness, the light that shines in him. What then does it shine on? What are the grounds on which it is appealed to?

This work of Thomas Mann, this discourse of an old humanist, this serene late bloom of spirit working through the discourse, is meant to stand for the possibility of an answer. The tireless spirit remains even after the most exhausted animals are gone. This is the spirit that was always there even in the worst moment of the war of the journey and the pity when the scum of the earth in each of us—Thomas Mann's phrase for the Nazi regime—put in power the dictatorship of the scum of the earth all the more scum for the memory it soiled, the tradition it debauched.

But what was the war; what extreme form of what perennial war? It is interesting that Dante did not have to ask that question. His memory knew that answer, and knowledge of it was implicit in his genius; but for us it must be made explicit, and it troubles us almost more than the question that we are driven to ask it. It is as if, by a change in the *phase* of consciousness (which we call self-consciousness or sometimes heightened consciousness) we had acquired a new possibility, however threatened, of choice: as if we had found some new way of tragic aspiration, some new perspective of intolerable failure, to compel us to new efforts of assent and dissent. The new occasion here—the extreme form of the perennial war—is the occasion when those so nearly without mind that their memories lie, take charge, like the Nazis in Germany, of those who still live and still woo—not the folk and the mob—but the Muses.

This is not a change—only a reversal of phase. We find in control what had been the object of control. We heighten the old techniques of imagination weighted by memory with the *élan* of our fresh freedom from purpose. The forces which we tried to understand overwhelm our understanding. Yet those forces, where they still move in the human animal, still crave to be understood—still crave to acquire the nobility of memory. The long human howl, the cry of infants, the naked human voice, will be music yet: though the whole world howl before it happen, and if in the process it seem to come to destruction.

So the humanist faced with the Faustian image must believe, and that is what the passage from Dante gave Serenus Zeitblom the strength to believe while he passed through the war of the journey—the Germany of the last sixty years—and the war of the pity—the life of his friend the great German musician, Adrian Leverkühn. So, as in the first chapter we found the whole theme of the work announced in terms of Faustus, in the second chapter we find that theme repeated and strengthened, counterpointed, with another strain. Here the Faustian image is put to music, and in that music we hear the classical tongues of human reason and dignity over against that other language of tones, a language not humanistic, not reliable: both living by contradiction in human nature; the one nobility of mind, the other peril of spirit, here joined in new service to the deities of the depths. It is as if the humanist insisted that it is the function of his culture, by piety to his memory, to regulate and propitiate the entrance of the dark and uncanny into the service of the gods.

It is in the service of the gods, then, that this life of a great musician is written under the double image of a new Faustus and old Memory; and it is the role of artist—that characteristic hero of the high literature of the last seventy years—and the music he creates which press together to combine the image. So much for the statement of the theme; interpretation may come later; meanwhile we remind ourselves of the material through which it is worked and of the techniques or forms to which it takes for expression.

The material is of several kinds. There is the immediate biography of the young genius capable equally, at twenty-one, of experience, of music, and of theology. He withdraws from experience and theology and dedicates himself to the composition of music which is a further reach of both: his withdrawal is perfected after a single sexual contact which leaves a secret syphilis to combine with a hereditary migraine, and after, also, a single hallucinated interview with the devil. He is by nature one not to be touched, to be adored not loved; and he becomes by consequence of his disease and his compact with the devil free, or almost free, of the obligations that go with human contact and love, and is bound only, and almost wholly, by the special obligation to mocking laughter—which is response pure, response without sharing. That is, he can sink unimpeded into what underlies all experience—what is in the self *no matter what* is taken away: the revelation of the equivocal without any control or standard except for those of the process of revelation. Thus, having no connection with experience, except through daemonism and disease, he can afford that ruthless irresponsibility of the artist which is in the end responsibility plain, full response *away from* the truth, *under* the truth, *without* truth. In other words, he is asserted to have in fact that absolute mastery of experience which every adolescent requires himself to see as the immediate, or at least the next possibility of his own genius: surely the oldest imagined role, older than Faustus, older than Memory. In his life itself he succeeds in his withdrawal, his dedication, and secret power till near the end, when life strikes him two blows. The first blow is the murder of his one personal friend which he brings on by expressing a desire for marriage. The second is the death of his darling and beautiful nephew Nepomuk or Echo—the echo in infant form of the life he never lived. From the second he never recovered except for the moment of his last composition. Finishing that—the lamentation of Dr. Faustus—he collapses into idiocy, his work done, and the life he never lived still to be begun, if at all, by those who are to come after him.

Against the biography of Leverkühn there are three critiques: the critique of the social history of the German haut-bourgeois from 1885 to 1940, the critique of German national history in the War from 1939 to 1945, and the critique of Adrian Leverkühn's principal compositions, all told in the increasingly desperate humanistic tones of Serenus Zeitblom. Altogether, the three make a single critique of Europe as the forced sell-out. Let us say that the critique of the Nazi war is of the ambience: it is the horror in our nostrils, and it is there in the book; and saying that let us have done, for it is only the holocaust of what had been long on fire. But let us think of the critique of society over against the figures of the composer and the scholar, each further ahead of his society and deeper in it than anyone, as the artist and humanist ought to be—and each misunderstood or ignored by the society he expressed. The artist expresses what the humanist must understand: man's disobedience to his own nature. Only here in this time, 1885–1940, instead of a tension, a precarious balance, between expression and understanding, which hold society together, we find society tearing itself apart. We get expressionism and authority, not balanced or related, but identified, confused, a matter of random because indistinguishable resort.

This we see wonderfully in the careers of the lesser characters, particularly in those of Clarissa and Inez Rodde, ending for the one in blackmail and suicide, for the other in drugs and murder, the one caused by shame and failure of talent, the other by distrust of suffering and cultivated infatuation. We see it in the aesthete who bought bad pictures and loved the beauty of bloodshed, and in the poet who wrote no poetry but invoked violence. It is in Schildknapp, the cadging translator and anglophile, who never got his own work done; in Rudi Schwerdtfeger, the fiddler, the victim of his own coquetry. Above all it is in the discussion club of the 'twenties where because all the horror of the 'thirties was seen as *possible* it was adopted and wooed as a *necessity;* but it is no less in the writhing reptilian eloquence of the impresario from Paris. What we see is the moral suicide—not simple viciousness or ordinary depravity—but such confusion of order with disorder—such failure of memory—as is tantamount to the moral suicide of bourgeois society. No wonder the chattering terror became the only mode, first of expression, then of action. And for final commentary there is the hideous and gratuitous death of little Echo. It is always the gratuitous that reminds us of the essential.

There remains the third critique which is of Adrian Leverkühn's music: *Love's Labours Lost*—a mocking opera bouffe of Renaissance Humanism; the *Gesta Romanorum,* a parody of the daemonic element in medieval Christianity; the Oratorio of the *Apocalypse,* where the howling glissando of the human voice, moving from the bestial to the sublime in mocking imitation parodies the musical styles of hell, reaching finally the "inaccessibly unearthly and alien beauty of sound, filling the heart with longing without hope"; and lastly the lamentations of Dr. Faustus, written after the death of Echo, which we now see was a parody of the life of Leverkühn and his society. Of this last piece, here is the humanist's description:

> We children of the dungeon dreamed of a hymn of exultation, a *Fidelio,* a Ninth Symphony, to celebrate the dawn of a freed Germany—freed by herself. Now only this can avail us, only this will be sung from our very souls: the *Lamentation* of the son of hell, the lament of men and God, issuing from the subjective, but always broadening out and as it were laying hold on the Cosmos; the most frightful lament ever set up on earth.

So the humanist, Serenus Zeitblom; and saying that, he forces himself a little beyond his humanism: out upon the base on which humanism is built, and which it denies and shuns, avoids and rediscovers at moments of outward catastrophe or inward "breakthrough." It is always the task of humanism to break through itself *again* to reality, whether by reason or image. That is what that early humanist, Marco Lombardo, whom Dante found untying the knot of his anger in Canto XVI of the Purgatorio—that is what Marco meant when he said Man has a mind of his own.

> A maggior forza ed a miglior natura
> liberi soggiacete, e quella cria
> la mente in voi, che il ciel non ha in sua cura.
>
> Però, se il mondo presente disvia,
> in voi è la cagione, in voi si cheggia. . . .

("Ye lie subject, in your freedom, to a greater power and to a better nature; and that creates in you mind which the heavens [i.e.

the influence of the stars, mechanical law] have not in their charge. Therefore, if the world today goeth astray, in you is the cause, in you be it sought."—Temple Classics edition.) *The Divine Comedy* is among other things a great exemplary break-through by reason and image to the base of the human. Adrian Leverkühn's *Lamentation of Dr. Faustus* is an image, an idol, an invocation for such a break-through; a supplication which, if we could only hear it, might enact itself in our contemplation. It is the human voice at the crisis of phase: at the moment of reversal or renewal; and it is in this light that the remaining comments of Serenus Zeitblom ought to be read. He is asking us to hear. To hear all modern music as lament and *lasciatemi morire*. To hear *this* putative music as Echo, "The giving back of the human voice as nature-sound, and the revelation of it *as* nature-sound . . . essentially a lament: Nature's melancholy 'Alas!' in view of man, her effort to utter his solitary state." He asks us also to hear this music as complete, as saying "nothing and everything," as creating a universal identity of the blest and the accursed, in which the freedom is so wholly expressed that it is wholly subject to the form—*a maggior forza ed a miglior natura*. The intention is again Dantesque; for it is Dante who is the most deliberate and the most complete of all poets; it is in his work that everything is taken care of, and something else besides; and so we are meant to hear the evoked music of Adrian Leverkühn—both as to the deliberateness and as to what is deliberated: the liberation of maximum expressiveness in the condition of maximum control. The *Lament* is written in twelve tones (the chromatic scale of Arnold Schoenberg) on the twelve syllables of the words "For I die as a good and as a bad Christian"—good by repentance, bad in that the devil will have his body. "It is the basis of all the music—or rather, it lies almost as key behind everything and is responsible for the identity of the most varied forms—that identity which exists between the crystalline angelic choir and the hellish yelling in the *Apocalypse* and which has now become all embracing: a formal treatment strict to the last degree, which no longer knows anything unthematic, in which the order of the basic material becomes total, and within which the idea of a fugue rather declines into an absurdity, just because there is no longer any free note."

What this form controls in absolute liberation is the last change of mind—"a proud and bitter change of heart!"—in the "speaking unspokenness" of music, whereby final despair achieves a voice, and the consolation of the voice, the voice for the creature in its woe, and whereby "out of the sheerly irremediable hope might germinate . . . a hope beyond hopelessness, the transcendence of despair." . . . The end is the high G of a cello. "Then nothing more: silence, and night. But that tone which vibrates in the silence, which is no longer there, to which only the spirit hearkens, and which was the voice of mourning, is so no more. It changes its meaning; it abides as a light in the night."

That is how Serenus Zeitblom would have us hear "the most frightful lament ever set up on earth," and a little later, when before the final wail of his own voice, Leverkühn mangles and eviscerates himself in words ("one's fellow men are not meant or made to face such truth") Zeitblom makes the following observation: "Never had I felt more strongly the advantage that music, which says nothing and everything, has over the unequivocal word: yes, the saving irresponsibility of all art, compared with the bareness and baldness of unmediated revelation." And in this observation is clarified the mystery why it is music, in the absence of religion, that makes the break-through into reality tolerable as truth and viable as image. Dante would not have needed it, or would have used it—indeed he did so use it—as a compensatory weight; but this other age has need of it: "the saving irresponsibility of all art," clearest and most nearly credible in music.

It is this evoked, this putative music, its working presence to the good will of our belief, that transforms the critique and the anecdotes and the biography into something we can call a novel; of two composers whom I know, one insists he wrote Leverkühn's music, and the other hears it completely; as for myself, with less skill, I hear it incompletely; but I know how everything works into what I hear and do not hear. But if the novel is governed by the music, we must emphatically remember that all the music, except the last piece, is parody and that the medium of the parody is that echo of nature the naked human voice, and that it stands in analogy and parallel everywhere to a series of critiques of individuals in their history. The notions in these words, parody, critique, and the naked human voice, taken under the image of Faustus and Dante, represent the means by which the work was composed, and also both qualify and limit the meaning—the music—which goes on when the book has stopped.

Of these three notions, the naked human voice should be familiar: its presence, real or invoked, has always worked as a great force; it is the substance of poetry so far as we can read it and of music so far as we can play it; and it is the one daemonic force in which we all have some skill at heightening ourselves, by which, in ourselves, we call on something beyond ourselves. Parody and critique as serious means to artistic purpose, especially in the novel, are relatively new, and are without rules of thumb; and what makes them interesting here is the sense that Mann was driven to employ them by a combination of the limitations of his talent and the cultural conditions of our times. Parody is the form of this novel and critique one of its developments. Let us see.

If parody is the right name for the form of this novel it cannot be unique and is not likely without a common cause; which may well be some inability to create individuals along with an unwillingness to resort to type in the use of the age before our own. Gide, Kafka, Joyce, Eliot, Mann—even Yeats and Proust—have none of them had the gift of creating individuals or composing in sustained narrative. Each has lacked power of objective creation; each has depended in high particular upon his own biography. Individual character reached its height with Shakespeare and Rembrandt and Tolstoi, and, if you like, Beethoven. It may be that harmony is needed to create character, vital and cultural harmony, and that in a polyphonic age only parody of character and the individual is possible to express. Private life disappears either into public life or into itself and is in either case, when expressed, only a parody of itself. But if I am right I do not see that parody is any less expressive than the epic. And I suggest that "myth" in the lauding sense we use it of Joyce and Kafka can only be a parody, so self-conscious it is, of what we mean by myth in Greek drama.

A few claimers and disclaimers as to the meanings and uses of the word are in order. Parody is something sung beside the main subject. Parody is not caricature, not satire: it is a means of treating reality so as to come short of it either on purpose or through necessity. Parody emphasizes mechanics, especially prescriptive mechanics in executive technique, and greedily fastens on the merest possibilities in the material. In our day, every man is a parody of his moral self. Parody is our ordinary means of judging men and events. Music alone parodies the rest of humane culture: which is why it frightens us and how we put up with it: we know what is parodied. Because it involves, points at, and limits, what it parodies, parody is a good name for a means of getting at material that—in our state of belief—does not submit to existing system. Parody is arduous, rigorous, and establishes relations in its own way. It makes possible the free use of dualisms—the oldest technique of Yin and Yang, Up and Down—for parody is free of single beliefs and is bent on the object.

In Mann's chapter of the corrupt bargain with the devil we have precisely an example of parody freely resorting to dualism, for here Mann parodies both his own book and the humanity the book was meant to re-discover. But I do not know that Mann parodies himself. For him parody is a way out, and he can be objective about it—as Leverkühn in his opera bouffe of *Love's Labours Lost.* He can submit all his desperate material to the arrogant, debasing parody of itself. That is the advantage of the bourgeois turned artist. It is the rebellion of the bourgeois against himself in a created self. Only the bourgeois understands Bohemia (his slipping) or needs the devil (his climbing); or at any rate, the bourgeois is in the gulf between his slipping and his pride—which is why he adapts to himself the notions of birth and breeding: that he may somehow reach irresponsibility and dishonor. He is like Pascal in this, who saw that birth and breeding save a man twenty years. And it is the devil who lets the bourgeois parody himself; the devil is always what happens to the ideal: the dishonor and irresponsibility of practice carried to an extreme.

What is the temptation to the young bourgeois composer, Leverkühn?—That the presumption of total and absolute guilt—of the sin so great mercy is impossible on it—gives absolute knowledge and with it the nearest approach to absolute redemption. It is the lust in the brain, not the lust in the flesh, that is tempted. As if, thus renouncing love, the human touch, the fraternal, and thus assuming the great human cold (that is, by deliberately parodying our inadequacies), we could somehow come on the elemental and the actual, and, however intolerable themselves, communicate through them a joyous life to those who come after: an ambition, surely, of love and touch and brotherhood. It is the temptation "within"; it has nothing of the temporal power about it. It is the right temptation for the time held to be sterile in its technics and techniques: in a time of asserted omniscience and the mechanization of crafts. Adrian Leverkühn strove for that illumination by which he could restore assent to the conditions of human life by himself, in his genius, first escaping or denying them; and to do this required a compact with the devil: at any rate a confusion between the daemonic and the diabolic. He parodied his humanity in order to find it: at once an affair of pride and force and a protean cheapening of himself: the lout, the merchant, the familiar—above all the lout—in which forms the devil made his apparitions. The parody points, terribly, at the reality, as the devil points at God; and it is one of the possibilities of the humanist in our time so to point.

It seems to be not a possibility but a necessity for the humanist to resort also to critique, to carry his critique along with him and make it a part even of his most imaginative works. Partly he does this to make present what he cannot create, partly to explain what his audience will not understand in what he has created, and partly in the effort to make up for the lack of a common background—the lack of the Great Memory which mothered the Muses—in even a small and select audience. As Shakespeare had to bed down his play about *Troilus and Cressida* with images of lechery and insurrection, a novelist like Thomas Mann has also to bed down his work with a critique of present history and character and surviving memory. If we can think of *Troilus and Cressida* as the train of its images, we can think of *Doctor Faustus* as the train of its critique; both trains are employed for the same purpose: to unite disparate elements, to order inchoate elements, and to mark the vitality of what is united and what is ordered. The image and the critique are what the works are about; and in the case of Mann this is what separates him from Fielding's Lucretian inter-chapters in *Tom Jones* and the essays on the theory of history in Tolstoi's *War and Peace,* where the critique was on a parallel intellection of the subject: In Mann's *Doctor Faustus,* as in *The Magic Mountain,* they are central to the subject and reveal it.

Thus, in *Doctor Faustus,* when we come to Leverkühn's next to last piece *The Apocalypse,* we feel the excitement of a real thing in the critique by Zeitblom which alone presents it to us. We feel all three of our themes: the artist, the humanist, the naked human voice—together with their rigid correspondences in the world of history and the world of critique—all these themes have merged, or at any rate they give voice to one another in one organized place in time. We see, or hear, in the *Apocalypse,* that the music is about all these, and so makes the one "critique" that unites the intellect in the feeling, transforms the feeling in the intellect, and makes of the whole, as Croce would say, an instance of theoretic form. Art has itself become critique.

So it has with Gide: in the various journals for *The Counterfeiters;* with Joyce: in the polylingual multi-myth of *Finnegans Wake;* with Proust: in the "Place Names" and the "social history"; and, perhaps, with Kafka: in the creation and distension of a pseudo-mythical world to explain "K." It is merely because Mann is so much more explicit than these others, and wishes to make his critique stand for so much more of ordinary life in present history than they do, that he stands out as a novelist of critique, and has made more to do with it than they have. But he is not alone; and what he has done with critique, like what he has done with parody, is a reflection of the cultural conditions of the times. Granted that he intended great work, the resort to critique in the novel of the individual as humanist beyond himself was inevitable. For one thing, the horizon of the humanist had stretched enormously with the divisiveness of modern knowledges and their incongruous techniques; for another thing, even the best humanist finds his own Great Memory failing, let alone that of his audience: he must tell himself as well as his reader what he has in mind; and, for a third thing, the impulse to set the individual in his milieu, his history, and what Erich Auerbach calls his "moving background," has run out, along with its dividends, and there has been a renewal of the older impulse to create the individual in terms of his type, that is to say, in terms of the critique of the individual and his "moving background." But since the humanist here is imaginative, the critique itself must become art: which with Mann is the art of music.

There are many ways of saying it. We can think of the novel as the characteristic art of the modern individual and his world; and it may be that the world in which that individual is lodged has so changed that the art of the individual can no longer redeem the sense of the individual, nor the intellect that of the intellect. Critique would then be the last gasp: *Doctor Faustus* would then be the bonfire of the daemonic. Our great hope lies in our consciousness of terrible loss in our inability to portray the individual. Knowing the loss proves the individual still exists, we still hear his music and in the music his voice. In our sense of loss is our right to that music and our new sense that the music is somehow a critique of the reality. Critique is the mind turning to parody because it must; and music is the imperative of the turning.

Parody, then, is what art must do when it has become critique, when in it the individual becomes biography and anecdote; parody comes about because art can no longer be pious to either the journey or the pity in the old forms, and has not yet found the means to settle on new forms. Parody is a form for transition, and in the interim of transition can well lean on music for its models. If music is equivocal and is also the organization of sound, then it is the art both most apt to parody and the furthest from it. It parodies what it is and it reaches what it is through parody; as the later quartets of Bartók show more clearly than any music of Schoenberg. It reaches the naked human voice and—in that—the absolute irresponsibility of art.

Above all it is parody that rescues us from the curse—we cannot be rescued from the burden—of critique and the false escape of anecdote. It is parody that makes it possible, in such an age as ours, to seek what we must shun; makes it possible to see the elements of the substance of our ordeal not in logical or statistical but in organic opposition; and so, after the break-through, make something out of them. Parody brings us to the voice and the irresponsibility.

Let us return with all these provisional and, in all the old senses, disheartening terms to Thomas Mann's book itself. This great man and German and composer, Adrian Leverkühn, is above all a parody of the human. Standing between the dictatorship of the scum of the human race and the folk who threw up the scum; or, not standing, let us say bestriding them, Adrian Leverkühn is that parody of all the bourgeois humanist held dear which shall restore him: he is what is in the names of his principal works—*Love's Labours Lost, Gesta Romanorum, Apocalypse, Doctor Faustus.* He is that terrible parody of the bourgeois, the "break-through" by which he may yet be re-created, only in another image. Only the idol is dead. Parody is a means, no matter how hard to take still a means to touch the understanding, which might, for practical purposes, reach further than the everlasting mercy—at least when, like Leverkühn, we must pass through the daemonic to reach again the human.

If that is true—if in any sense we must pass through the daemonic to reach the human—we can take that truth as the clue to *Doctor Faustus* at its most serious level: which is the level where we identify Faust and Leverkühn. Adrian Faust Leverkühn is the daemonic scape-goat for humanity. He comes to his destruction, is absorbed by the devil, precisely at the moment when he has understood the sins of mankind by re-enacting them in that mood of the mind which is both most human, in that it stirs, or touches, the deepest human places, and, also, is most removed from the human in that it touches directly upon none of the ordinary concerns of men. Faust has sold his humanity in order to come upon understanding of the force which keeps humanity alive and perennially on the edge, in the maw, of suicide. And this Faust, this Leverkühn, achieves his understanding by creating its image in the most equivocal language available to man, which is the image of music: the naked human voice. But there is no redemption here, no Christ, no Cross, only destruction. Our Christian religion has at its heart the image of a perfectly good man who takes up the evil that breaks life into his goodness, taking it to salvation in a mystery. The image of Faust as Leverkühn is not a mockery of Christ but a reversal: it works back into the conditions from which Christ is the redemption. It reminds us in its own way, and in another language, what the European Christ is for. The devil is always the other thing than God, like God; the devil is God gone to the devil; the man possessed of the devil is the man stripped of everything human except the elementally human: those very elements out of which, after each catastrophic slump to gulf-bottom, the human can be re-born, re-made, re-created.

That is why Adrian Leverkühn is cold—the coldness of the human; why he is mathematical—the sequence of the heart-beat; why he is aloof—the loneliness of the human; and it is why he is proud—because of the great human pride, the temptation to re-create himself in his own fastness. He is cold, mathematic, aloof and proud; but he is neither a good man nor a bad man. He is neither above nor below good and evil; he is both good and evil in the culture of 1900 to 1950, and being both he is apart from either. He is the image—the idol or eidolon—to which good and evil happen, and he is required to be enough deprived of ordinary humanity to meet the truth of that image: the truth which he devoted himself, with a devotion constantly on the edge of infatuation, to create. And for this devotion, this infatuation, he must be the man without God; for if he thought he had God, if he felt he were the man-God, he would have been the god who gave in to the temptations on the mountain, he would have been the god become—as Hitler and the others—the dictatorship of the scum of the earth: the debasement of the divine, or the daemonic, in the human. No; Adrian Leverkühn is the man become the devil on behalf of the divine; the man become the devil insofar as the devil is a parody as a means of access to God: Thomas Mann's limit of human approach.

There is something absolutely irresponsible about any image which is perfectly evil, perfectly good, or perfectly apart from both; but of the three images, the human imagination in our day, having too much experience of the first, and too little of the second, can attempt to create only the third. This is no time for Cervantes to create Don Quixote; and anybody who tried would make a worse failure of the perfectly good man than Dostoevsky did with that haunting failure Prince Myshkin in that great book *The Idiot.* Thomas Mann was right. In line with Cervantes and Dostoevsky, he yet followed Goethe, who struggled to make the very Europe live which we wish to re-create, and like Goethe Mann chose the image of Faust as his weapon. Only in the image of Faust can Thomas Mann's understanding, lacking the everlasting mercy and the living grace, come upon "the hope beyond hopelessness, the transcendence of despair" which may yet break through to mercy and grace because they are the naked human voice itself, the voice crying in the dark always there. But the voice is the voice of the Muses.

PART TWO

STUDIES IN DOSTOEVSKY

CRIME AND PUNISHMENT: *Murder in Your Own Room*

Crime and Punishment has upon most readers an impact as immediate and obvious and full as the news of murder next door; one *almost* participates in the crime, and the trivial details become obsessively important. It has besides a secondary impact, by which, as one feels it, one discovers that one has been permanently involved in the nature of the crime: one has somehow contributed to the clarification of the true residual nature of crime in general through having contributed to the enactment of this crime in particular. It is the feeling of this impact that leads us to say our powers of attention have been exhausted. But there is a third and gradual impact, which comes not only at the end but almost from the beginning to the end, creating in us new and inexhaustible powers of attention. This is the impact of what Dostoevsky meant by punishment. The three impacts are united by the art of the novelist, and they are felt simultaneously. It is only that we are not aware at the time of the triple significance, and must, when it does transpire, rebuild it analytically. Thus we may come to estimate what it is that we know—what it is that has been clarified in the history of Raskolnikov which we had known all along in ourselves without being aware of it: we estimate our own guilt.

A crime is above all an act against the institutions of human law, custom, or religion; and there is a sense in which any act may be understood as criminal, for if the institution cannot be found against which it is committed, then it may be called an anarchic act—against some institution that has not yet come to exist, but which will exist because of the crime. This notion comes from putting Rousseau's dusty vision in reverse. If, as Rousseau thought for one inspired moment, the evils of living come mostly from human institutions, it is as likely true, though not as inspired, that our institutions arise out of the evil that we do. It is LaForgue who has said it best, and without any but poetic logic to blister his cry:

> Allez, sterile ritournelles!
> La Vie est vraie et criminelle!

This cry of LaForgue represents the lyric sense that must inhabit every criminal who truly imagines his crime, if only for a flash, *before* he commits it to act. What the criminal imagines afterwards is another thing and we shall come to it. Here it is the crime only that has been imagined, and the promise of liberation in the cry within.

So it is with Raskolnikov. If we feel his case in terms of the LaForgue lines we can understand both the motivation of his crime and the external logic of most of his conduct afterwards. It is the story of *Crime and Punishment* at the level of its immediate impact. We are very near it; it is the murder that only by some saving accident we did not ourselves commit—as we did not make a million, win a race, or conquer Europe, all the things it is still not impossible to do, and which, because we have not done them, may yet tempt us to murder. Between temptation and deed there is no distance at all in symbolic meaning. With that symbolic strength in mind, the story of Raskolnikov becomes not only possible but probable, and, as we attend it, not only probable but proved. Let us look and see.

How easy it is to believe that this young, handsome, proud, and sensitive boy might be drawn *first of all* to the possibility of murder as the way out of an intolerable situation. It is the situation of poverty, debt, starvation, shabbiness, sickness, loneliness; for Raskolnikov has reached such a stage of privation that even thought has become a luxury—a kind of luxurious hallucinated hysteria; an extremity in which only the rashest dream seems a normal activity. It is the situation of the sponge, too, for Raskolnikov has come to depend on his mother and sister for help they cannot afford to give, for help they can give only by prostituting themselves in marriage and servile relationships. The sponge who is aware that he is a sponge is in an awkward situation; the pride of his awareness deprives him of the use of the exactions he makes; and that is how it is with Raskolnikov, as he lies in his attic committing symbolic murder. He deceives himself, proudly, that he has conceived murder to symbolize his mother's and sister's freedom as well as his own. He lends his dark motive the external colour of a good deed, and then identifies the colour with the motive, and forgets what the murder, dark within him, really is. But to starve and be a sponge, that is not all Raskolnikov has to put up with in his pride; he is in the situation, too, of the proud man of intellect who has as yet done nothing and who is afraid that there will be nothing for him to do unless he invents it. Not only can he do nothing for his poverty or for his family, he is in the terrible position of being unable to do anything for himself. Such is his pride, that none of the ordinary things men do will be enough; and such is his pride, too, that none of the things ordinary people—his mother, his sister, his forgotten friends—can do for him are tolerable to him; he is the man for whom no one can do anything. Deeper still, he is that part of all men which cannot be touched, but which must create an image of itself in some extraordinary deed, some act against ordinary people and against the ordinary part of himself. The extraordinary wells within him and inundates the ordinary self with its fever. And in that fever, which never leaves him while we know him, the possibility of murder becomes the necessity of murder.

What is fully imagined as necessary has goodness and freedom at the very heart of its horror, a sentiment which may be interpreted in different ways, having to do either with the tearing down of order or with the envelopment of disorder, or, finally, with the balancing of several disorders so as to form an order. At the level of immediate impact, Raskolnikov's story is concerned with the tearing down of order; that is the melodrama which carries us along and exhausts our attention. What Dostoevsky does to that story, the immense clarification of secret life and intimate impulse which he brings to it, composes the secondary impact of the story, and brings us to the second stage where the disorder brought about in the first stage is enveloped by the created personality of Raskolnikov. Actually, the two processes go on at once, in the sense that no matter how far into the second stage Dostoevsky leads us, the first stage is never left behind, but is rather always present, a frame of action and image, to carry the significance of the second stage. This is to say that Dostoevsky never fails of the primary task of the novelist; if his story seems for the moment to have been left behind, it is only that in reality it has got ahead of us, and when we catch up we see how much has been done without our noticing it. The story of the Crime is blended with the clarification of the Punishment; the actor creates the role which expresses the nature and significance of his deed; Raskolnikov, in the end, becomes the product of his crime, but still depends on it to command our attention.

That is how Dostoevsky envelops the disorder consequent upon Raskolnikov's attempt at the destruction of order. With the third possibility, whereby the imagination not only envelops disorder—our substantial chaos—in a created personality, but proceeds to balance the sense of several disorders—the tensions of chaos—against each other so as to form a new order; with this possibility Dostoevsky has little to do. It is not that he was necessarily unequal to the task, but that the nature, source, and direction of his insights did not lead him to undertake it. His view of necessity was simpler, and his sense of possibility more simplified, than the task would require; his vision was that of the primitive Christian, and that vision was so powerful within him that it blinded him to everything else. To him the edge of the abyss of sin was the horizon of salvation by faith, and suffering was the condition of vision. Sin was the Crime, and the suffering created by faith was the Punishment.

If we push the operation of this insight one step further, it becomes evident that the act of life itself is the Crime, and that to submit, by faith, to the suffering of life at the expense of the act is to achieve salvation—or, if you like a less theological phrase, it is to achieve integration or wholeness of personality. It is only dramatically true that the greater the sin the greater the salvation, and it is only arbitrarily true that any one act is sinful more than another act or than all acts. The crime of Raskolnikov, and its punishment in created suffering, could have been as great if he had never stirred from his room, if only the novelist's imagination could have conceived them. But the imagination requires images, as vision requires fables and thought requires formulas, before conceptions can be realised; which is to say that the faculties of men are not equal to their needs except by the intervention of symbols which they discover rather than create, and which they discover best of all in stories of violence, or of the sense of violence, or of the promise of violence.

So we watch, with the immediate attention which discovers meaning, the process of Raskolnikov trying to make a hero—a complete man—of himself by committing a foul and frivolous murder. Any animal might strike another down without need when the odour of blood is thick, and it means nothing. But we are shown how much this murder of an old and malevolent pawnbroker, ripe for death, as Raskolnikov says, ripe as a louse, is not meaningless but huge with meaning. The meaning begins with the stench of Petersburg, the stench of the detailed plans, the stench of pothouses, the pervading sense of the filthy possibilities of the human heart, and the glittering eyes of the victim peering through the slit of the door. The meaning grows more meaningful, irretrievably meaningful, when in the second chapter we are exposed to Marmeladov in the stinking tavern and hear his confession of drunken humiliation and of what it has brought upon Katerina his wife in the way of sickness and shame and anger and hairpulling, and brought upon his daughter too, in her glad submissive acceptance of the humiliation of prostitution. It is impossible to *say* how this adds to the richness of Raskolnikov's motive, but like the general images of stench and violence and drunkenness, it is impossible not to *know,* and very precisely, how much it does add. Let us say that it exposes Raskolnikov, and through him the reader, to a kind of dead-level human degradation in terms of images which revolt him as he assents to them.

At any rate they fit him—for the purposes of the story—they fit him to see as further degradation the events which his mother's letter reports to him. Before he opens the letter we see his cluttered mind in his sleazy room trying to work around the idea of a "fortune all at once"; and in the letter he reads how indeed that is precisely what Douania his sister is about to get by selling herself to Luzhin. Douania has permitted herself or has been driven to do just the practical, ordinary thing which Raskolnikov, the extraordinary man, is unable to do, and which—as it is being done for *him*—is the more intolerably humiliating to him. Her marriage is like the prostitution of Sonia. Thinking of it, Hamlet-like, the idea of the murder rediscovers itself most naturally in his mind, and he finds that he had *felt beforehand* that it would come back; it has begun to acquire a kind of reality quite independent of him except that it requires to be completed.

Your ordinary novelist might well have now proceeded to the completion of the deed, but Dostoevsky saw deeper into the nature of the deed and knew that it required further preparation, so that it might be as ripe as the victim. Raskolnikov goes out for a breath of air and to escape the pressure of his dilemma. But there is no escape, except from one level of intensity to a deeper level. Walking on the boulevard the double pressure of Sonia and of Douania springs upon him in the shape of the drunken young girl, with the torn dress, and indecorous posture, evidently just seduced and then discarded, who is being pursued by the plump gentleman. In his shabby and dishevelled pride, and with his uprooted and irresolute mind he first attempts to save the girl and then gives it up as a bad job; he revolts against his revulsion, reminding himself of the percentage theory of vice whereby "a certain number" are bound to go that way, and resolves forthwith to go see Razumihin, that simpleton of a man who takes things as they are. But again he changes his mind; he cannot see Razumihin till after "It." The image of the debauched girl has set the murder to pursuing him still more closely. He contrives for himself, as he thinks, an escape in the green islands of the Neva, where there is no stench, no drunkenness, no human filth. The human filth is stronger. He first buys himself a glass of vodka, and then walks out exhausted, turning aside on the way home and falls asleep in the bushes, where a dream assaults him with a fresh image of the little sorrel horse beaten to death because it cannot pull all humanity. In the dream he rushes to kiss the bleeding face of the horse as it dies, and at that moment wakes. The moment of waking is the nearest he comes to renouncing his crime before committing it, and it is the nearest, too, that he comes to realising its nature before the event. "It was as though an abscess that had been forming for a month past in his heart had suddenly broken. Freedom, freedom! He was free from that spell, that sorcery, that obsession!" He had reached the point which Shakespeare, in his own play of Crime and Punishment, *Measure for Measure,* calls the point where the two prayers cross, where, in the human heart, good and evil are created in the one gesture.

It was coincidence, you will remember, that decided the event. Raskolnikov happened to hear, on his way home, that the old pawnbroker would be left alone at seven the following evening, and he heard it at precisely the moment that he had given up the idea of the murder, when he had, in fact, begun again to use his reason and will. But the other thing had grown in him like a disease, and feeding on the coincidence, was able to destroy his will and reason, that is to say his sense of propriety in the social order. It may be observed, for those who carp at the use of coincidence as belittling the probabilities, that on the contrary the use of coincidence in art, like the sense of it in life, heightens the sense of inevitability; for coincidence is the artist's way of representing those forces in us not ourselves. Coincidence, properly dealt with, creates our sense of that other self within us whom we neither can ever quite escape nor quite meet up with.

In this case it is the perfected chain of coincidence, upon which Dostoevsky lavishes so many pages, that builds up the murder so that it is a kind of separate being existing between Raskolnikov and his victim. As he climbs the stairs, he feels that Alyona Ivanovna ought to be ready for him, ready to be murdered, for he feels that the murder is somewhere between them, other than either, but equally accessible to both. It was in the nature of Dostoevsky's insight to see always that the actor and the patient are both implicated in the deed, and that they are joined by it. The actor, in this case, has more consciousness than the patient of the implication; in *The Idiot* it is the other way round, and Myshkin, the patient, is shown as more conscious, or more representative, of the deeds that are done to him than the doers of the deeds can possibly be. In *Crime and Punishment,* it is Sonia who is perhaps the counterpart of Myshkin, for to her all deeds happen whether the doers realise it or not, and they happen, moreover, completely. It is perhaps because Raskolnikov is the other sort, the sort who requires of a deed that before it is credible or fully significant he must do it himself. He does not believe in the murder until he has done it, and not altogether even then. Constantly it slips away, a thing he realizes that he has forgotten, or a thing he has to re-enact, to emphasize, and so a thing that tends to lose its meaning except as he identifies himself with it; whereas to Sonia, once she has learned of it, once she has submitted herself to the idea of it in him, she has no doubts about it and it is entirely meaningful. Nothing herself, Sonia is able to contain everything; while Raskolnikov, who must be everything himself, can contain nothing for long. Dante would have known how to punish him, looking for a mirror through an eternal hell; but Dostoevsky has rather to transform him in order to save him, or more accurately to show him as about to be saved in Sonia's eyes.

But he is not transformed for a long time, never permanently in the book; never can he leave the murder which fixed him, nor the images of which it was made: the images of stench, poverty, drunkenness, vanity, sick-hunger, lechery and intellectual debauchery, through which the murder comes to be a deed in being, with the double power of invocation and growth. At first, indeed, he forgets it for the images and the sickness which went with it, and when he wakes to it he finds that instead of feeling it behind him it has somehow got ahead of him and he is driven to catch up to it. Instead of freedom, power, completeness, he is more at loss than ever, and more incoherent, there are only "scraps and shreds of thought," suspicions, excitements, alarms, and fresh temptations to extraordinary declarations of himself. This is, of course, the first phase of the Punishment for the Crime, that having striven by the crime to reach a complete solution of his incomplete life, he should find himself not only less complete than ever and more wayward but actually perilously incoherent, with a personality on the verge of dissipation. He lives in a haunted vertigo, into which for the time he can invoke only the shrieking phantoms of rage and dread. He is in the position, so humiliating to his continuing pride, where he is completely powerless as the perfectly good man, as powerless as Sonia. There is nothing he can yet see to do for himself, and nothing any longer that he can do for others. When the police send for him about his IOU which his landlady had sold, he feels himself possessed by "a gloomy sensation of agonising, everlasting solitude and remoteness," and knows that it will never be possible for him to appeal to anyone in any cirmustance of life. There is a sense in which Dostoevsky might have stopped at this point, for he had put Raskolnikov on the path at the end of which lay the meaning of his Crime as Punishment. For as in the Christian psychology no man may complete himself in deed, so the meaning of a deed can never be completed within the history of the man who enacts it. Only the judgment completes either the man, or his deed, or his meaning.

But both the deed and the meaning can continue in their course of meaningfulness. The growth of meaning is infinite. At the moment he feels his agonising solitude form consciously within him he hears the police discuss the murder; that is, it is given to him from outside for the first time, and as not his murder, but as an object in no one's possession; at once he is driven to confess, to seize it for his own, but a combination of the fumes of paint and the pang of creation cause him to faint. When he comes to, he goes out leaving a strange impression and a potent silence behind him.

Out of that strangeness and silence grows the pursuit-game which occupies the rest of the book, for Raskolnikov having decided that suspicions may have been roused about him from his peculiar conduct, begins playing a complicated and eccentric game, or rather a set of games. He pursues the police, eggs the police on to pursue him, and himself both pursues the murder, the acknowledgement of it, and denies it whenever he comes face to face with it. The result of all this rash, tortuous, and vain activity is that he creates such an image of the murder that at last it overwhelms him. He plays his hands so that others play to him. In the event, there is nothing for anyone to believe about him except the extraordinary reality of the murder. He could not have made more certain of his arrest and imprisonment had that been his entire object. Only he delayed it, played with it, encouraged it to develop, in order to get the full savour of it and of himself.

First he rouses unconscious suspicions in Razumihin, then in Zossim—of the doctor in whom the suspicions may have been quite conscious, for he looked at Raskolnikov "curiously" whenever there was opportunity, and especially after that scene where Raskolnikov himself first realises the murder in a parallel and arbitrary image which brims and trembles as you look at it. It is that image which comes when Raskolnikov lies abed listening to the doctor and Razumihin talk of the murder, and how a house-painter has been mixed up in it. Nastasya, who is present, bursts out that Lizaveta was murdered, too.

"Lizaveta," murmured Raskolnikov hardly audibly.

"Lizaveta, who sold old clothes. Didn't you know her? She used to come here. She mended a shirt for you, too."

> Raskolnikov turned to the wall where in the dirty, yellow paper he picked out one clumsy, white flower with brown lines on it and began examining how many petals there were in it, how many scallops in the petals and how many lines on them. He felt his arms and legs as lifeless as though they had been cut off. He did not attempt to move, but stared obstinately at the flower.

It is so that the murder is brought home by the housemaid's first mention of the other and incidental murder of Lizaveta. We feel what passed in Raskolnikov's mind, and feel it as if it passed in his face, and in his hands, too: quite as if he had plucked the scalloped petals of the clumsy white flower off the wallpaper. Razumihin, who was simple, may have seen nothing, but the doctor, looking at this dissenting soul, surely saw what Raskolnikov saw in the flower even if he could not then have named it. The blankest or the most conventional image is, as Dostoevsky knew, the best to hold the deepest symbol if only there is enough tension present when it is named. It is only another instance of this device that when Raskolnikov is about to go into the bar where he meets and gives himself away to Zametov, he first sees a good many drunken women, some of forty and some of seventeen, almost all of whom "had blackened eyes." Raskolnikov, who had gone out to end *this,* as he put it to himself, reflects upon this bevy with blackened eyes and pocked cheeks, that even the worst life is precious.

> "Only to live, to live and live! Life, whatever it may be! . . . How true it is! Good God, how true! Man is a vile creature! . . . And vile is he who calls him vile for that," he added a moment later.

Whereupon he proceeds to risk his life, to make it precious, by playing like Hamlet on Rosencrantz and Guildenstern, upon the suspicious nerves of Zametov the police clerk as he drank tea in a restaurant. This scene, like the two great scenes with Porfiry, and like the last scene with Svidrigaïlov, show Raskolnikov clinging with a kind of ultimate shuddering tenacity to his original proud role of the extraordinary man, the role of Napoleon within the little man, and clinging the more desperately because in the act of playing it he sees the role is false, the role of the condemned man whose life is thereby sweet.

What else happens at the same time, the history of the growth of the Punishment along with the realization of the Crime, is of course present in these scenes, but it has been instigated in other scenes—those with his mother and sister and Luzhin and Razumihin and the Marmeladovs; and it is perfected in other scenes still, those with Sonia especially, though these scenes might well be lifeless and pointless without their counterparts with Porfiry and Svidrigaïlov. There is a synergy—a working together and back and forth—between these counterparts much as there is a synergy between the two parts, the proud, self-willed part and the meek, submissive part of Raskolnikov's character. This working together takes place, and the resultant unity is seen, not because there is any logical or organic connection between the parts, but because, quite to the contrary, the conflicting elements are dramatised in association, in parallels that, as they say, never actually meet except as opposites. The more nearly they seem to be forced into meeting, the more disparate they actually show themselves to be. The fusion, if it can be called a fusion, is in the dramatic *product* of the conflicting elements, not of the elements themselves.

It is something along these lines, I think, that the theory of the "doubles" in Dostoevsky must be approached, and this whether we think of single characters or of whole books and the doubleness of the conflicts within either. Let us look at Raskolnikov, who is usually thought of as a typical Dostoevsky Double. He is self-willed and will-less, he is proud and he becomes humiliated, he loves Sonia and hates her at the same moment, he is fond of Razumihin and cannot tolerate him, he is both on the edge of confession and of anathema all along, he is good to the point of giving all that he has and evil to the point of taking life; and in short there is neither certainty nor limit to any of his moods or acts; any role is dominant for the moment to another role that may at once take its place because it has been really dominant underneath. But he is not these roles in turn, he is the product of all their playing taken together. In any pair, the one may be taken as the idea of the other, and the other the reality of the idea, and the only alternation is as to which, at a given moment, is idea and which reality. The relation is rather like that between the idea of murder and the image of the white flower on the wall-paper, where we can reverse it and say it is the relation between the idea of the flower and the image of the murder. What we get is a kind of steady state precariously maintained between the conflicting elements. The balance tips, but it recovers in the act of tipping. We should feel it as we feel similar physiological states in the body—only as the disturbance and forward drive of life—were it not that the language itself and Dostoevsky's taste for seeing the opposite to every presented element have together a tendency to formularise pure types, and then to ignore for the moment what does not exemplify the type. What happens is, by language and its dialectic mode, that Dostoevsky's imagination arrests, for the maximum possible amount of attention, the moments when the balance does tip from love to hate, from pride to humiliation, from idea to deed, from image to tension, and by the arrest, by the attention which is bent upon the moment of arrest, we see how the one in each case fecundates the other. We seem to see deeply what they make together by seeing wilfully what they are apart.

By a little progress of this notion, we can say that Raskolnikov is balanced in turn against the other characters in this novel, and that the other characters and their stories make something with Raskolnikov which is quite different from anything found in them as types, though there would be no product of their whole conflict if there was not a great deal that was living within each type, from Razumihin to Porfiry to Svidrigaïlov to Sonia, and all the rest. As illustration, let us take first the Marmeladov family, and consider by what astonishing luck it was that Dostoevsky thought of putting them into the history of Raskolnikov and the punishment of his crime. They were to have been, the whole little crowd of them, a novel all to themselves called "The Drunkards," a novel showing, no doubt, all the ills and humiliations that can come from the head of a poor family who has given over to heavy drinking. The luck is that Dostoevsky had them all going, with past and present and future, when Raskolnikov happened to meet old Marmeladov in the tavern and heard his humiliating confession with such apparently inexplicable sympathy. The truth is that he has something deeply in common with him, and again that Marmeladov has something which he has not yet but which he must have. What they have in common comes out when Marmeladov says that he has *nowhere to turn* except to his sick and somewhat crazy wife. Raskolnikov sees that it is not Marmeladov the good-natured drunk that turns, but Marmeladov humiliated, on hands and knees, with his hair pulled, Marmeladov in the mud which he Raskolnikov has not yet reached, but will reach in good time. Man grows used to everything, the scoundrel, says Raskolnikov, and adds: But what if he is not a scoundrel?

The scene is something like the great scenes in Dickens, caricature by direct observation, with the difference that Dostoevsky—and this is perhaps the way Dostoevsky himself read Dickens—replaces zest of observation for its own sake with the severity of attention that is based upon zeal, and replaces the anguish of social consciousness with the dignity of religion. Marmeladov, like Micawber, is able to represent much beyond himself because he is something of a buffoon; he can talk and act for talking and acting's sake; and he can be honest, and let himself go, just to see what will happen; he can see himself at his worst in order to be at his best. And so he does; he produces, to show himself at his utmost, and for the sake of Raskolnikov, for the sake of this new strange novel in which he unconsciously finds himself, the character and personality of Sonia, whom Raskolnikov needs as complement and salvation, and whom the novel needs for mechanics and plot. And not Sonia only, he also produces, by just the agency of his being, scenes in which all manner of things which bear on the novel can take place. His death, his funeral, the lyric insanity of Katerina his wife and her death-dance in the streets, all these are provided with new and enriched context by the accidental meeting in the tavern of the *distrait* Raskolnikov and the drunken buffoon Marmeladov. And not only Marmeladov himself, but each of his family, as he precipitates their fates through his drunkenness and buffoonery, add to the context of Raskolnikov's growing fate.

Together they furnish him with his own opposite. As he is the person who above all must act, they are the persons who must be acted upon. He is the criminal, and they are the victims, victims generally and all the way through in much the same way that the old pawnbroker was in Raskolnikov's eyes "ripe" to be murdered. No degradation is too great for the old drunkard who has nowhere to turn; you have only to put fresh degradation in his way and he will take it up with gusto. Katerina, too, eager to find insult in everyone's speech, in his absence or in his presence, imagines insult and injury upon herself at every opportunity. The children, even, with their illness and their rags cannot be treated except with brutality. And as for Sonia, she is not only eager and willing, she fairly demands further humiliation. By prostituting herself, this thin, bird-like creature, almost without a body, shows herself as inviting at best further depravity; for surely no one not depraved, no one not desiring to sack the *last* citadel of integrity, would have any use for her. Sonia had to come from such a family, for only out of the experience of such utter humiliation could her own perfect humility grow. As they are damned so she is blessed, by the enormous shift in significance caused by the shift of a single syllable. It is Gide, who knew his Dostoevsky well, who observed that where humility opened the gates of heaven, humiliation opened those of hell. Sonia's blessedness is built upon the bottomlessness of their hell. She accepts, and makes into inner strength, a worse stage of the experience which tore them apart.

Thus, as Raskolnikov comes into contact with Marmeladov and his wife, as he probes them with his intellect, they absorb his sense of himself into a kind of private hell, an abyss beyond soundings, quite off the continental shelf of consciousness which his intellect, however demoniac, can reach. But Sonia, and this is the secret of her personality, can no more be penetrated by Raskolnikov's intellect than her soul can be ravished through the degradation of her body. That is her attraction as a prostitute: that she cannot be prostituted in anything that she has to offer; and that is her power over Raskolnikov, the power of perfect submissiveness which in another place Dostoevsky calls the greatest power in the world: it is the power that he cannot attain by any deed, but that can be attained by imitation, by suffering what she has suffered. It is the power of her suffering, the happiness of it, that not so much overcomes him as it infects or fecundates him. For he is not overcome, though it is promised that he will be; he fights back, the very feeling of her goodness, his very sense of the stigma of her faith, aggravates his pride and the intellectual structure upon which his pride is built, so that when he goes to her for comfort and strength he finds that he has to torture her, and repel her at every level. The love he feels for her is also and simultaneously hate, and there is no difference between the emotions as he feels them, only as he intellectually knows what they are. And this is an example of the profound psychological rightness of Dostoevsky's judgment, for surely it takes only a pause for judgment to see that as hate or pride is the burden Raskolnikov carries so love or humility is the *burden* of Sonia's life. If she feels his burden as love and accepts it as of nature, he must feel the burden of her love as intolerable. He is indeed a kind of Prodigal Son who finds the love with which he is welcomed the very burden from which he ran away in the first place. It was not of Sonia that he made the following remark but thinking of her and just before seeing her, so it fits all the more: "Oh, if only I were alone and no one loved me and I too had never loved anyone! *Nothing of all this would have happened.*"

It will be remembered that earlier in the book Razumihin has explained to Douania that her brother is perhaps a person incapable of love. Razumihin may have meant only that Raskolnikov is a lonely fellow, but he was literally right as well; no one can be said to love who does not feel as acceptable the burden of love in return, and who does not feel, too, that in loving someone positively, he is imposing the most difficult of human burdens. Sonia knows this in herself, by intuition directed inwards as well as outwards, as a condition of her being, and it is to that double burden that she submits.

Like the crime which existed *between* the old pawnbroker, so between Sonia and Raskolnikov there exists her intuition of love, which she feels so strongly that he *must* know, that gradually by a contagion from her understanding he does know it. It is a love, this unassailable love of the unsmirchable prostitute, that has nothing to do with sex. Not that it might not have been sexual, and even might have taken the means of a kind of ultimate lechery of the spirit, and still have been within the Christian insight, but that Dostoevsky was unable ever to create a character or a mood which showed more than the most superficial aspects of sexual awareness. His people were not eunuchs or in any way deprived of sex but they were born without it. It is love *manqué* that Dostoevsky deals with, love *malgré-lui;* and it is for this reason perhaps that Dostoevsky is able to show love as pure spiritual renunciation. That is why, too, in what was to others the romantic fancy of purity in a prostitute, he sees a kind of exorbitant and omnivorous reality: a true dramatic enactment of the idea of purity. That is why, again, he so often concerns his characters with the idea of debauching young girls, girls before puberty, in whom sex as anyone else would have understood it would not have ripened, so that the debauchery would be of the actor alone.

If these remarks help explain the character and power of Sonia who is of the character of the saint, they help with the others as well, most particularly with the riddle of Svidrigaïlov, to whom we shall come in a moment for his own sake, but whom now we shall consider in his relation with the character of Douania, Raskolnikov's sister. This young lady is painted as all abloom with normality; she and her mother belong in Dostoevsky's long gallery of simple, intelligent, sincere, generous, impulsive, and dependably decent women, young and old, of whom there are samples in almost every one of his novels—as, to give but one example, Mme. Epanchin and her daughter Aglaia in *The Idiot*. Always they serve the same purpose, to act as foils or background for the extraordinary actions of distorted or driven individuals, such as Raskolnikov and Myshkin. They preserve their identity and their normal responsiveness through every form of violence and disorder; it is their normality which, by contrast, promotes the meaningfulness of the good and bad angels, the light and the dark angels, whose actions make the stories. Nothing in themselves but attractive types, they come to life in terms of the protagonists.

In *Crime and Punishment* they represent the normal conduct from which Raskolnikov departs; they represent the order of society which he tears down and envelops; it is they, their lives, to whom he gives meaning. In the same way Luzhin, the bourgeois on the make, and Lebetziatnikov the nihilist reformer, are caricatures, the one malicious and the other kindly, of normal types of eccentricity within the ordered society which produces at its extremes the super-egotist Raskolnikov and the super-reformer Sonia. But these figures gather part of their meaning from the driven, demoniac, "secret" character of Svidrigaïlov, the lecher of women and debaucher of souls: the mysterious figure whose evil is concentrated in what is asserted to be, but never shown, his intense and overweening sexuality. As an example of sexual behavior, Svidrigaïlov is incredible. Sex is Dostoevsky's symbol for a diabolic, destructive power, which he can sense but cannot measure, and which he cannot otherwise name. This aspect of the Svidrigaïlov type of figure is Dostoevsky's attempt to explain, to dramatise and invoke, a force which he does not seem ever to have understood but which he knows must exist. It is a lonely, awkward, proud sort of power, hovering always on the brink of suicide; it is haunted and haunting; it is the power of the "Other" thing, the other self, the dark side of the self, the substance and drive of that secret world in us which the devil creates, the power which in conventional life—the life which we mostly live—we successfully ignore, so that we tend to estimate its presence in others rather than in ourselves—as if others were our othermost selves. Thus Douania's soul had been imperilled by Svidrigaïlov's attempt to seduce her, and imperilled precisely by Svidrigaïlov's technique, which he outlines to Raskolnikov, of assaulting her through purity. He has caused her purity, not her baser emotions but her purity, somehow to desire him, and she had been rescued, in the first instance, in the nick of time: by the confusion, in Marfa Petrovna's eyes, of her purity with her lust. Raskolnikov understands well enough what the risk is—that his sister may be contaminated, that her decency may somehow come to absorb the temptation which Svidrigaïlov affords her in the new terms of his generosity. What he does not understand is the means by which the contamination, the trespass, will take place, which is by the frustration of violence on Douania's part when in the lonely room with the locked door, she tries so hard to shoot him. She is left by the desperate effort—by the fruitless tumescence of her spirit—in a very ambiguous state, which the story of Raskolnikov's Crime and Punishment did not have time to develop. One is not sure whether in that scene Douania has absorbed something from Svidrigaïlov, or whether Svidrigaïlov has absorbed what he wanted from Douania. Something has passed between them, at any rate, which leaves Svidrigaïlov either done for or contented, either vastated or fully occupied. In either case his remaining hours are justified—his visit to his little girl fiancee and his farewell present, the adventure in the hotel-room, the mouse in the bed, the five-year-old girl whose smile turns in his dream to a harlot's grin, the dream of the flood, which is to say the coming of judgment, and the suicide at dawn. We feel that the enigma of Svidrigaïlov has either been solved beyond our understanding or that it did not really exist—quite the problem of the devil. At any rate, his function has been fulfilled for everyone but Raskolnikov.

His relations to Raskolnikov have gone beyond those with the others, both in scope and intent, however much they may depend for their actuality upon the others. For Svidrigaïlov is a foil for the whole story. He comes before the crime, in a way induces the crime to come into being, is the first to perceive the crime, and in a way *finishes* the crime without (since he does not have Raskolnikov's luck in finding Sonia) reaching the punishment. He *is* Raskolnikov in simpler perspective, he is Raskolnikov's other self, a mirror of being into which Raskolnikov never quite dares to look. He is the mystery of Raskolnikov's other self. The sense of him is symbolic, as it always is with mystery. Because he is a mystery beforehand, and exhibits himself mysteriously and providentially, he gathers meaning as he goes along, but not too clearly. He has the advantage of being not well understood, the figure grasped at but not caught, whom we are always about to understand. In fact we have frequently the sense of understanding him perfectly until we stop to query what it is we understand, when we find only that he represents precisely that secret life within us which drive us into incomprehensible actions. Like the character of Stavrogin in *The Possessed,* of whom Dostoevsky says in his notes that he was not *meant* to be understood, but was meant rather to be a reservoir of the portentous, the possible, the mysterious, he is the symbolic clarification of that which cannot be expressed other than symbolically. He is the promise upon which we lean, knowing that it cannot be kept. He recedes like the horizon that follows us, only when we look.

Perhaps we may say that Svidrigaïlov envelops the disorder brought about by Raskolnikov's crime by imagining a kind of order which we cannot reach but which is always about to overwhelm us. He is a symbol of the mystery of the abyss, and it is a great witness to the depth of Dostoevsky's imagination that he is able to create in the flesh, with eyes too blue and flesh too youthful, such figures at will.

It is no less a test of Dostoevsky's skill—not his depth but his skill—that he is able to employ the one remaining major character in the book without, as it were, creating him at all. I mean, of course, that thirty-five year old roly-poly of the disengaged intellect called Porfiry, that man whose life, as he insists to Raskolnikov, is already finished, who has no other life to live, and nothing to do with what remains to him but probe and prance intellectually. Porfiry is so much a victim of moral fatigue that he is beneath every level of being but that of intellectual buffoonery. He represents order; he understands desire, ambition, all forms of conduct, but he knows nothing of the sources and ends of conduct, except that he can catch at them, in the midst of the game of the drowning man which he plays so long and so skilfully, like so many straws that only just elude his dancing fingers. But he is unreal, except as an agency of the plot, something to make the wheels go round; he is a fancy of the pursuing intellect whom Raskolnikov must have invented had he not turned up of his own accord. As Svidrigaïlov and Sonia between them represent the under-part, and the conflict in the under-part, of Raskolnikov's secret self, so Porfiry represents the maximum possible perfection of the artificial, intellectual self under whose ministrations Raskolnikov *reasons* himself into committing his crime, and who therefore is the appropriate instrument for driving him to the point of confessing it. It is Porfiry, who has no morals and no faith, who is all the proud game of intellect, who whenever he comes to sack Raskolnikov leaves him in a state of collapse, just as it is either Svidrigaïlov or Sonia who gives him strength. Porfiry knows what he must do, and can point it out to him in the example of the peasant who came forward to take the suffering of the crime upon his guiltless shoulders, he knows all the intellect can know, and perhaps knows that it must collapse, but he cannot push Raskolnikov over the brink, because he knows it only conventionally, by rote. He understands the Crime, because he represents that against which it was committed, and knows with what it was committed, but he cannot touch the Punishment, the completion of the Crime, because it must take place in a region of the soul beyond his grasp, the region which reason, argument, all the armament of order only clutter up and from which they must be swept, the region where the assumption of guilt by all that is innocent within the self takes place through the submission of the sinful, acting self to the faithful, waiting self, which waits, in Dostoevsky's primitive Christian insight, only to be created.

I think we have touched both upon the elements that go to make up the obvious and immediate impact of Raskolnikov's crime and its consequences in action, and upon the elements which as we understand them as exhibited in the various characters leave us all—not Russians, not fanatics of humiliation, not the distorted shadowy figures of Dostoevsky's novel alone, but all of us without exception deeply implicated in the nature of the Crime. A word remains with which to fasten upon the nature of the Crime an indication of the nature of the Punishment. I do not know that there is a word ready to hand, for we have fallen quite out of the way of thinking in insights and images with the simple, direct intensity which was Dostoevsky's second nature. We lack the anterior conviction, the conviction before we begin to think, with which Dostoevsky mastered the relationship of man to God. But at least in saying that, we state Dostoevsky's major and abiding theme. To punish Raskolnikov, to bring him to retribution, to atonement, Dostoevsky had only to create his relationship to God, and to show at the same time how that relationship sprang from the nature of man as a creature of God quite apart from the structure of human society as an institution of men's minds. Dostoevsky believed that as Christ the innocent one took upon himself the suffering of all the innocent ones in the world, and so redeemed them along with the guilty, so the individual man has in him an innocent part which must take on the suffering caused by the guilty part. As he saw it, in our crime we create our guilt. Perhaps the commonplace example of false arrest will begin to make an analogue for what he meant. Which of us, falsely arrested, would not at once begin to assess his guilt, even for the crime which brought about the false arrest? And you would assess this guilt the more clearly because you were aware of the haphazard, the hazarded, character of your innocence. Similarly, the depth of your guilt would be measured by the depth of your faith, which would then, if you had imagination enough, transform you.

It should be emphasized that it was transformation, not reformation, that Dostoevsky envisaged. Reformation would have dealt with the mere guilty act against society. Transformation, through suffering, is alone able to purge the guilt of being.

Finally, we may draw some comparisons, in this search for means of clarifying the nature of Dostoevsky's notion of punishment, from recent history in our own country. When Mooney was released from his generation of false imprisonment, it soon turned out that he had no symbolic dignity, but represented rather a mere miscarriage of institutional justice; and so with the Scottsboro boys; so, too, with Dreyfus in the last century, for Dreyfus had no dignity. But if we think of Sacco and Vanzetti, does there not arise within us at once a sense that their great and terrifying symbolic dignity is due to Vanzetti having assumed, with profound humility, the whole devastating guilt of the industrial society which killed him? Whether Vanzetti was innocent or guilty in law has become an irrelevant question. But the guilt which his last words and letters, his last conduct, somehow expiated, which was our guilt, remains permanently in question; for Vanzetti, like Raskolnikov, showed himself in the humiliation of his punishment, in humble relation to God.

THE IDIOT:
A Rage of Goodness

We have here, almost plumb in the middle of Dostoevsky's work, a novel which in its major intention tried to dramatize God's gift of the good and perfect individual man beating down the proud evil of all human society by his mere example. The rest of his great work may, with a little stretching, be described as quite the opposite, as the attempt to dramatize the substantial goodness in human society beating down the obsessed pride, either carnal or intellectual, of evil individuals—or of individuals who, if not evil, were in their confusion dominated and driven by evil. We think of Raskolnikov and Svidrigaïlov, of Stravrogin, of Ivan and Dimitri Karamazov and how all of them are driven to find goodness in the lacerated, the injured, the insulted, the humiliated—in the sink and sewage of human society. Here, in *The Idiot,* we have Myshkin, a hero of another kind, whose heroism consists almost altogether in his lack of it: a hero who makes no effort to show himself and what he feels: that is to say, a positive hero, a hero who is already there, and who has therefore nothing to do, a complete image, idol, or ikon, before whom others, as they are drawn to him, must in the end abase and humiliate themselves. That Myshkin, the positive hero, is himself engulfed in the process, and indeed destroyed beyond human redemption, is a natural and necessary result. The fault of the positive hero is the most fatal of all faults, that he has none. He has no being, no existence, apart from the vision of those who believe in him. He is ideal only, an insight or aspiration divorced from the human soil out of which he sprung. You cannot uproot goodness and have it live any more than you can altogether eradicate evil.

This is not how Dostoevsky meant, intellectually, for the history of Myshkin to come out, but it is how, imaginatively, it had to come out. The conception of goodness out of which he worked offered no other possible solution; and his conception of goodness was lodged actually, like his conception of evil, in the image of its own double: which is to say, its own ruin. He was mistaken in thinking that the idea of pure goodness could be dramatized so as to dominate the kind of good and evil men and women he could create; but his imagination went beyond the mistake of his intellect and overwhelmed it. Thus we have a double, perhaps a triple, drama in the finished book. There is the drama of Dostoevsky's own conscious attempt to create his positive hero. There is the dramatic fable of the good man in an evil society. And there is, as it were creating itself underneath and absorbing the others, the drama, the immitigable and inexhaustible drama, of the good man who, in submitting to evil, is doomed not only to become evil but to enact evil without losing a jot of his goodness. No wonder, thinking of Myshkin, Dostoevsky thought that submissiveness was "the most fearful force that can exist in the world."

Let us explore the three dramas and the relations between them, uniting them first, as they are united in the book, by some consideration of the title. I do not know how Dostoevsky came to call his book *The Idiot,* but I do know that playing with any of the other obvious titles only increases the inevitability of his choice. The book tried of course for the title that all Dostoevsky's books tried for, The Life of the Great Sinner, but it had too little scope, as even *The Brothers Karamazov* had too little scope. Yet the flavor of that alternative should be kept in mind as the activating flavor of consciousness almost all Dostoevsky's characters come to in their moments of crisis: they regard themselves as living the lives of great sinners. A more likely title might have been The Epileptic, for the moment of vision and the scream that plunges the vision into intolerable darkness is in the recurrent heartbeat of the book as it is the recurrent clarifying *and* mutilating fate of Myshkin himself. Epilepsy is Le Grand Mal in the simple medicine of the past, as we should say that his goodness is Myshkin's Great Ill; for indeed the two are in the final drama of the book united. But such a play on words would have furnished an under-title at best, a quicksand of a title in which the book would have sunk two-thirds out of sight. *The Idiot* has advantages that none of the alternatives possess, and has besides a certain necessity *vis à vis* the *good* man in action—again, and always, having reference to Dostoevsky's deliberate idea of goodness. The word *idiot* is luckily the same in English as in Russian, with much the same history and much the same meanings. Fundamentally it means a private person or a layman, and by development a person who does not know what he is talking about, a fool in word or action, though with no sense that either word or action lack significance or responsiveness. It is the name we give the sense of incapability, of impotence, that attends some of our deepest responses. We all of us feel a sense of kinship with idiocy which in moments of peril we actually sometimes recognize, as when we say of a man in great terror that he was a chattering idiot, and know exactly what he felt like. Or again we use the word to measure the limits of intellect, as when we say of a problem that is beyond us that it has reduced us to idiocy. Beyond that, or on a good level rather than a bad level, we ally idiocy with kinds of generous or unthinking folly, as when we call a man an idiot for giving either his money or his mind away without thought for himself, and in calling him an idiot mean to praise him for what we would ourselves do were we less selfish. Still higher in our levels of meaning, or still deeper in our instincts, we often believe that acts of folly, of rash courage, win through at least as often as acts of thoughtfulness. In fact, the ancient beliefs that fools and madmen bear the wisdom and prophecies of the gods, have not at all died out with the gods but have survived them. We believe, for example, that he who speaks without thinking may at least speak what he feels or even what he "really" thinks.

Similarly, as any practicing spiritualist and many surrealist poets will tell you, idiocy, or the dive beneath the syntactical mind, is the only available credible vehicle for second sight and intuition and feeling. All these levels of meaning return us to the idea of the idiot as the lay or private substitute for God who is blighted in the attempt to do God's work. That is the role of the idiot as Myshkin, and that is the fate of Myshkin as idiot.

So much for the advantages of *The Idiot* as title; they rise from long and vital associations and flow naturally through the symbolic reaches of the reader's mind. But there was a necessity in the title, too. Only by making his positive hero an idiot in the eyes of the other characters (and in some degree in the eyes of the reader) could Dostoevsky envisage, that is, give face to his goodness. Only so could he make credible in a created figure the kind of goodness that Myshkin exemplified. You cannot make a man talk or think like God, because your reasoning powers are clearly inadequate: they will miss the point and involve you in all sorts of inadvertent blasphemy. This is not from lack of knowledge of God, or even from lack of skill in that knowledge; it is due rather to the nature of the medium in which that knowledge comes to you: the medium of feeling, direct perception, intuition: a medium which unites itself with the whole sensibility which it expresses. You become a submissive, a receptive agent; you feel God as goodness within you and within what you suffer, and the love you might otherwise (in the absence of God) build with pride, becomes pity which builds within you at the expense of every possible humiliation of spirit and every possible ignominy of mind and body. It is only the idiot Christ, the mind reduced to childish directness of perception—the perception of goodness through the means of pity—that the individual man can reach. That is, the man who is to be the purely good man, must divest himself not only of the love of created things but must also divest himself of those attributes which he has created in himself and by which he competes with God. He must get down to instinct, which God gave him, and which reason only impairs. Idiocy is the condition of the great divestment; for in idiocy instinct is set to operating with the least possible impairment by reason; or at any rate idiocy is the condition which we are most likely to accept as the limit at which, as it is approached, instinct works best, and at which, as it is reached, it is obliterated. Idiocy, then, is the very condition of dramatic necessity for the novelist who would, like Dostoevsky, attempt to dramatize instinctive goodness and pity as the essence of Christianity.

How far Dostoevsky would have accepted this argument is doubtful; he would most likely have objected that it reasons too much, and insisted that what he had in mind goes without saying; yet it is only by following some such argument that his figure of Myshkin becomes dramatically credible within the limit of Dostoevsky's declared intention. To support my argument I would cite the following items from the book itself. There is, first, the story Myshkin tells in Part I of the persecuted Swiss girl Marie, who thought of herself as a great sinner but who had been actually only greatly humiliated—by her mother, by her church, by her community. Myshkin, taking pity on her, "corrupted"—that was the community's name for it—corrupted the children of the village into attending her through her mortal illness. Thus she died happy, saved by pity. The children seemed to her "like birds beating their wings against her window and calling to her every morning, *'Nous t'aimons, Marie.'* " Myshkin goes on to relate how after this, Schneider, the doctor who had been caring for his idiocy, told him that he was a child. He told me, says Myshkin, "that I was a complete child myself, altogether a child; that it was only in face and figure that I was like a grown-up person, but that in development, in soul, in character, and, perhaps, in intelligence, I was not grown up, and that so should I remain, if I lived to be sixty." Myshkin says he laughed very much, but added that in one thing Schneider was right. "I don't like being with grown-up people . . . Whatever they say to me, however kind they are to me, I always feel somehow oppressed with them, and I am awfully glad when I can get away to my companions; and my companions have always been children, not because I am a child myself, but simply because I always was attracted by children."

Secondly, there is the anecdote Myshkin tells Rogozhin about the woman who crossed herself at her smiling six-weeks old baby, and who when he asked her what she did answered him: " 'God has just such gladness every time he sees from heaven that a sinner is praying to him with all his heart, as a mother has when she sees the first smile on her baby's face.' That," Myshkin went on, "was what the woman said to me almost in those words, this deep, subtle, truly religious thought—a thought in which all the essence of Christianity finds expression; that is the whole conception of God as our Father and of God's gladness in man, like a father's in his own child—the fundamental idea of Christ." It is not for nothing that directly after this Rogozhin exchanges his gold cross for Myshkin's tin cross and takes him to his mother—herself an idiot, understanding nothing of what was said—to be blessed. Only an idiot can bless an idiot.

Thirdly, there is Myshkin's outburst against Catholicism just before he breaks the Chinese vase at the Epanchins' party, an outburst which is about as near as Myshkin the idiot or Dostoevsky the author can come to an intellectual expression of what is meant by fundamental Christianity. What his outburst amounts to is a plea for revolt against intellectual authority, against grown-up pride of all sorts, and an insistence on the meekness of the child, the submissiveness of the idiot. "O, we need to have resistance at once, at once! Our Christ whom we have kept and they have never known must shine forth and vanquish the West." The depth to which Dostoevsky believed this is attested by the epileptic fit into which Myshkin falls immediately after his declaration. The moment before a fit was for Myshkin the highest clarity man could reach and was worth all the rest of life; and this particular moment does indeed reflect the central illumination of Christian meekness in about as passionate language as Dostoevsky was capable of. Nor should we complain that a plea for meekness, for submissiveness, for non-resistance to evil in the physical sense, should be expressed in violent and intolerant terms. There is no fanaticism so violent as that of humility cornered, humility humiliated by outward oppression. Christ ended in bloodshed, no less violent in that it was his own; and no Christ was more violent than the meek and childlike Christ Dostoevsky saw—in life visibly, in himself incipiently, and in the created figure of Myshkin the idiot potentially.

It is because of that violence, perhaps, that Dostoevsky is sometimes thought of as a Russian version of the Pauline Christian. Certainly Paul and Dostoevsky shared a violent eloquence; certainly both insisted on the charity of understanding as a prerequisite to salvation—both making their insistence in such violent and fanatic tones as to obscure their argument in the vehemence of its expression. Both in short were Protestants. But I think their similarity ended there. It is true that the ideas of Paul might have developed into those of Dostoevsky, but it would not have been the Paul that we know. For us Paul united spirit and intellect, whereas Dostoevsky united spirit and feeling. Pauline Christianity —western Christianity—imposes an order on human society capable of making room for the disorder of human lives. Dostoevsky's Christianity works rather the other way around, and would limit the possible order of human society to its capacity to submit to the disorder, as it must seem, of feeling and instinct and intuition. It is thus that Dostoevsky identifies Roman Catholicism with socialism, and sometimes with liberalism generally; he saw that it ought to have been so identified as a matter of logic. And it is thus that he identified Russian Orthodoxy, and its emphasis on suffering as the *condition* of salvation rather than, as in western Christianity, merely incidental to it, with the extreme conservative form of the state of the Tsars. For him, in his extreme moments, a society must needs seem to totter with corruption in order to prepare for the ordeal of salvation. He needed confusion and dismay and general gross unnecessary suffering, and not only in the heart where these things always are, but in the society around him; he needed them as a forcing bed in which his insights became images. As both a novelist and a prophet must, Dostoevsky took what he needed, insisting it was all there was.

We must say that for him there was nothing else; but we cannot say it was Pauline; it was too single a theft for Paul. Paul was a dualist in the lasting sense, or at any rate up through the dual mystery of the resurrection of the dead; for he saw always opposed man's higher and lower natures, spirit and flesh, god and devil, the heavenly order and the worldly order. If you think that Dostoevsky saw these opposites also, you have not clearly looked into the soul of the idiot.

The idiot is the living image, not of Pauline, but of primitive Christianity, the Christianity of a world ignominiously on its knees, knowing only that the next moment the face is in the mud. Dostoevsky's dualism—his doubles of the self-willed and the meek, of the intellectually proud and the spiritually humble—is only the dramatic prelude to a monistic collapse into an undifferentiated groveling humiliation. Thus the two Christian fables he was never tired of rehearsing were the fable of Christ and Mary Magdalen (in *The Idiot* the story of Myshkin and Marie) and that of the childlikeness of Christ, which is the general fable of Myshkin as it is of Alyosha in *The Brothers Karamazov.* For Dostoevsky as for Yeats Christianity "brought a fabulous, formless darkness in." It is not that Dostoevsky saw men and women in action with the oneness of the Essenes; he saw and felt them in sufficient variety; but that he tried to bring them back to that oneness, and tried especially so in *The Idiot.*

The trial was made by exposing a series of characters—Nastasya, Rogozhin, Ippolit, Aglaia, Ganya, Keller, Radomsky, Lebedyev, and General Ivolgin—to the fearful force of Myshkin's submissiveness and to the creative force of his instinctive judgment or intuition: his reaction as he felt them press upon his submissiveness: their reaction as they feel the goodness of his presence and beyond it. All these characters are haunted by their other selves, which Myshkin brings into action, for good or for evil, for pride or for humility, as the case may be. This Myshkin is able to do because he alone is without a ghost. His submissiveness brings *him* nothing, because he is already there; yet to the others it brings everything. He exists to drag out of them, to absorb, their other selves, to perfect them, so to speak, by mutilation and deprivation.

We shall see in particular how these matters proceed with the different characters; but we have first to set up some sort of images for the submissiveness and the instinct that Myshkin uses to go along with the images of Christianity out of which they sprung. The submissiveness in Myshkin may be characterized as having the attractive force of the abyss; it is a version of that gulf which Pascal, as Baudelaire's poem says, always carried within him. It is the abyss of insensibility for which acute sensibility always hankers; it is the haunting possibility. But, not only a gulf of emptiness, it is also a dreadful reservoir; there is something positive to be got from it: precisely the sickening fall into salvation, that fall in which one leaves everything behind except the self, in which one arrives, still falling, in the vertigo of paradise. Who would know better than an epileptic what that fall was like? Epilepsy is not only the Great Ill, it is also the Falling Sickness; and the great scream of the fit is wrung out of the victim at the moment of falling. It was to the possibility of that scream, as much as anything, that Myshkin's friends reacted, as it was more than anything to that scream that Myshkin himself submitted and which he also invoked as a matter of course.

He invoked it, because it set him free. Like Ivan Karamazov, Myshkin was one of those to whom all things were permitted, and indeed Myshkin is in the writing of his drama much more like Ivan the damned than like Alyosha whose goodness he superficially resembles. If we think of Ivan and Myshkin together we shall see that the permitted pride of the one and the permitted instinct of the other come to much the same thing, intolerable suffering and humiliation, ending for both in the obliteration of sensibility. The man who acts out of pride and the man who acts out of instinct are equally driven and deprived creatures to the extent that they act purely. The damnation of the one is equivalent to the blessedness of the other, at least in this world. Each is beyond the possibility of balance or sanity, and each therefore comes to humiliation. There is another consideration, too, which but perfects the equivalence of pride and instinct. Both the wholly proud man and the wholly instinctive man are adequate only to those situations which are prepared for, patterned, and petrified:

situations to which one needs to make no adjustment, which one does not need to reason about. How can one *not* see either instinct or pride except as brought to confusion? The great naturalist Fabre gives an account somewhat as follows of an experiment with the Pine Processionary Caterpillar. Noticing that like many caterpillars this species followed the silken track laid down by the leader in the procession, and returned over it to their nest after feeding, he induced a short train of them to venture upon the rim of a round bowl, and when all were upon the rim cut their backward track. Not till many hours of steady marching had passed did the leader by accident leave the endless rim of mounting humiliation. Which was it, the obstinacy of pride or of instinct, that led them so fruitlessly to exhaust themselves? Had it been men rather than caterpillars we should conclude for pride, but that is only because we have a terror of distrusting instinct. The advantage of imagination—and I mean the artist's imagination—is that it is quite oblivious to such fears, quite superior to such temptations, and will conclude for images of both in so far as either is capable of being imagined—that is, dramatized—for all they are worth in the vast immediate field of the actual.

What Dostoevsky thought as a man is of only preliminary importance, but what he enacted as an artist is of great importance. What he thought was only the conventional machinery by which he put his imagination to work in a given direction. What he thought initiates movement and establishes connections on a social level. Both the thought and the plot will commonly operate as heresies; they will exaggerate the force of insight and intrigue in order to put the mass of imagination—what actually happens to the characters in the novel in motion. Thus the opposition of pride and instinct will seem to us a dramatic dodge, a device by which we get at, say, the relations between the instinctive man Myshkin and the proud man Rogozhin, or between Myshkin and the two women Nastasya and Aglaia. We still value the insight precisely as we value the device, by how much it frames those relationships, and in the end by the degree in which the imaginative experience of those relationships replace the insights. Because of the profound inadequacy of the imagination before the actual—it is only a version of the actual—the replacement will never be complete, which is why the machinery must be used in the first place in any art more complicated than the lyric cry, but if successful it will move in the direction of completeness.

Very much the same rule applies to Dostoevsky's substitute for the classic devices of tragic catharsis which he could not use since they involve the notion of a stable and completely human society. I mean his emphasis on humiliation as the necessary preface and absolute condition of humility, an emphasis which involves the conviction of a society with a drive towards collapse whether into the arms of God or the embrace of the devil, a society held together only by violence, with an operative discipline—to use Dostoevsky's own words—of laceration, insult, and injury, alleviated only by the individual humanitarian gesture. Whether looked at spiritually or politically, as an idea of society I cannot think of anything more repulsive; it is fascist society *in extremis.* To me such humiliation is not the prelude to humility, it either precludes it, or extinguishes it, or reduces it so far in the human scale that it is the desperate virtue of idiots or of the damned. We have seen recently M. Laval commending such humiliation to the people of France as humility before the facts; and we can say that Hitler has no doubt provided many people with the temptation to be true to the Dostoevsky type of character. It is for that reason, if for no other, that however repulsive we may find Dostoevsky's "humiliation-humility" sequence as an ethical idea, we must yet concede that it is an excellent focus for dramatizing at the highest possible tension a common and profound aspect of the human scene. If you believe that great sin must come before great salvation, that great extinction must precede great creation, then you will be exemplary as a dramatist if you insist on humiliation as the means of humility.

But you will most likely come on such heresy, as Dostoevsky did, by accident, and like him you will overcome your heresy to the degree that your power of imagination is more faithful than your power of thought to the actuality of life. It is imagination, not intellect, that is the charity of the understanding. That is one point at which we can use Dostoevsky's language. It is the intellect that sins and the imagination, by creating the sin, by making it actual, that redeems. Pushing the notion one degree further, we can say that so far as the arts are concerned the movements of intellect are accidental and intermittent and in their attempts to solve our problems cause most of our conflicts, whereas the imagination, so to speak, is the will of things and continuous, so that it is able to absorb the problems of the intellect by showing their counterparts in action. With the intellect we agree or disagree; the imagination either rouses our dissent in part or exacts our complete assent; in other words, the intellect of the man often sets the imagination of the artist to work at a job very much like purgation.

So it was with Dostoevsky and *The Idiot.* He made eight plans for the novel before he came on the idea that finally put him to work. These plans survive in the Dostoevsky Archives at Moscow and are described in Ernest Simmons' admirable study of Dostoevsky. It is upon his study that I here depend. At its inception the story was to have been of a family drama based upon a court trial. The three principal characters were to have been the Idiot, Mignon, and the Heroine, all of whom were violent characters given to extreme and passionate actions. The two women bear some resemblance to Nastasya and Aglaia in the finished book, but the original Idiot has nothing in common with Myshkin but the experience of epilepsy. He is rather a Byronic hero, self-willed and criminal, sensual and extravagant, egoistic and proud: a pure type along the lines of Svidrigaïlov and Stavrogin. He is called Idiot principally because he is strange. On this basis Dostoevsky invented various combinations of chararcters and various romantic intrigues which would bring them into relation. "Situations involving murder, suicide, rape, incest, and diabolical hatred," says Mr. Simmons, "give a vivid impression of the confused drama of violent passions that agitated his brain as he sought for the artistic constants that would bring order into the chaos that he had created." What he principally lacked was a governing idea, something both general enough to make a large novel and specific enough to give the largeness focus. His first ideas were all too general: a struggle of love with hate; or, endless pride and endless hate; or again, endless idealism with endless sensualism. And so on. The one constant he had was the image of the character who finally became Nastasya, and the one near-constant was the theme of the radical generation, the young reformers, nihilists, socialists whom he feared and distrusted, and this theme was more a preoccupation and a hindrance than an active obsessive theme, and so remains in his finished novel. In the third plan there is a single phrase about the Idiot which belongs to the finished character: "He ends with a heavenly deed." Then in the fourth plan a new character begins to emerge, a meek, simple, and charming person, but nothing is done with him and he disappears. In the fifth plan the Idiot is still possible to identify with Rogozhin, but there is a description of a character named Ganya who has a Christian nature and in whom feeling predominates and whom he wants to be the most powerful figure in the novel. In the sixth plan this character becomes identified with the Idiot of the earlier plans. He differs from Myshkin, however, in being a Double, like Raskolnikov or Ivan or Dimitri Karamazov: he is both submissive *and* brutal; he has "The dualism of a profound nature." Dostoevsky has now, as Mr. Simmons observes, merely "to push the development one step further to arrive at the image of Myshkin—The Meek opposite of the Self-Willed type." In the seventh plan he is made a Prince and associated with children: Myshkin is in sight. In the eighth plan the whole work is brought into relation to this new conception of the Idiot as the simple-minded Christian. "Dostoevsky plunges into the details . . . as though he were feeling the greatest satisfaction in ridding his imagination of the former proud, vengeful, and passionate Idiot." The beginning of the first draft was unsatisfactory and he "threw it all to the devil." Beginning once more he wrote the whole novel, with many interruptions, in the space of about a year, which as it runs about a quarter of a million words was fast work.

Despite the trouble he had in getting under way, in arriving at a means of composition, at a governing idea to transform into imagination, the idea of the Idiot Myshkin, once it came, set him free to work out what he claimed was an old ideal—as different from a more operative idea—for a great theme. The following passages are extracted from a letter which he wrote to his niece Sofya Ivanova, after the first part of the novel had been finished. They will serve as text both for Dostoevsky's intended relations to the rest of the novel and for what he was actually, as a novelist, compelled to do with his material. After describing how difficult a job it is for a novelist to tackle the ideal good man, he goes on: "There is only one positively good man in the world—Christ, . . . I recall that of the good figures in Christian literature, the most perfect is Don Quixote. But he is good only because at the same time he is ridiculous. Dickens' Pickwick (an infinitely weaker conception than Don Quixote, but nevertheless immense) is also ridiculous and succeeds by virtue of this fact. One feels compassion for the ridiculous man who does not know his own worth as a good man, and consequently sympathy is invoked in the reader. This awakening of compassion is the secret of humour. Jean Valjean is also a powerful attempt, but he arouses sympathy by his horrible misfortune and society's injustice to him. In my novel there is nothing of this sort, positively nothing, and hence I am terribly afraid that I shall be entirely unsuccessful."

It should be emphasized that this was written after the first part, only, had been finished. The author is right so far. Myshkin is introduced with a description that makes him look like the typical Christ in the art of the Eastern Church: as "above the average height, with very fair thick hair, with sunken cheeks and a thin, pointed, almost white beard. His eyes were large, blue, and dreamy; there was something gentle, though heavy-looking in their expression." Mr. Simmons, after quoting this passage, adds that "in the manuscript notes his name is frequently coupled with that of Christ, and in one place he is called 'Prince Christ.' " For the rest, all through the first book, Myshkin is very kindly dealt with, laughed at a little only because he is strange, called an idiot only now and then to get the reader used to it, but generally arousing a mixture of admiration and compassion and respect. His unusual powers of direct instinctive perception are recognized at the Epanchins', at the Ivolgins', and at Nastasya's party. His opinions are asked, his judgment sought, and he is even required to decide Nastasya's marriage for her. As for himself he sees into the centres of people without managing to understand much of their outsides. He becomes attracted deeply, but in a mysteriously limited way, to the two proud and beautiful young women, Nastasya and Aglaia. By a combination of his judgment and his character and his feeling of attraction—by his deep but limited seeing—he precipitates the lives of most of the people with whom he comes in contact into new and intolerable forms—forms for which perhaps the goodness in them was ready but for which their living complexes of good and evil were not ready at all. The speed of this part of the novel is great; it is tight-woven and wide of scope, both with regard to the theme of Myshkin and with regard to the affairs of the Epanchins, the Ivolgins, and Totsky. It reaches a preliminary climax or crisis when with the fire of the roubles Nastasya goes off with Rogozhin, leaving Ganya in a swoon, the company shocked, and Myshkin deeply dismayed, but not at all troubled by what he has so evidently done. It is almost as if Dostoevsky had composed a dramatic fable of the alternative obedience and rebellion of these people to the sudden felt presence of their own conscience, with Myshkin, the simple, the innocent, acting the part of conscience.

The second part, after the first five chapters which proceed in a direct line and to which we shall return as the most powerfully composed single segment of the book, begins to show confusion of novelistic purpose, a mixture of themes, unexplained and unprepared for, incredible actions, and a more than occasional prolixity and positive redundancy of treatment, all of which last till at the very end Dostoevsky once again seized hold of his Idiot-Christ theme with complete imaginative power. It would seem as if Dostoevsky had partly relied on discarded bits of his earlier plans, partly let his pen run where it would in the hope of something turning up, and partly perhaps surrendered himself before the importunate assault of his mere ideas. The affair of the blackmailing nihilists, for example, is superfluous to the book, is dealt with at too much length as a side issue, runs off into Dostoevsky's emotional-intellectual dialectic against atheism and socialism, springs an incredible surprise (in Ganya's knowledge and proof of the falsity of the claim), and is saved, if it is saved, only by the outbursting character of Mrs. Epanchin or perhaps a little by the symbolic character of "Pavlishtchev's son" Burdowsky. There is something intriguing about a man who claims to be a bastard only to be proved legitimate; and it is surprising that Dostoevsky does not again return to the theme of the false bastard in connection with the main theme of Myshkin.

As a result of this confused and even bewildering treatment, the sound and clear things tend to lose some of their native force. I think particularly of Aglaia reading Pushkin's poem "The Poor Knight" with the initials transposed to make those of Nastasya—which is the last place in the book where Myshkin is seen as arousing laughter. Or again, there is the affair of Ippolit's attempted suicide which instead of being given the freed, independent treatment it deserved, was by a false economy fastened onto the tail of the blackmailing scenes. You have to think back, to feel back, later, to see what the scene ought to have meant at the time of its delivery.

The explanation of these confusions is predominately to be found, I think, in the intrusion of Dostoevsky's *ideas* upon his story. The middle areas of the book lose sight of the image of the Idiot in a maze of undramatized notions about the Russian soul, the east, the west, atheism, socialism, drunkenness, and so on, plus casual, almost spontaneous efforts to introduce complications of plot and character which might relieve the main theme from going where it is now clear that it must go—towards the collapse, focussed in the figure of Myshkin, of the ideal of positive good. There could be no clearer example than this of a great sensibility violated by an idea, no sharper case of a theme being surrendered by the author to a mere thesis, and then wrenched back by violence to safety.

Whether Dostoevsky—whether any novelist—could have done otherwise with a theme so intractable because initially so alien, is doubtful. We can defend him (or label his intentions, which is a form of defense) in two ways. It might have occurred to him that a major part of the material of character and event and intrigue in the central portion of his book had of necessity to be fortuitous. It is possible to hold that many of the items handled could as well have been others, and are themselves, and justified as themselves, all the more for their air of expressing mere casual possibilities. It is because they are immediate possibilities, perhaps, that they do their work; their fortuitousness is what makes them fatal—as, for example, General Ivolgin's probable theft of money from Lebedyev. They are the right objects for the Idiot Myshkin to affect precisely because they are unpredictable and superfluous. Myshkin is one of those who must have every sort of grist, the unexpected even more than the expected.

Again, there is a kind of rightness to the disordered apparitions of undigested material which becomes apparent if we think of the book as a fable, a sermon, a parable of the good man in an evil world. The good man will by his presence call forth exclamations and cries of both good and evil, as in all of us our conscience, when we think of it, creates qualms of ill deeds not otherwise remembered. We may say that Dostoevsky did not so much sympathize with disorder; he felt the roots of it, in himself and others, both clutching and pushing. Thus his primitive Christianity, his ideal of submissiveness, was always on the point of disclosing itself as a matrix of disorder. The man of instinct, of feeling, is always nearest to the underlying dark disorder of things, just as the man of pride, of intellect, always is found, at his focal moments, creating disorder in the name of the order that turned him loose.

But, having once acknowledged the morass of form in the middle parts of the book, let us proceed to acknowledge some of the things that emerge from the morass, and especially those things that emerge in relation to the theme of the Idiot Christ at large in the actual world. Taking the smaller things first, one of the ablest things Dostoevsky does is to show the immediate effect that Myshkin has on the footman at the Epanchins'; he allows Myshkin to smoke, to break artificial rules, and he listens to what he has to say. Similarly with Keller, where the process takes a little longer. Keller is the hard-drinking, bellicose ruffian, with a chip on his shoulder, not to be taken in by anybody; yet as soon as he has a chance to see what Myshkin is like, he becomes a good egg, even a good friend, and offers to second him in a duel. Totsky and General Epanchin, being men of the world, make allowances for Myshkin; they understand that there must be such people. Mrs. Epanchin, a sensible, direct, warmhearted woman, knows Myshkin is a fool and a great causer of trouble, not at all a safe man to have around, but she not only puts up with him and forgives him, she finds that she must seek him out. Lebedyev, the drunken buffoon and vainglorious sponge, deeply enjoys being seen through by Myshkin, even enjoys bringing each fresh rascality out in the open. Radomsky, more a man of intellect but goodhearted and on the right side, cannot help trying to confess himself to Myshkin, and goes out of his way and without reason to corroborate to him his father's thefts of public money and ensuing suicide. General Ivolgin, the constitutional liar and idler, similarly resorts to Myshkin with almost perfect candor because he feels that Myshkin alone knows that he is essentially an "honest" man. Kolya, too, the precocious child, the very one who ought to have stood aloof because he saw so much, and with so little reason, makes himself a follower of Myshkin. None of these persons loses anything to Myshkin; neither do they gain anything materially. They are the "ordinary" people who make up the world, and they have the same deep but slightly uneasy and superficially indifferent regard for Myshkin that such persons have towards their own conscience; and indeed that is what Myshkin is for them, an easy, objective form of conscience, to whom they can appeal without harm.

On a somewhat different level come Ganya Ivolgin and Ippolit Terentyev. Ganya is the man of vanity and ambition, but without pride; Ippolit is the man of overweening pride and intellect, but almost without vanity. To each, in a different way, Myshkin brings doom. His mere presence destroys first the possibility of Ganya's marriage to Nastasya, and second, indirectly, he prevents the possibility of his marriage to Aglaia. Further, he is present at, and is partial cause of, Ganya's supreme humiliation over the affair of the fire of roubles. Yet Ganya becomes Myshkin's man, and where he might have played Iago with cause, shows no slightest trace of jealousy after the beginning. As to Ippolit, Myshkin crushes, though by *tour de force* and not even eloquently, his Nihilism and makes a good deal of a fool of him in public, yet it is to him, and in his house, that he brings his death. Perhaps Dostoevsky arranged this in order to furnish a contrast to Myshkin of a kind not offered either by the girls or by Rogozhin. Ippolit is the man already maimed, diseased, lacerated by life, and as a consequence has rebelled against God. Redemption is not in his line; he is the Poor Knight Don Quixote *manqué,* mutilated even; and there is nothing he can rebel against except the God who has condemned him. He is a kind of sink of personality on the point of turning into a fount. To whom can he bring his rebellion, on whom can he pour forth his fountain, except Myshkin, the lay Christ of the God whom he wishes to deny? Myshkin was responsible for the material failure of Ganya; and he is morally responsible for Ippolit's realization of the doom that is upon him. Again he acts as conscience—this time not as the friendly conscience, but as the insuppressible and insupportable conscience.

With Rogozhin that is the role he had always played, but with him it was the role of a full person and not that of a mere fabulous figure. It is in relation to Rogozhin, even more than in relation to Nastasya and Aglaia, that Myshkin comes alive, moves, has his being, and suffers. This may be because, in the history of the eight plans for the book, he is a split part or double of Rogozhin; if so, that is an accident in the creative task but it is the central fact in the created product. If we turn to chapters three, four, and five of the second part, which begin with the conversation between the two men about the nature of their respective loves for Nastasya—Rogozhin's being hate and Myshkin's pity—and end with Myshkin's saving epileptic fit just as Rogozhin is about to stab him, we shall see what Dostoevsky was really capable of as a poetic novelist dealing with the desperate theme of the good man in action. One way of defining the effect of these chapters would be to say that it did not matter what theme Dostoevsky was dealing with, for the theme, whatever it is, disappears into the texture of the images of insight and wrestling contest in which they are delivered. They are *made* things; the poet is operating as *maker,* and operating inviolably. The atmosphere, which is the air in which the scenes actually breathe and not backdrops laid on, was first set when, that morning, Myshkin had seen "those eyes" staring at him on the crowded platform of the railway station. He was sure enough in a half-conscious way that they must have been Rogozhin's eyes, but they seemed also like his own eyes, and he kept the memory of them boring within him all day, while he searched for Nastasya, for Kolya, and for Rogozhin himself. It is as if he has been himself hunted and cornered when finally he comes to Rogozhin's house; he is full of extraordinary and inexplicable emotion and knows the house by instinct, by its largeness, its gloominess, its frigid, inhospitable, and hidden air. At the street level there is a money-changer's shop owned by a member of the sect of Skoptsy—one of those who practice self-mutilation for religious purposes. The gloom of the house and the presence of the Skoptsy are brought in again and again through the following scenes; darkness and self-mutilation become virtually parts of the psychological image of the whole scene. They make the right background for both men, for both surely mutilate themselves spiritually in the darkness of their own souls, Rogozhin out of passion and Myshkin out of goodness. In this dark place they understand each other. "When I am with you," says Myshkin, "you believe me, but when I am away, you leave off believing me at once and begin suspecting me." To which Rogozhin responds, "I believe your voice when I am with you. I understand, of course, we can't be put on the same level, you and I." In this dark place they understand also what must happen, that Nastasya, though she loves Myshkin, will eventually marry Rogozhin in order to be murdered by him, and that she will do so because of Myshkin. This prophecy is enforced by the seven-inch horn-handled knife, a new and unused knife, which Myshkin picks up unconsciously off the table, and which Rogozhin seizes from him. To complete the symbolic significance of the scene, there is next introduced Holbein's picture of the dead Christ, of which Rogozhin has a copy hanging among portraits of bishops and landowners. It is the one picture Rogozhin likes to look at. "At that picture!" cried

Myshkin. "Why that picture might make some people lose their faith." Some two hundred pages further on in the book the full meaning of the picture is made plain in Ippolit's description of it. It lacks the spiritual beauty found in most portraits of Christ, he says. "It's the face of man *only just* taken from the cross—that is to say, still bearing traces of warmth and life. . . . It is simply nature, and the corpse of a man, whoever he might be, must really look like that after such suffering." The portrait is a temptation for Rogozhin, a doubt for Myshkin, and a symbol for the reader. For us it is a judgment, focused in Rogozhin's eyes, upon Myshkin as the idiot Christ. And for Myshkin, in his turn, after he has changed crosses with Rogozhin, been blessed by his idiot mother, been refused the embrace of brotherhood, and left the house, Rogozhin becomes, in terms of "those eyes," of the knife, and of the picture, first the pursuing demon, and lastly an accuser and a judge. When Myshkin discovers him at Nastasya's house, he exclaims, "With what eyes shall I look upon that man for the rest of my life!" The self-knowledge is not, however, perfected until Myshkin's epileptic fit supervenes upon Rogozhin's attempt at murder, and it endures only for the single moment in which his soul is "flooded with *inner* light," and which is terminated by the "first sound of the fearful scream which broke of itself from its breast." In that scream, says Dostoevsky, "everything human seems obliterated and it is impossible, or very difficult, for an observer to realize and admit that it is the man himself screaming. It seems as though it were someone else screaming from within the man."

So beautifully composed, so intensely felt, are these chapters at all three levels of meaning—the intellectual, the narrative, and the imaginative—and so united on the imaginative or symbolic level, that one feels Dostoevsky has created enough mass in momentum to carry through to a fitting end even his difficult and desperate theme of the ideal man; and so far as the novel *is* completed, it is the imaginative energy of these chapters that supplies the momentum. But unfortunately Dostoevsky had conceived his drama in terms of Myshkin's further relationship with Nastasya and Aglaia, for which he was unable to provide images deep enough and grasping enough to *deliver* the combination of idea and act as drama. Nastasya is carefully and imaginatively built up off-stage so that when she appears she is actual enough, and Aglaia is observed and made to act on-stage sufficiently to make her actual as a person; both women are created full of possibilities; and the reader is ready to believe not only that anything may happen, but that the right and justifying things *will* happen inevitably, out of the momentum of the characters. Yet at the crisis they are forced, and being forced they are not so much incredible as inadequate. Both women rage too much, and rage vainly, because Dostoevsky has not provided a focus for their rage in the *created* character of Myshkin, and, at the same time, because he has provided too much focus in his *idea* of that character. The inadequacy is Myshkin's, not the women's; he has nothing within him capable of satisfying the passionate desires which dominate both Nastasya and Aglaia in their feeling for him. Whether Dostoevsky deliberately omitted all sexual being from Myshkin's nature, or whether he simply was by his own nature incapable of deep sexual experience and so could not envisage it either in Nastasya and Aglaia or in Myshkin except as an idea, it was that lack, that incompleteness as a man in Myshkin, which brought on the downfall of the women, and transformed what ought to have been the tragic triumph of the good man into his reduction to complete idiocy. You cannot transmute what does not exist; you can only rage at your disability and end in ignominy and humiliation. Thus in Dostoevsky the mighty attempt to create always becomes involved in sin or ignominy and ends in humiliation and obliteration. The deprivation of his nature like the privations of his life led him to envisage emotions as released either as an ecstasy of rage or as a rage of ecstasy. The emotions do not express the people, they take them over. There is always, in the great creations of Dostoevsky, "someone else screaming from within the man." In *The Idiot* it is the rage of goodness.

THE POSSESSED:

In the Birdcage

During the months when Dostoevsky, homesick at Dresden, was fishing about and making notes for a novel—to be short, to be quickly written—which he owed his publisher in satisfaction of an advance, what was known as the Nechaev Affair blew up in Russia and gave a special transformation to Dostoevsky's obsessive but unrealizable theme: The Life of a Great Sinner. The Nechaev Affair precipitated out of that theme a political novel, a novel about the Russian polity of 1870; but it was a polity seen as shaped, or misshaped, by the force of his unrealizable theme. If we are to think that *The Possessed* is a political novel, we must think so only in the sense that a man can have politics whose way of dealing with life rested on a fundamental belief that a true rebirth, a great conversion, can come only after great sin. It is a politics that goes with an extreme case of this kind of mind; a politics which cannot only afford to be hopeless but which delights to be hopeless because its rewards are all outside politics; it regards politics as one of those necessarily evil avenues through which the rewards may be reached. That is to say, politics is a transgression against the good to come—but only as life itself is; to a novelist especially as life itself is. In *The Possessed,* life as transgression turned up its political aspect to the attention of Dostoevsky the novelist; and it did so by the accident of the Nechaev Affair.

Nechaev was a young revolutionist on the Bakunin or absolutist model, who believed that the ends justified the means and that the more criminal and immoral and violent the means were, the better the ends. Claiming to represent the central authority of an international revolutionary movement, he gathered about him a cell—presumably one of thousands of similar cells—of five students sworn to his personal authority. Becoming suspicious of one of these students, or at any rate saying that he was, he brought about his murder and had his body dumped in a pond on the Moscow university grounds. There it was found. Nechaev and the others were arrested and brought to trial. There was no international movement, no central authority, and no other cells; but there was a great scare in Russia. The essence of the affair, as it unfolded, was that something false in fact was true enough in effect to make a great stir, and was indeed a trial for the country at large, leading to excesses of opinion, of censorship, and confirmed the policy of wholesale exile of intellectuals to Siberia. It was a ripe subject for a novelist like Dostoevsky, even without the murder, and with the murder thrown in, it was a subject that fell into his lap. It gave him a story to go with his obsessive theme. What appealed to him must have been the fraud behind it and the treachery within it, where the fraud was authority and the treachery was power. The strength or momentum that kept the conspirators faithful to Nechaev was drawn from an organization that never existed, not even in Nechaev's mind, and it was maintained or solidified by a treachery otherwise frivolous. Yet by a fraud in Nechaev's mind, a great stir could come about. Nechaev was a small fellow with a small mind. To a novelist the question would be: what would happen if a real energy should go to work, with help from some other appropriate, always available energy, on the basis of a fraud equally hollow but with a more desperate because more deeply generalized intent than anything Nechaev showed. What reality would that make? What fraud how deep in what heart? At any rate, one way of looking at *The Possessed* is to conceive that these are the questions that it asks. What motives does Dostoevsky create?

At first, as is common with "serious" artists, Dostoevsky thought he was dealing with motives outside his art, the presence of which might ruin his art. In a letter written in the spring of 1870, when the novel had not yet shaped itself, he wrote that he had great hopes of it; "I don't mean as a work of art, but because of its tendencies; I mean to utter certain thoughts, whether all the artistic side of it goes to the dogs or not. The thoughts that have gathered themselves together in my head and heart are pressing me on; even if it turns into a mere pamphlet, I shall say all that I have in my heart." That is to say, he had the ordinary man's instinct for decisive judgment and fulfilling action; it was only the habit—the clothing and characteristic stigmata of the profession—of the novelist that prevented him, in his eight hundred odd pages, from writing a bloated pamphlet. The habit of his calling overcame the need of his emotion; he overcame, by writing a novel, both heart and head, and transformed decisive judgment into the judgment of the looking-glass, fulfilling action into the dramatic image of the stresses of things upon which, in exigence, action is made. The "tendencies" and "thoughts" which in his letter he asserted to be his subject became qualities, clues—even keys—to his true subject, the question: how does it come about, beneath both heart and head, that such things can be?

We have as much right to the clues and keys as Dostoevsky had. Even the novel most wholly a novel is both full of the ikons of mysteries still pressing and cluttered with the debris of mysteries no longer experienced; without "thoughts" and "tendencies" we should be overwhelmed by undifferentiated emotion. The thoughts and tendencies stand between us and the raw force of emotion which is the vital part of the novelist's material, just as for Dostoevsky the thoughts and tendencies were tools for focussing, for converting from one phase to another, more available to the lasting transmitted part of the mind we call the intellect, that same raw force. In life we tend to forget the nature of the force in anxiety over our conversions of it; but it is the rational purpose of the novel to remind us what the force is, throughout its phases, which we have converted, and it does so by showing the experience of those who have mistaken the mere conversions for the thing itself. That is what happens in *The Possessed* at a number of levels, not all of them levels which Dostoevsky recognized in his own consciousness, some of them being indeed at the level of mistaken conversions unwittingly made by Dostoevsky himself; for the novelist can never avoid dramatizing himself, and can never be more objective than when he does so. It is precisely by dramatizing himself into the situation he sees, and his ideas into the raw force he feels, that he comes nearest to answering the question which is his subject: how comes it such things be?

That is how we have the same right to the clues and keys of thoughts and tendencies that Dostoevsky had; they have for the nonce of the novel become absorbed into the subject, and they are made to seem to grow out of it, like vital dogma, in so far as they are, by the process of the novel, conversions from one phase to another of the raw force of emotion. The relation is not obscure, but it is the reverse of theology and of most philosophy; here, in the novel, the dogma gives the raw force one among several possible purposes, and the raw force enlightens the dogma no matter which purpose is chosen. The relation is not obscure, it is clear; it is the relation in which we understand why we must love our enemies, not that they may cease being our enemies, but because God loves them without regard to the enmity between them and us. It is in the novel, more than in any settled form of art, that our thoughts and tendencies—the dogmas by which we catch momentum day to day—come into their only true concert, the concert of conflicts; and it is in Dostoevsky's *The Possessed*—because of the sharpness of the dogmas, the extremity of the thoughts and tendencies—that of all novels this is most clearly seen to be so.

It is with this in mind that the present essay means to add to the task of seeing what human motives Dostoevsky could create by turning the fraud of the Nechaev affair into a novel, the further task of seeing what happened to the thoughts and tendencies in Dostoevsky's mind under the pressure of that novel. What happened to The Life of a Great Sinner when told as the tale of an extreme, but fraudulent, nihilist conspiracy? Pushing the question one step further, How does it come about that the one theme is the double—the other self—of the other? Is there after all only one effort in which man can dramatize his evident need as vital purpose? Is there in the end no difference between the effort to be a superman and replace god and the effort to find god in man? Whatever the reality, are the god-man and the man-god in actual experience the same? Is actual experience always hallucination with respect to the real? Which, finally, is more wholly hallucination—the extreme of self-will or the extreme of submission to the will of God,—the shambles of pride or the glory of humiliation? To ask both sets of questions is the novelist's only answer to either.

To have these questions in mind—in whatever version seems the most appealing idiom—is to be in sufficient knowledge of Dostoevsky's clues and keys, the thoughts and tendencies he meant to write about when he began *The Possessed,* but which got transformed by what invited a focus for his attention as soon as he had got going, the force of the Nechaev Affair. The attractiveness of the Nechaev Affair, the reader should be reminded, had special features for the Russian novelist of 1870: the novel was the only relatively free form of expression a Russian could use; the novelist had, and was expected to have, the force of the publicist, the prophet, the preacher, and, above all, the reporter. Every other form of expression took more or less the avenue of conspiracy or of secret force, both autocratic. The weak or reformist liberalism of the 40's and 50's which had had immediate ends in mind, seemed to have been replaced by a violent and revolutionary anarchism which had destruction as immediate end and a secular millennium as ultimate end. The shift in attitude would seem to have a relation to the precipitation upon the cities and towns, partly because of the liberation of the serfs in the 60's, of a socially rootless and impoverished intellectual proletariat; a shift that was only sharpened and emphasized by the state policy towards that proletariat. *The Possessed* was published serially between January 1871 and December 1872; and during that period the educated proletariat whose image it projected were being sent to Siberia at the rate of a thousand a month. When the intellectuals become predominantly a proletariat it may well be that they respond to the horror of their unreality with positive terror; it is their remaining actual weapon. Dispossess a man of mind and sensibility and he is likely to become possessed; that is to say, he is likely to be invaded by those forces which, by encompassing his own detruction, would strike a blow at the immortal part of society: which is, however it is phrased, the characteristic temptation of the possessed: the temptation of suicide to become murder, of politics to become anarchy, of man to become god.

All three are phases of the one temptation, and the people who inhabit *The Possessed*—all but one—are given over and come to their ends through one or another phase. The exception, Stepan Trofimovitch Verhovensky, stands as much as anything for the immortal part of society against which the blows of the nihilists are directed; he dies, but only what is mortal and mistaken in him; he is incorrigible, he is guilty, he is beaten, but he will come again: he is the eternal possibility of the man clothed and in his right mind. He is the man who *knows* that he sits on his own bottom, no matter what pomp or servility he may pass through. Perhaps that is not how Dostoevsky thought about him, but that is what the novel made him come out in the aspect which is clearest to the west European and American mind. He is the foil—the background and future—against which the incommensurable nihilism of his son Pyotr gathers meaning. Stepan Trofimovitch is the justification of the mottoes which Dostoevsky prefixed to *The Possessed* from a poem of Pushkin and the Gospel of St. Luke.

The motto from Pushkin is about riders who have lost their way because demons have bewitched their horses, and the question that asks itself is about the dirge the demons sing: whether it celebrates the birth or the death of evil. The motto from Luke is about the man who, having been possessed by demons, has lost his way and recovers it by exorcising them into swine who at once "ran violently down a steep place into the lake and were choked"; after which the man sat "at the feet of Jesus, clothed and in his right mind"—at which the swineherds were afraid. There is an ambivalence from the motto from Pushkin which, so to speak, Dostoevsky's novel—not his thoughts and tendencies but his novel—forces into the motto from Luke. We know we deal with the cycle of evil, but we do not know at what point in the cycle we are, and therefore cannot tell by what expense—or whether we can afford it—we can exorcise the evil and come out clothed and in our right mind. If we think of Dante, who also dealt with a situation where *la diritta via era smarrita,* alongside Dostoevsky, we shall see what the ambivalence in *The Possessed* has to do with our sense of what is possible to the imaginative mind. Dante, in *The Divine Comedy, knew* that his concept of order would encompass any disorder the nature of man might provide. Dostoevsky *knew* something very different, that his insight would surpass any anarchy in which man's nature might end. In Dante, man remains intact. In Dostoevsky, there may be nothing intact.

II

In *The Possessed,* it is the purpose of things to get out of hand; they are then pursued as far as the limits of Dostoevsky's vision could reach within the form of the novel as he understood it. The limits of vision were radical, in the character of his sensibility. The form of the novel was accidental, both as he stretched it and as he failed to take up its possibilities. In between, affecting each—by constriction and by propulsion—his thoughts and tendencies maintained, and above all picked up when it slacked off, a mutual relation between vision and form. The vision is of an intolerable society which most men are incapable of rejecting though the means are at hand to do so, and which they are therefore bent on destroying; this is because the vision of Christ, in the minds of those unequal to its burden, creates the vision of anti-christ: which is, so to speak, the precise measure of their inadequacy. The form of the novel is the form most appropriate to an intolerable society: it is a serious use of the form of crime and detection generalized, universalized, and then again specified. It is a form that controls only one aspect of the force it releases. In it the great affairs of men in society are carried on as if they were so many intrigues, puerile and degrading farces, childish conspiracies: as if, that is, the affairs of men could provide only so many opportunities for private crime and general guilt. Neither the corrective force of observed manners nor the richening force of daily preoccupations, as in Tolstoi, bring the form of crime and detection to anything like liveable proportions. Thus Dostoevsky had chosen a form which made life itself fit all the negative aspects of his vision, meanwhile adding to rather than diminishing the dramatic interest of the form; it was the right form for his leading thoughts and tendencies about the world of the anti-christ—it was the very form of life that prevented the continuous revelation of Christ, or, failing that, his second coming. It gave him a chance therefore for prophetic rage and apocalyptic insight; it gave him a chance to dramatize the positive side of his vision rising out of the negative side as its drama got out of hand—not as a contradiction nor as a new saying, but as an inevitable growth. This was the opportunity that his thoughts and tendencies made to seem spiritually possible. It would almost seem that the whole of Dostoevsky's thoughts and tendencies can be summarized in the single idea that, whether for the individual or for all mankind, the cost of the real vision of Christ was the previous, actual experience of anti-christ. No experience other than absolute guilt—and perhaps not even that—could create the utopia of forgiven man.

If this sketch of the relations between Dostoevsky's vision, form, and leading ideas is approximately correct, we can see why the politics in *The Possessed* is a non-social politics, why its principles are conspiratorial, why the conspiracy fixes upon a hallucination, why the hallucination spreads through society. We see too why this hallucination can not pass off by daylight, but must be exorcised either by the god-fearing Russian people (that is, the peasants) or by saints (those who have passed through the hallucination). To Dostoevsky, exorcism and conversion are political instruments, because the only true politics is in religion, and the image of the true society is that of a theocracy of saints which has engorged the state. Again, if we remember that to Dostoevsky moral freedom was always the great objective for the individual, and that to him the great gift of Christ was moral freedom, we see why in this world of the anti-christ—whether political or social—the possibility of moral freedom without God could only show as the possibility of sin. We see why crime had to be construed as sin, and we see why Stavrogin was raised *as a sinner* in his crimes to the status of a god. If we had ever been able to complete his role as Great Sinner, we would have seen too how he could have stood as exemplary witness to the god-fearing Russian people.

But Stavrogin did not complete his role—even less than his counterparts Myshkin in *The Idiot* and Alyosha in *The Brothers Karamazov* completed theirs. It was not only that Dostoevsky could not construe his positive vision beyond its conventional prototypes—Tihon in *The Possessed,* Zossima in *The Brothers Karamazov;* it was not only either, that no writer has ever fully portrayed any greatness save his own, and that by his style—which is why we *know* so little and believe so much of Christ. It was not only these; it was also partly that Dostoevsky was, at the crucial point, always a little heretical in his orthodoxy; the crucial point was in his psychology—in his sense of the relation between the ideals in the mind and their corresponding actions in the soul. He could not bring himself to envisage as united what he felt as separated by a great gap; he wanted so desperately to do so that he would do so honestly or not at all. He not only gave the devil his due; he knew that the devil lived in his own heart unexorcisably, whether by saint or peasant, certainly not by thoughts and tendencies. At any rate, that was what his working imagination proved in the fact of his novels: that there was a terrible gap between the actuality of spiritual experience and the ideas by which he got at it. It was as if he knew that his ideas, like the saint and the peasant who symbolized them, were institutions that like all institutions compromised reality in the interests of mere getting along and killed the living faith in the interests of certainty. Thus Dostoevsky was more Western than he thought, and a child of the French Revolution and brother to the Commune, beyond his power to realize except—since he had no classic irony to support him—with horror and repudiation. It is lucky for us that this is so; it brings his whole predicament nearer our own if we can bring the range of our common ancestors nearer. Why can not we say that Dostoevsky too had experienced Rousseau's vision on the dusty noontime road? He too saw that all that is evil in man's life comes from the institutions he has created to prevent—or to forestall—a continuing revelation. For Rousseau his vision meant a point of departure, for Dostoevsky it meant an ambiguity so great and so terrible that he was condemned by the persistence of his means to the deprivation of certainty in his chosen end. The nearer he got to it, the nearer he got also to the ever-present alternative of its opposite. Nevertheless, the two men were on the same track—or lost on the same track—and we can understand Dostoevsky better by remembering it.

Both men were adepts in the prepotent disorder which existing institutional orders only hold in check for the moment. Both were skilled in their fuller works at setting afoot outbreaks and contagions of disorder which any acceptable order must in the end encompass if it is to survive to cope with the next batch of disorder. Both knew that true order was something continuous that happened to disorder. The temptation in Rousseau is to assert panacea in popular sentiment and popular will, which, since none can conform to them, leaves every state illegitimate. Dostoevsky's temptation is to assert panacea in popular sentiment guided by absolute authority reached by conversion and faith; which leaves every government not a theocracy illegitimate. Both carried their assertions far enough to risk the exclusion of the disorder they meant to encompass. They forgot its prepotency in doctrine, though they returned to it in experience. Yet each was a good prophet, and both became so by two means: by bringing images of the underlying disorder in man's life into the open in terms of the existing order of their times, and by asserting an ideal for its control alien to any possible politics. That others *therefore* corrupted their ideals is the matter of our history. That they themselves—and particularly for us, here, that Dostoevsky—never in the end drove the ideal through against the force of actual experience is the mark of their greatness. In Rousseau, it was as if the honesty of common sense entered and weighted his emotion. In Dostoevsky it was as if—a much rarer thing—the honesty of raw emotion, the force of the things he was, entered and bent his will.

It is at this point that we can actually re-enter the novel. It has been with us all along, closing round us, with a motion which we may hope is analogous in our terms to the motion with which it closed round Dostoevsky, that is with the motion of a thing possessed, to which it is only possible as it is only prudent for the time being, to give in. We see at once a darkness, with fractions of light, the splinters of things in motion; an uncomfortable darkness, with motions as unmotivated as they are disorderly, as consequential in fact as they are frivolous in inspiration. You have an idea that when people disappear they descend into some degraded form of themselves, into their own soil, where they absorb their peculiar strength to return. No common knowledge of them is possible which is not scandalous; no ultimate knowledge is probable which is not catastrophic. They are swine and their throats will be stuck—or if not, there is a steep place at hand. Destruction is all that they can come to.

Such is the atmosphere of the provincial capital where the natural disorder of things gets out of hand, and it is created by a "vast conspiracy" of thirty people, a conspiracy thought to be nihilistic but actually a clique of run-out higher liberals, without aim and without a leader. They are flunkeys in thought, but without a lord; for whom their nearest substitute is Stepan Trofimovitch Verhovensky, a day-dream glamor boy of progressive patriotism, a Gulliver home from Lilliput, who has written a noble letter of self-defense but cannot think whom to send it to. He is a fiasco, altogether in the power of Varvara Stavrogin, whose son Nikolai he has in the past tutored. He has also a son Pyotr, due to arrive soon after years of absence to claim the inheritance Stepan has wasted. Varvara, the great lady of the town, has "the cruel and insulting despotism of a crazy woman." Knowing Stepan loves her, knowing also the impending scandal about his son's money, she orders him to marry her ward, Dasha Shatov, with dowry enough to pay off the son and something besides. Stepan drinks too much, gambles too much, dreams too much: his future is to him a "colossal ordeal," and he tries vainly to build up enough will to reject it and go forth naked in his old age. Besides this harmless old gull, there are many others: Liputin, an elderly official, an ex-general, perhaps an atheist, certainly a scandalmonger; Shatov, born a serf, an expelled student, sullen and violent, one of those who is shamed because unequal to his own ideas; Virginsky, a pathetic poor man who has all the latest ideas and convictions in their crudest form; Lebyadkin, a dubious buffoon and cad, who sleeps with Virginsky's wife and eats his food, but who, as the story goes on, has a house of his own and unexplained money; Lebyadkin's sister, the crippled and half-witted Marya whom he beats when drunk; Kirillov, an engineer interested in the ratios of suicide, an objector and dissenter, with a dark, muddy-colored skin and lustreless black eyes, another Raskolnikov whose crime is against himself; Shigalov, the rigid doctrinaire reformer. There are others in the group or near it or who become attached to its contagion—Gaganov, Drozdov, Lyamshin, Erkel, and Fedka. Altogether apart from the group but affected by it are such people as Karmazinov the run-out author, Governor Von Lembke and his wife Yulia, Shatov's wife Marya, "Stavrogin's woman," Lizaveta Tushin, and Mavriky her faithful lover. The list is long, and there are others not named. They represent the town; all are in disorder; and in the lump they are rather like a slice of Dickens' society seen out of kilter through dark glasses.

To them come Stepan Trofimovitch's son Pyotr and his pupil Stavrogin, the one an unknown, the other a known mystery, and because of their coming the town is changed from a scandalized community, to an hysterical community, and then to a place—not a community at all—of the possessed. Their power lies in their personalities and in the mystery of their personalities, which both tempt others to make more of them than they are, and (thus) to find motives for themselves in the mystery. Dostoevsky is here depending on the great truth that, though most people desire serious motives, they do not ordinarily have them in anything but a routine sense. By presenting his conspiratorial group as sunk to the routine of scandal he has laid them open to the full hallucination of motive at the hands of any energy greater than their own, however itself in fact unmotivated. This is sometimes called the attractive force of leadership instead of personality; and it helps explain the power which gathers to every heroic and priestly class. Dostoevsky made use of this force not only in these two figures in *The Possessed,* but in such other figures as Svidrigaïlov in

Crime and Punishment, Myshkin in *The Idiot,* Versilov in *The Raw Youth,* and Alyosha in *The Brothers Karamazov.* In fact none of these novels could have acquired and heightened their momentum without the force of these figures. They not only cause things to happen initially but they set up trains of contagions of action; contact with them crystallizes emotion into motive; and they seem either to have the power to create or obliterate personality in their followers or their victims. Whether such figures exist in any statistical sense is immaterial; we like to believe that they exist and to act as if we were in contact with them. The demimonde of our culture is full of them: sibylls, witches, fairies, poltergeists, great detectives, and the supermen heroes of our comic strips, all belong to the family. They represent the inexplicable and uncontrollable power which, as we believe we have it—or as it possesses us—moves us without penalty of personal responsibility. The interpretation of the social sciences as an absolute determinism is a secular hocus-pocus which corresponds to these figures, whereby we go to ruin, or have our way, in complete freedom. No matter how they may appear, these mysterious figures are among the favorite hallucinations of our mortal lives, and equally whether they work for good, for evil, or for both.

Once Dostoevsky set them up, all he had to do to get them going was to draw lines of initial relation to certain characters in the group. For Pyotr, aside from his relation to his father, the political relation was enough: the intellectual proletariat in the town was already rootless enough to believe in the coming terror; Pyotr had only to say that it was on its way, that he represented its secret leadership, and so take charge. Beyond that, he does three things: he stirs up malice in the community from top to bottom; he tries to solidify his position in the group by a common crime, the execution for treason of one of its members who had merely wished to leave the group because of a change of heart; and, third, he tries both to get Stavrogin in his hands by a combination of blackmail and crime and to make Stavrogin the chief or leader of his conspiracy and so make it real in the ultimate sense as well as actual in the immediate sense. He is an enthusiast and like all enthusiasts requires a force not his own and beyond his understanding to keep his enthusiasm alive. He depends on Stavrogin, as a man depends on his property; he must add to it to keep it, and must put it to use in order to add to it. On that basis all Pyotr's actions become understandable.

Stavrogin needs more attention, if only because he has to stand behind Pyotr; but also because he has to stand behind, in different ways, a great many other people: he has to contain in himself, in perfected, ordered form—that is to say, with order and disorder balanced on the knife's edge—the disorder of the whole town. He has to be a hero and come to tragedy, where Pyotr has merely to succeed and come to failure. Stavrogin has to remain a mystery and to do so by taking on himself the mystery of other things. Both the people in the book and the readers of the book must know a great deal about him and be the more mystified the more they know. In his notes for *The Possessed,* Dostoevsky, according to Simmons, was acutely aware of this. "Very important," he wrote, "the prince reveals himself to no one and is everywhere mysterious," and he reminded himself "to keep the reader in a quandary." This he did, but he shows a great deal of what he fails to reveal. Perhaps Stavrogin's essential mystery is that he has led a part of the life of a great sinner and is seeking, to the last act of his life, to lead more of it. If so, it makes more rather than less of a mystery to give it its name; just as the maximum mystery of any life in which it happens is the mystery of a change of heart and the assumption of a new life. At any rate, in the book, a part of his mystery is shown in his relations to Shatov whom he has made a believer; to Kirillov, whom he has made an individualistic nihilist, to Marya Lebyadkin the crippled imbecile whom he has secretly married as a gratuitous stroke in debauchery, to Liza whom he loves in a way intolerable and inadequate to her, to Pyotr whom he has inflated to an intolerable predicament by false assurances, no less pervasive for being largely tacit, and to the Elder Tihon to whom he confesses his ambiguous debauchery, ending in her death, of a little girl. (Though many have argued the contrary, the originally suppressed chapter in which this abortive confession is related does not clear up the mystery of Stavrogin but deepens it. It is an abortion, a failure in birth, in the life of a great sinner: it shows Stavrogin *unable* to break through into a new life, but condemned instead to insult again the society by which he would be saved.) These are all episodes which show the creative power of the mystery in Stavrogin's personality; and the credibility of that power to the reader will depend on how far he "believes" in the effect reported on each of the characters, and on how far he accepts the verisimilitude of the change, in his presence, of the general situation as it is reported directly to the reader. Stavrogin tells us nothing himself.

We know him only by what he rouses in others, how he appears to others, and, to a certain extent, how he appears in contrast to others. As we reflect on this system of representation and its intensity, we begin to see that he is intended to be one of those creatures of man's mind which are their own meaning: a symbol from which one takes what one brings. That is why, at Tihon's, he breaks off his evident effort at regeneration by physically breaking an ivory crucifix: he breaks, or creates, in each person with whom he deals, the sign of what that person is in himself. That is why, too, Dostoevsky had to prepare so carefully for his first appearance on the scene of present action by giving a history of his previous appearance, three years earlier. He had come then with a reputation ahead of him as savage, reckless, brutal and callous: a debauched bully, fresh from living deliberately in rags in the dregs of Petersburg. Yet when he arrived, instead of a sodden drunk, he was an apparition of elegance, a man with a fateful secret, by rumor a murderer. The ladies were wild about him, either in adoration or hatred. He had light-colored eyes, his cheeks were too red, there was something repellent in him that suggested a vampire. The stories about him turned out probably to have been true: he pulled an old man by the nose as a "calculated and premeditated indecency," and instead of explaining his actions he bit the governor's ear; after which he relapsed into a brain-fever, or as we would say, had a breakdown, recovering from which he went away for three more years. When he reappears in the midst of a scandalous scene at his mother's, he is in the company of a strange young man, Pyotr Stepanovitch Verhovensky. Pyotr enters first and refuses the embraces of his father. He is described as one who suggests ill health but is well, round shouldered but strong; too articulate; not ugly, but no one liked his face; with a tongue of special shape with an everlastingly active little tip. In contrast, when Stavrogin follows him in, it is said of him that he is unchanged, except that a mask-like quality to his face is gone and that he is now incontestably beautiful, shining with the light of some new idea. His first act is to lie when his mother asks him if Marya is his wife, and then to speak gently to Marya. His second act is to take a blow in the face from Shatov's whole fist: merely staring Shatov in the face, holding the white-hot iron of his revolting, terrible, *reasonable* anger. Thus he begins his work.

He begins it 180 pages into the novel, at the end of the first Book. He could not have come earlier because neither the reader nor the novel would have been prepared for him. Most of all, what we call in translation of a phrase of Dostoevsky, the underground man would not have been prepared for either Stavrogin or his self-appointed lieutenant Pyotr. When they come, many things have been set in motion—by scandal, by spite, by the sense of the man under the bed, most of all by the underground man: the verminous cockroach sort of man who comes up through the cracks from between the floors; precisely the condition of the intellectual classes turned proletariat, but not limited to them. It is among people who have turned to the underground phase of themselves that Stavrogin appears. The odor of lice is thick. It is only concentrated in the buffoons, Lebyadkin and Liputin; it is only pitiable in Stepan Trofimovitch; piteous in Marya; desperate in Shatov; absolute in Kirillov. Against them the underground man in Pyotr is reckless and enthusiastic, in Stavrogin ambiguous.

It is from his ambiguity that Stavrogin gets what Shatov calls his immense power, by which he can raise Shatov from the death of nihilism at the same time that he confirms the living nihilism in the heart of Kirillov. It is by communicating the shadow of this power, too, that he raises Pyotr's "extraordinary aptitude for crime" to enthusiastic action, making of him a madman engineering chaos out of hysteria. Indeed, in the second Book of the novel there is a progressive laceration of the underground man to the point of private hysteria. Only Stepan Trofimovitch, the fiasco of the old liberal, gains through these lacerations; most of what is false in him is lacerated away, and he has the special sad strength of feeling that his die is cast—*Alea jacta est.* All the rest come nearer that breaking point when private hysterias burst into the open and become public disorder. The promise of what is to come shows in small incidents where what is revolting excites mirth: the substitution of pornography for tracts in the gospel woman's bag, the secretion of a live mouse in the ikon of the Mother of God, Liza giving her diamond ear rings for alms, the unseemly behavior on the expedition to the saint and prophet Semyon Yakolevitch, and the two scenes between Stavrogin and his double Fedka, the peasant murderer. Everybody is going against each other and against himself at the same time. It is the immense power of Stavrogin that presides over all this, both as creator and creation; and it is his image, as the true arrogance of man, that gives whatever unity of impression the novel has. His image makes it possible for the reader to tolerate the breakdown of form and uncertainty of intention in the middle of the book, where what seem riddles are tensions, where blows in the face become holy burdens, and where also there is a vast deal of high jinks, Dickensian, Quixotic, and perfectly hellish at the same time.

This account of the power of Stavrogin should not be taken as implying that Dostoevsky failed to carry along the political side of his tale. The politics is what Stavrogin enlightens and obscures, first one and then the other. The political side of the novel is kept going at three levels. Pyotr's conspiracy is made to gain momentum, a quintet is formed out of the group of thirty, and the quintet is first inured and then pushed to violence. The fête for the new governor and on behalf of the nurses goes forward in confusion, incompetence, and in the growing certainty of fiasco as well as failure: it is known beforehand the buffoons will get the upper hand and the riff-raff will take it over. Furthermore, there is an account of administrative breakdown and corruption at the centre and a rise in crime, cattle plague, and cholera in the whole area of the province. The combined momentum—intelligible, desperate, mad—is irresistible. The conspiracy ends in murder, the fête makes fiasco, the people make a mob, all at once.

But, to repeat, if we grant the momentum, it is only Stavrogin's image that makes it understandable, makes it human—the kind of humanity Nietzsche was to find all too human. Let us take two examples. One is in the chapter called "Ivan the Tsarevitch," where Pyotr makes his last bid for the support and leadership of Stavrogin, offering to do murder for him, and indeed afterwards procuring murder for him. "The Pope shall be for the West, and you shall be for us!" he cries. "You are beautiful . . . you are the sun, and I am your worm." Here Pyotr kisses Stavrogin's hand, and goes on, that without him he, Pyotr, is Columbus without America; that Stavrogin is the hidden God, the *Deus Absconditus,* into whose hands it is so fearful a thing to fall; more Russian than that, Stavrogin is also identified as Ivan the Tsarevitch, Ivan Filipovitch, the God of Sabaoth. Finally, this criminal enthusiast cries out: "There's no one on earth but you! I invented you abroad; I invented it all, looking at you."

There is one image for Stavrogin. Here is another, from the suppressed chapter, "At Tihon's." Stavrogin has gone to the holy man to find a means of playing the martyr at the heroic level, and when they have had some discussion to the effect that atheism is preferable to believing in the devil without God because "the complete atheist stands on the penultimate step to most perfect faith," Stavrogin asks Tihon to recite from the Apocalypse the passage about the luke-warm Laodiceans, and in the midst of the recitation interrupts to say, "I love you very much," to which Tihon answers, "And I love you." Exactly at this moment of *rapprochement*—what he had come for—Stavrogin becomes difficult again, is *irrité,* rates and mocks Tihon, saying that he needs no one and can shift for himself. Yet precisely because of the nature of his independence (that it must affect others like an immense power), and at the moment he is about to assert it most brutally, he requires of himself that he demand the mercy of Tihon. Unlike Shatov he does not entreat mercy but demands it; unlike

Kirillov he cannot make greatness of soul express itself in an unbelief which is the equivalent of death. Nor is he lukewarm; his ennui is positive and frightful. He hands Tihon the written sheets recording his debauchery of the twelve-year-old Matryosha, whose tiny shaking fist he by his own will keeps still before his face. Why does he make this confession?—because he wants to exchange one kind of suffering for another, to substitute the cross for the devil, but also because to make his sin public would be "another way of nipping the governor's ear"—another way to challenge society, to find an enemy, to express his power in such a way that it would work. There lies the true arrogance of Stavrogin, that his force must work, that he must degrade his power in use. His role in its purity is intolerable to him, because there it would do no work; though he wants the purity, and knows what it is in the sense that the complete atheist knows what faith is, he must nevertheless cripple it, degrade it, so that it will do work—and must at the same time chastise himself for doing so. Since he cannot be a saint he will be heroic among the enemies of what he cannot be. That is why, though he scorned it, he did not reject Pyotr Stepanovitch's invocation.

Stavrogin, then, is one of those symbols through which men merge their thwarted selves, and find such a momentum of action as carries them to the brink of rebirth and to the suburbs of destruction. They are the momentum of that part which is hopelessness in the human enterprise: the hopelessness that shows most, and as a terror, at those times when the intellectual classes have become, as they had in Dostoevsky's Russia, a proletariat. It is the kind of momentum we feel in society when everything in politics and religion expresses itself as a form of power. That is the situation meant by Lord Acton's phrase, that "power tends to corrupt; absolute power corrupts absolutely"; the momentum is what is corrupted. It is characteristic of Dostoevsky that he should have begun, as he says, by taking Stavrogin out of his heart, a typical and tragic figure, in order to break that momentum in an image of rebirth; it is even more characteristic that when in the honesty of his imagination he discovered that his tragic figure could not go beyond the momentum of his sin, he surrendered him to that momentum. Stavrogin hanged himself, in sound mind, afraid of sham greatness. He could not find God in man; he would not become a god-man.

On that, Dostoevsky ended his book, but it was only a formal close to go with another, less formal, just behind it. In the next to last chapter, "Stepan Trofimovitch's Last Wandering," we find that there had been another momentum at work all along, another inertia than that uncopeable inertia which Stavrogin presided over. It shows in the apotheosis of Stepan Trofimovitch, father of Pyotr and tutor of Stavrogin, from the flunkey into the Don Quixote; and in the apotheosis we see an *éclaircissement* of the text of the swine which Stavrogin's death could not give. What has happened to Stepan Trofimovitch? Beginning with the casualty of "culture," the parasite of progress, the mere creature of Varvara Petrovna, a man given to hysterias, vanities, unmoored allegiances, we proceed through a stripping which becomes a devastation, a vastation, a rehabilitation, an apotheosis. In detail there is nothing not taken from the twenty years of romance and fiasco, but in substance it is all taken from the reality of which the romance was the protective lie, the *Bovarysme,* the protection put on, like the French language, the love of Shakespeare, Raphael, brandy, and champagne: the great protection of *The lies I have told all my life.* But there is a truth in the protection as there is a truth in the lies: in the reasons why these lies are told rather than other lies; and perhaps they are not far different from Kirillov's reasons for refusing to invent God, or from Shatov's reasons for holding that viable faith depends on keeping connections with one's country. Stepan Trofimovitch, as he lies dying, is the old Westerner, and all he sheds of the west in his apotheosis is enough to show that he is a rooted Russian after all, at bottom, at the end: of his "cause," his course, his romance, his life. He *recurs* to his different selves; but as Varvara Petrovna tells the priest who has just confessed him, Wait: he is such a one as must be confessed at every hour.—What does that mean, if not that he is permanently alive; permanently on the edge of resuming the "lies" he has told all his life—just as permanently on the edge, if only he could, of ceasing to lie.

This old liberal is one who teeters between the gospel and champagne; between a great tenderness and a great folly, between a blessed revealed order and an anarchic rejection of all imposed order. But he is not the teetering; he is the living thing that teeters. He is the obstinate finality in human nature that needs both gospel and champagne. He is that immortal, hopeful part of man, with shifting but unarrestable momentum, that has never needed either a hero or a saint; hubris is not in his line; he is Don Quixote without Sancho Panza, and he tilts at real things. On his deathbed he hears by accident the passage about the luke-warm which Tihon had quoted to Stavrogin; it is new to him and he rejoices that it is better to be cold than only luke-warm. Then he asks for the passage about the swine, and, after hearing it, makes his own wholly unheroic attestation. Russia, he says, is the great invalid, and a great Will from on high will enter into her and cleanse her as in the lunatic possessed of devils. They will beg to enter the swine. "They are we, we and those . . . and Petrusha and *les autres avec lui* and I perhaps at the head of them." His last words were that "The Infinite and Eternal are as necessary for man as the little planet on which he dwells." He says nothing of the hero and the saint.

It is not that Dostoevsky asks his readers to choose between Stavrogin and Stepan Trofimovitch; how could he ask a choice where he could make none himself; but he set them side by side, each impervious to the other, each lost in his own temptations, those of hopelessness and those of hope, with a kind of incommensurable equivalence in their disparate momentums. You cannot create, you can only bring destruction, by Stavrogin's kind of momentum; you cannot destroy, you can only go on, by Stepan Trofimovitch's kind of momentum. The one is necessary to conceive against the other as life is necessary to conceive against death. Each "possesses" the other, unawares.

It is only because Stavrogin and Stepan Trofimovitch Verhovensky inhabit the same novel and are forced together in the same country house called Skvoreshniki that their absolute disparity could seem to have an ambivalence. The name of the country house means in English a birdcage. Verhoven means supreme, and supremacy is what Stepan Trofimovitch could not undertake. Stavros means cross (in Greek of the kind that Russians know) and his cross is what Stavrogin could not take up. By the politics of the birdcage, in the prison of life and looking to liberation, these seem much the same.

THE BROTHERS KARAMAZOV:

I. *The Galloping Troika and the Momentum of the Underground*

Dostoevsky is the great master of the unmotivated and nowhere more so than in *The Brothers Karamazov:* in him you see how hard it is to achieve lasting or adequate motive, how almost impossible to escape from evil into the good and yet live, but also how deep is the affliction of hope within us that we may do so. You see action, whether of the Psyche or of the hand, that springs from random hope—from the general fund or stream of hope gone random, *driven* random, usually by some suffering, or by some simpleheartedness. One should remember that to be simplehearted is either to be without motive or to be almost perfectly united with motive. The wicked are like that, says Dostoevsky, and adds "We ourselves are, too." That this notion should be at once linked to caprice (in the person of old Karamazov, as the first of many instances in the persons who inhabit this book) indicates the depth of the force here called random hope—the depth of the unexpected, the unpredictable act that seizes on and hauls on the hope like a hook. It is this force which this novel transforms, through suffering and the conscience of sin, into motive. This is why in so many of his books Dostoevsky wanted to write The Life of a Great Sinner—as if only the Great Sinner could achieve ultimate motive. That he could never openly use the title does not greatly matter; we feel the intention behind the titles we do have: *Crime and Punishment, The Idiot, The Possessed* (or, if you prefer the title some translators use, *The Devils*), and most of all *The Brothers Karamazov;* we feel also why Dostoevsky could not use his chosen title. The intention got lost in the rush and momentum of what in life escapes intention and surpasses motive altogether. The man from underground—the man in the very cellar of the soul—is the driver of the galloping troika, which is, I take it, a name for the vehicle of our behavior.[1]

Yet there is always the loom of motive, a kind of receding loom, with which we may yet catch up.

So it is with Fyodor the father, him who is murdered. He is given at once as a senseless fellow but shrewd in instinct, a sensualist who makes of his shame his sentimentality. He is a buffoon for two reasons: because it is expected of him and because he likes to make buffoons of others; and perhaps for a third reason:

[1] Several times during these remarks I use the phrase "the Galloping Troika," sometimes coupled with "the Momentum of the Underground," and use them without explanation in the hope they might gather meaning as they went along. The Underground refers to Dostoevsky's *Notes from the Underground* and its nameless inhabitant. As for the Galloping Troika, it is from Gogol and is used by the prosecutor in Dmitri's trial and is afterwards used as a title of the chapter which ends the prosecution. Here is part of what the prosecutor says in the first instance. "A great writer of the last epoch, comparing Russia to a swift troika galloping to an unknown goal, exclaims, 'Oh, troika, birdlike troika, who invented thee!' and adds, in proud ecstasy, that all the peoples in the world stand aside respectfully to make way for the recklessly galloping troika to pass. . . . [If] the troika were drawn by his heroes . . . it could reach no rational goal, whoever might be driving it. And those were the heroes of an older generation, ours are worse specimens still. . . ." At this point the prosecutor's speech was interrupted, but the book goes on for him and his plea.

that buffoonery is a good medium in which to get random things done—in which to snatch up a windfall of possibility. He plays, and knows that he plays, one of the most tempting of all rôles: the man of whom no one knows what he will do next: except that it will be unpleasant, or vicious, or senseless: somehow against any cultivated order of things. Such a fellow is bad enough on the street corner or in a parlor game, but at the center of life he makes pandemonium and himself a natural subject for murder. He is also the drunkard beside himself; he is beside his sanity and is thus unlike the ecstatic, the fanatic, or the anarchist—whose sanities are not there. He is all of a piece and of earth-energy: which is why, for the time being, "such creatures are let live." He is the unmotivated out of which motives are made (the disorder in which order is seen necessary); he is also the fellow whose portrait appears: the bloated figure with the pendulous Adam's apple, the slobbering speech, and black tooth stumps who likes to think of himself as a Roman patrician of the decadent period. He is your own picture of his picture of himself: a cynosure of every thought of parricide; you can't keep your eyes off him.

He is perhaps in his fifties when the story opens on the eve of his gloomy death at the hands of his sons, Dmitri, Ivan, and Alyosha and his bastard Smerdyakov. He is their father, and he makes them a family, a family of ugly ducklings, which is precisely the Karamazov breed. None of them, taken separately, has an adequate motive to murder their father, but taken together in each other's light, confronted with their father's buffoonery, and under the blessings of the Elder Zossima, an ample and powerful sense of motive is achieved. We see now without recognition what we will learn later: that none are guilty and all are guilty. It is true that Dmitri is jealous of his father and is at his wits' end for money; so Ivan also perhaps needs money and is strangely at the early end of his own kind of wits; and Smerdyakov, the young man with a guitar, is already in the terminal state, as we say of those with whom we tamper although we cannot save them, of needing need, of desperately desiring desire: he is a lackey to every motive of money, flesh, or pride, but only the lackey. Nothing that he is or does is his own: he makes a servile double or mask for every true need or desire. As for Alyosha, he has no use for money, and unless he wished to avenge his mother whom his father had driven to her death he has no proper motive. It is more likely that, without a motive, the incipient love and untrained goodness in him—his drawing power—make him a motor, and that in his presence the others are motors, too. As Alyosha in his power of acceptance or love, so Ivan in denial and pride and Dmitri in the bounty of his body and elation of spirit are all forms of what is merged and debased in their father—degraded and lacerated in Smerdyakov, their bastard and lackey brother: the Karamazov quality, the Karamazov idiosyncrasy: vitality no matter what. In any going society they are all equally unseemly, but necessary, and enormously attractive. We cannot say them nay except with respect to the degree with which we say them yea. As they attract others, so they attract each other. They cannot let each other alone, nor can we. By a kind of random inevitability, a fortuitous possibility is roused in each of us by them, as for each of them by each other, which once foreseen only an exhaustive act of will can reject.

Separately they are nothing, it is the bringing together that counts. All the brothers have been raised apart, each has been educated as his variation warranted, Dmitri in the army, Ivan at the university, Alyosha at the monastery: old Karamazov in debasement, Smerdyakov in degradation, Dmitri in the pride of body, Ivan in the pride of intellect, Alyosha in a humility which comes close to acting like a pride. With respect to each other, each has passed twenty years in the desert. When they come together, though each is also himself, they unite and break in a single storm on the community. Under the genius of the family they make, as Brutus says in *Julius Caesar,* an insurrection in the state of man.

There could have been no dramatic media better than those Dostoevsky uses in which to represent the storm: murder, money, and sexuality whether in love or lust. Money is the nearest form for the terrible hope of freedom, sexuality the most interior form, and murder is the climactic form. Among them they make the commonplace of obsesssion, the cellarage of action, the requirement of the psyche to breed spirit and its annihilation. Thus Ivan argues that all have the right to wish for another's death. Thus Dmitri tells us of the hatred which is only a hair's breadth from the maddest love. And thus old Fyodor creates his own murder in that revenge of buffoonery which he takes upon his own unseemliness: he debases himself so far that he is there only to be squashed. Thus, too, Dmitri considers that crime is inevitable to the infidel—and in saying so seems to imply there is a shortage of the faithful, which is why he can also say that for the immense mass of mankind beauty is found in Sodom, or of Katerina that "she loves her own *virtue,* not me," and of Grushenka that she "has a supple curve all over her body. You can see it in her little foot, even in her little toe. I saw it, and kissed it, but that was all, I swear!" Murder and sex are instruments of assessment: of nihilism and creation. Money is in this sense an indifferent instrument; but money is also an instrument of conversion. It itches in the pocket, your own or some one's else, to become or make another thing. Money converts sex into murder.

Money, murder, and sex are all related to buffoonery in Dostoevsky's psychology, as buffoonery is also related to caprice and motive, with motive at the center—at the knot of each reticulation—as the absent or needed link. Take Dostoevsky's notion of the buffoon at its highest level, which is Alyosha explaining to the boy Kolya the mad behaviour of Snegiryov (the "wisp of tow"): "There are people of deep feeling who have been somehow crushed. Buffoonery in them is a form of resentful irony against those to whom they don't dare speak the truth, from having been for years humiliated and intimidated by them . . . That sort of buffoonery is sometimes tragic in the extreme." Grant a man his self-pity—grant him especially the pitiless eye of self-pity—and which of us is not at least secretly a buffoon. In Dostoevsky he bursts into the open.

Perhaps there is no principal character in *The Brothers Karamazov* who is not in some sense a buffoon except Alyosha and the presence who stands behind him, the Elder Zossima, and for them there are counterparts, "underground" forms, quite unconscious buffoons. For Alyosha there is, or was, stinking Lizaveta, whom everybody liked, and nobody mocked, and all the more so for her absolute unseemliness: she is a debased Alyosha. For Zossima there is perhaps Father Ferapont, who wore chains rather than grace under his habit; he is Zossima's underground monstrous form, the inescapable *other* thing than *this* thing; he too takes everything unto himself, but like a vacuum or a sponge or a trap, not as resource or renewal. Father Ferapont takes the wilfulness of the soul, not its will. This last Dostoevsky expresses another way when he concludes speaking of the absolute authority of the Elder: "This instrument . . . for the moral regeneration of a man from slavery to freedom and moral perfectibility may be a two-edged weapon and it may lead some not to humility and complete self-control but to the most Satanic pride, that is, to bondage and not to freedom." Buffoonery falsely bursts the bonds.

With this in mind, one asks at once about Zossima's successive blessings of the three brothers—Ivan for his requirement of an answer; Dmitri because he is doomed to suffer; Alyosha because he must go into the world and "bear all." Do not these blessings *bring*—as the wind brings rain—torture and despair on Ivan and Dmitri? Is it not only Alyosha—whose story we shall never know—whom it was right to bless? Or are we to think this blessing the invocation of tragedy? Or does the Elder recognize tragedy in the contortions of the fundamental Karamazov baseness?—and this for Alyosha, too. Remember that Alyosha sees that he is on the bottom step of Dmitri's sensuality and knows that he who has taken the first step will take the rest. When we hear old Fyodor assure Zossima that he must not invite him to be his natural self—"Don't risk it. . . . I will not go so far as that myself"—when we hear this, it seems to me we can envisage what would have happened to Alyosha in the world. Precisely he would have gone that far, to the limit of his natural self—and Dostoevsky must have given us this limit, not in the summary of anecdote as in our record of Zossima, but all the way in fully dramatized form. As we see later for ourselves, Zossima invokes for Alyosha the experience he himself has not had. He sees in Alyosha the innocence to which everything might happen. That is why Alyosha is "given" as more a realist than any one. The idea of the potentiality of innocence has always been very tempting to Christians and to the guilt-ridden Christian like Dostoevsky it is the greatest temptation of all: the temptation to another kind of murder. All his life Dostoevsky tried for the maximum in this line and got nowhere further than Zossima. (Tihon in *The Possessed,* the Elder in *The Idiot* are of the type but lesser.) That is why he had to create so many buffoons—to take up the slack of innocence. The buffoon is the underground man in a state of expression, on the go; the buffoon is the innocent man prevented from the created experience of his innocence—prevented, to use Dostoevsky's language—by injury, insult, and humiliation, prevented by pride; it is all the same. The rare man—the one or two in all Russia, as Smerdyakov says—erupts into sainthood. The labor of creation is either for the saint or the buffoon; and either of them can be *either* the perfectly good man or the great sinner. Dostoevsky seems to have thought each must be both, and even *ought* to be so.

These observations are meant to bring into intelligible relation Zossima's charge that "love in action is a harsh and dreadful thing compared with love in dreams" and Dmitri's charge that you may be in love with a woman and hate her, that beauty is a terrible and awful thing, that man begins with the ideal of the Madonna and ends with the ideal of Sodom. "What to the mind," he says, "is shameful is beauty and nothing else to the heart." And, to repeat, "Believe me, that for the immense mass of mankind beauty is found in Sodom." Both these charges are partially enacted in this book, both are responded to as experience; it appears to me that the two charges and the two responses are two phases of the same thing.

To go back now to the blessings and the charges. Is it not that Zossima, when he bows down to Dmitri as an act of his "unbounded and inexplicable authority," bows in truth to Dmitri's charge? He has thus taken the Karamazov soul and will into his soul and will after the paradigm of his being. That is his function: to satisfy the need for holiness in those who suffer injustice. So, too, is not the harshness of love in action what Zossima imposes on Alyosha when he orders him into the world, and, as a realist, to bear all? Again, he blesses Ivan because his mind and heart can bear suffering: he is the martyr who will "divert himself by his suffering" and with an aching heart mock at his mind. Pride of intellect, pride of meekness, pride of body—three modes of regarding the intolerable world—each requires a blessing because to each there will come a fall: a fall through dread privation into something else.

This is the true or valid preparatory force of Part I of *The Brothers Karamazov.* A pitch or level of approach and penetration has been set and the situation (with respect to the parricide, the relations of the brothers, and of them all to the monastery, and so on) has been given momentum *at that pitch or level.* It is the momentum and the pitch of the galloping troika. Nobody has a clear motive or a rational goal, but all have found a common reservoir of motive—a welling pool—to dip into; and there has also been developed a high possibility of available convertibility, of likely reversibility. The old man and his sons all have the potential of reversing without altering their rôles—whatever those rôles may be. Even Alyosha rests on the base of sensuality; he is not yet *low* enough—squashed enough—for a monk, let alone a saint; and as for the old father, his buffoonery is the very teeter of reversibility.

Of course we can say this is all machinery and vocabulary: mere emphases of form, psychological and fictional, emotional and technical, conceptual and executive, symbolic and phenomenal. They furnish out the plot. They are the means by which we get under the plot and, deeper still, under the language, so that we apprehend as emotions of our own the genuine actions of men. The torrent of words seems to be a torrent of individuals. What else should a novel be?

What we nowadays call "form" in the novel might economize these achievements, but it could not have provided them. Henry James referred to Tolstoi's novels as "loose and baggy monsters" and I suppose he might have had a worse phrase still for Dostoevsky's monsters. At any rate, thinking of *The Brothers Karamazov,* and thinking of either the James novel or the life-shaped novels that at present afflict us with the idea chiefly that they ought to be cut, there seems a kind of mutilating self-determinism about what we call form: a certainty or a spontaneity of effort which mechanizes sensibility and cuts the options. All our paradoxes become minor, all our ironies trivial, all our wit substitutive. We have the achievements of those who are content to come —or go—short of mastery. It would be desirable to give another accounting of form; it is probable that we have matured the "form of the novel" at a different rate and perhaps on another track from those of the imagination itself. Hence there is a kind of adolescence, a failure in generosity, in magnanimity, in the actions of the psyche at her work among even the most ambitious and talented contemporary English and American novels: the forms they use do not correspond to our visions or our interests well enough to provide us with either a new psychology or a theoretic form of life—whether to accept or to reject, at least to experience. The critic can do nothing but remind us of these provisions.

In Part II of the novel, the provisions are ample, too ample to deal with all at once, except to say that the death of the Elder Zossima presides over the whole part and supplies a kind of center for the murder which is being prepared and a setting for Ivan's poem of The Grand Inquisitor and Alyosha's reaction to it. What Zossima is and what he represents move beside the secular plot, or the story of the brothers. Dostoevsky makes a permanent analogy in images, to use Shelley's language, "which participate in the life of truth." It is not a question of belief but of seeing what happens when the two trains of images are put side by side. Zossima as Elder is absolute authority and absolute humility, for the monk is "lower" with each year of seclusion. In full lowness, he realizes that he is responsible and responsibly guilty of all human sins personally. This is the "eastern" notion of the scapegoat. If we grow, we grow in guilt, and there is no end to it. When T. S. Eliot, commenting on pacificism at the beginning of the Second World War, said that if we share the goods we must share the guilt of our society, he was perhaps illustrating the notion of the "western" scapegoat. But the "true" scapegoat by the harshness of love (to love *also* that which God chose: to love what one hates) wins the whole world: that harshness which asks no conditions of God. Only the extreme of humility can refrain from asking conditions of God without pride.

With the death of such a man, those who loved him expect attendant miracles, and so also those who feared or hated him. And as the force of the man was personal so must the miracles be personal too. It was therefore taken as a gratifying preliminary miracle at the monastery when, as the Elder had said, a missing son was suddenly restored to his widowed mother. Miracles are the temptation of personal faith, as they are the triumph of faith beyond the personal: compare the petty cures that abound in graveyards and dark corners with the "true" miracles of the decisions of Thomas Aquinas, the intuitions of Francis of Assisi, or the existence of great cathedrals. But at the monastery we see the other thing: the temptation to see a miracle which passes the limits of reason in the letter which reports the missing son's imminent return. Even Father Païssy, Alyosha's mentor after the Elder himself, scarcely believed his own disavowal. How could he, quite, in a monastery which contained also the crazy ascetic, Father Ferapont, with his visible devils and pusillanimous burdens—his reduction of life to the disappearance of faith: the crazy saint who sacrificed intellect for the glory of God? He was one of those who believe that since we feel within us a power not ourselves greater than ourselves, we will come nearer to it if we extinguish our only avenues to it, the powers that *are* ourselves. We would starve and see marvels, which is a great temptation to the man who sees that he has glorified his intellect because it *is* an avenue—until it is glorified. No wonder, to repeat, that Father Païssy hardly believed his disavowal of the miracle. It was part of the underground life of the monastery, and very near the surface.

It remains Father Païssy's function to remind Alyosha—who has been seeing and feeling all this—that the power not ourselves and beyond ourselves is at work just the same. He gives Zossima's life a rational parallel when he says that the Christian ideal works even in the hearts of atheists—that Christianity is, so to speak, antecedent to every vital purpose and that all attempts to replace it have resulted in grotesques; which I suppose must also mean that Christianity underlies and is even aside from any of the forms it has been given. Book IV of the novel where these scenes take place is called "Lacerations." To follow and assent to Father Païssy's argument is easy if all you want is indifference or inertia, but very hard if you want to pass beyond tolerance into the harsh and dreadful thing which is active love. Perhaps this, as well as the parting from Zossima with which it ends, is the laceration of this chapter.

Certainly the laceration in the next chapter, "At His Father's," lies in the criticism in the parallel text to Father Païssy and the Elder which old Karamazov's remarks supply, with the teeter of reversal being imaged in the glass-and-a-half of brandy he consumes. He too wants a miracle: to be as capable a whoremaster at seventy-five as he is at fifty-five, and he finds the means to his miracle in money. He knows that sin is not only original and inherent but is also sweet. It is as if he were the figure of a man who had found a new and contrary way of saying "sin is behovely" and was himself a second and contrary form of mystic. He declares that the sweetness of sin is as much a means to being as is the penitence of Zossima. Both sin openly. If you have either faith or money you will win the world: the partial objective is the same. He breaks off his ranting boast to say he knows he is ill-natured; and Alyosha answers him, "You are not ill-natured but distorted," as he could have said to Zossima, or to himself, "Although you are good-natured you are distorted—or partial." (Dostoevsky's saints or good men are never *enough* so for their rôles.) The striking difference between the Elder and the father is that while the one prepares for death in faith, the other speaks of killing Dmitri as if it were squelching a beetle under his slippered foot, but he is alive in his baseness with a vigor faith could hardly reach.

As if the Elder and the father—a great death and a senseless murder—were not enough, the following chapter, called "A Meeting with the Schoolboys," introduces a laceration at first unintelligible but of which the consequences will furnish the countertheme of *The Brothers Karamazov* and will in fact bring the whole work to as much of a conclusion—the conclusion of what is inconclusible—as Dostoevsky could manage. As with Gide and Henry James, Lewis Carroll and Thomas Mann, Dostoevsky needed the young, needed children, to furnish both foils and support—needed the analogy of something earlier than adolescence to express the burden and content of maturity. Alyosha in his cassock, which he is that day to put off, finds himself among the violence and vice of a gang of boys stoning, humiliating, and insulting another boy. It is the class of humanity—children—whom he always likes. As he tries to break up the fracas, he is hit by a stone from the victim and is bitten by him hard in the middle finger of the left hand, near the base of the nail and to the very bone. It is an inexplicable interlude which worsens what surrounds it, merely, for the time being, because it is *there* and is in the pattern of things. Dostoevsky is always prodigal of the sufferings—here called "lacerations"—he gives his heroes, but he is very close to Pandora with Alyosha. After the stoning and the biting come the lacerations he receives in the hysterical mockery of Lise, the crippled girl to whom he is engaged—she makes a joke of his feelings—and the further horror, in the same house, of the bitter and mutually destructive relations between his brother Ivan and Katerina, as he watches the two of them degrade or immerse themselves in the rising tide of insulted pride. They, too, are throwing stones and biting fingers, as they erupt upon each other in darkening hysteria. It is as if every one said to the other what Mme. Hohlakov said to Lise: "You are not screaming. It's I am screaming." There is nothing these people—these lovers of life—cannot do to hurt each other in their actual love, and what they cannot think of doing each does to himself or herself. By making them realize this, Alyosha is one of the lot.

I do not say that Aloysha knows this, but the mode of that knowledge moves within him, as he carries two hundred roubles from Katerina to appease a man whom Dmitri had hauled by the beard, and who turns out to be father to the boy who had stoned him and bitten his finger. In their cottage he finds that family—Nina the crippled sister, Varvara the mad wife, Ilusha the sick boy, and the head of the household the cringing buffoon, Captain Snegiryov whose beard, if any beard must be pulled, must be pulled. The beard was not a very good beard—only a "wisp of tow," as the boys had cried after his son that day at the stoning—and hardly enough to pull a man out of the tavern by, as Dmitri had pulled him. The pulling had made the boy ill, and had made the captain spend his last penny on drink. "In Russia," he told Alyosha, "men who drink are the best. The best men amongst us are the greatest drunkards." This "wisp of tow"—with neither faith nor money—with only the impossible remnants of his captaincy—gives a tale of Injury, Insult, and Humiliation; to which his own response is buffoonery, that of his boy Ilusha a sickness at injustice and a mighty anger. Alyosha promises the captain Dmitri's apology and offers him Katerina's money. But the boy's mighty anger prevents him from taking the money and transforms his buffoonery for the moment into something better than dignity. The boy has a power over his father like that of Zossima over Alyosha. Would one judge of this? Or praise? The minor characters like the captain in Dostoevsky often tell us what the major characters are about. Alyosha "saw that till the very last moment the man had not known he would crumple up and fling away the notes." They were brightly colored notes. It is right that this laceration should have taken place, as the chapter title says, in the "open air."

Perhaps this series of Alyosha's lacerations—these steps and stages in his education as a realist and a sinner—these adventures among different momentums and surprising resemblances—these gestures from the underground that invigorate our chosen action with our random behavior—will ready us for the parricide, the murder of our father who impels and impedes us, in the dark place at the centre and quick of this novel. We are back at once among the immense mass of mankind who find—as the immense mass in each of us elect finds—beauty in Sodom and do not at all find that active love is a harsh and dreadful thing, but who do find that what was murder in the offing is now murder in the heart, what each of us would do if it were not so unlikely in the terms in which we conduct ourselves, and what each of us will not do individually because it corresponds so closely to what we do in the mass, as society in action; but which we do just the same. When we estimate Dostoevsky's account of it we see at once why the murder is committed "In the Dark"—in a gap of white paper in the black print of the book. We see why we are not given the mere deed. There was no "mere" deed. We see also why there is another chapter called "And There Was No Murder Either" though there was a man murdered who clung to life for direct reasons. We see that murder is only a name which in aggravated moments we give to the crisis in the storm when human patterns cross, breeding spirit and the annihilation of spirit. Alyosha's lacerations, which in our own milieus might have been our own, make us see how the murder was anonymous and communal (Thomas Mann's phrase), and our own.

Let us look how the thing becomes communal and how in anonymity we find our own name. Old Karamazov ripens his own murder by being himself, by being a buffoon, by taunting his sons, by his sensuality, by his money, by the insult of his creation of Smerdyakov, and by his rivalry with Dmitri over Grushenka. Katerina ripens the murder by her virtue and her pride and fanatic self-humiliation, by her love for Ivan, by tempting Grushenka with kisses, by tempting Dmitri with money, by heightening others' emotions, by eliciting judgment from Alyosha. Ivan ripens the murder by his contempt and pride, by envisaging and suggesting murder, by his *dealing* with Smerdyakov and his father, by his deceit as to where he is going on the fatal day, by his insistence that all things are lawful. Dmitri ripens the murder by comforting Grushenka and aiding her with relation to the lover who has deserted her, and by his quality as her conscience. Grushenka herself ripens the murder by being "on the market" and by her coquetry. Lastly, Smerdyakov ripens the murder because he is smeared all over; by his appeal to Ivan, the clever man, the appeal of the possibility; by his hatred of the legitimate; by his idiocy, contemplativeness, and epilepsy: that is, by his possibility of bringing together in anonymity the fragments of a general act.

He has all the defects of humanity but is incapable of virtues, vices, heroisms. He is smeared and smears, the very thing on the verge. Although, as we know, he "actually" performs the murder, he is the one person who cannot take on himself the guilt of it; the guilt merely demolishes him. We are glad he kills himself, because we could not have established his guilt either.

Why, with all these matters in mind, are we so ready to believe along with every one in the book except Smerdyakov, that it was Dmitri who killed his father? Why does the pyschology of his character grasp us so warmly by the hand? Is it because he dresses so well that we feel there is nothing within his clothes but him? Will he stand for us then as we should like to stand for ourselves? Or, to put it another way, why are we prepared (beforehand, from birth) to accept the peasants' verdict—the truesaying—of his guilt beyond above beside the law and the facts? Do we not ourselves occupy *in the shape of Dmitri* the darkness in which the old man was killed? Certainly we cannot so easily choose Ivan's shape or the shape of Ivan's devil; though it is an obvious possibility, it would not be right for the mystery that in the end alone seems live. There is also in the reserve part of our natures the possibility that we might occupy the darkness in the shape of Smerdyakov, just as we might in the uncreated part of our natures occupy it in the shape of Alyosha. We have the epileptic in reserve, who would take us over in his scream, and we have the saint to come, in whom we should disappear. Only in the shape of Dmitri can we participate in a mad but gallant action.

It is in Dmitri that we can accommodate ourselves to the Elder Zossima, to the Grand Inquisitor, and to the sweep or momentum of the story. And it is in Dmitri that we can believe for the length of the story that all are guilty and that none are guilty. Each of us can strike himself, as Dmitri did, "here," on the breast. Not only do the guilty flee when none pursue, the innocent flee so that all may pursue. It is a deep habit, either way; all are pursued, all are in flight. As with the murder, there is no mystification—only mystery: the mystery of any act done in common and in which, if we stop to breathe, we feel strangers in a new intimacy, that of action.

We the readers of course look even at the barest actions of Dmitri with knowledges he himself does not have but which yet affect the quality of Dmitri's action. I do not mean the "might-have-been's" which he misses but the "becauses" which give predominance to his actions, like the "becauses" of sunset and sunrise or the unnoticed witness of the sharply falling glass which was anterior to the immediate black sky. We know, for example, that Alyosha (whose movements are rather like those of the rising and setting sun) has helped drive Dmitri to his father by encouraging Grushenka to run off to her "first and rightful lover," the Polish officer waiting for her at Mockroe, and we know that the murder occurs while Alyosha dreams his vision of Zossima during the reading of the Marriage at Cana, and must have been finished pretty much at the moment when the boy Alyosha comes to terms with himself as a man. Perhaps more important, the murder takes place in the midst of the time when Alyosha learns that tragic phrases alone make grief endurable. To Grushenka, Alyosha had become conscience and, as conscience, had provoked as well as encouraged her flight, for conscience in its extreme apparitions often provokes sin. When Dmitri cannot find her he rushes to his father's house: which has been prepared for him and any deed he might do.

Prepared by Ivan, Smerdyakov, and the old man himself. This we learn mainly through Ivan's two conversations—with his father and with Smerdyakov—at his father's house, where he had gone after the long session of the Grand Inquisitor with Alyosha, with an inexplicable depression in his mind. He was preparing for an unknown future, but it was not that which depressed him, nor his loathsome father and the hateful house, nor his failure to "express" himself with Alyosha. No; the sickness in him was caused by some external object or thing. It was Smerdyakov whom his soul loathed—Smerdyakov, who was a parody of them all—but who was most, at this point, the degraded form of Ivan's self; and it was with Smerdyakov that he conferred, enraged, outraged, and at one with his boundless and wounded vanity, his "conspiracy" without object, his revolting familiarity, until there came to be a "compact" between these two clever people. For mutual laceration outside the field of love, this conversation has no equal in literature. It also prepared the murder—both the actual murder and that in which we participate with Dmitri. The sick actions of the psyche in their malevolent play make a guilt that requires a deed by some other hand.

Smerdyakov lays it out. Dmitri comes every night looking for Grushenka or the three thousand roubles his father has ready for her, and he has wrung from Smerdyakov the signals: two gentle followed by three quick knocks means Grushenka is there. Three more knocks means something very important. To leave the field open for Dmitri Smerdyakov will fall down the cellar stairs into an epileptic fit on the day when the old servants Grigory and Marfa take their "medicine"—a potion largely alcohol which puts them into profound stupor. Ivan has only to go away—preferably to Tchermashnya on an errand for his father—to let it all happen. To this Ivan says he would rather go to Moscow and, when Smerdyakov argues that Tchermashnya is nearer, laughs in nervous frenzy. That night when he retired he suddenly went out to the staircase and listened for five minutes to the movements of his father below, "holding his breath while his heart throbbed" —and all his life afterwards thought it the basest act of his life, which is no doubt why he listened a second time and why after a sound and dreamless sleep he woke in extraordinary vigor and agreed to go to Tchermashnya for his father on the way to Moscow. When Smerdyakov tells him, "It's always worth while talking to a clever man," he sends his father word he is going direct to Moscow and says to himself, "I am a scoundrel." During the day Smerdyakov falls down the stairs and into the scream of epilepsy. He is put to bed unconscious. In the evening, Grigory and Marfa are completely laid up. Thus the old man is left alone with the voluptuous hopes which steeped his heart to wait for Grushenka's knocks. We can see him sitting there till Dmitri comes.

While these conversations had been going on, Dmitri had himself been to Tchermashnya on a fruitless errand to see if he could claim an equity in his father's woods there. To get there he had pawned his watch and borrowed three roubles, and on the following evening, three hours before the murder, he pawned his pistols for ten roubles more. It is hard to say which troubled him more—the rivalry with his father over Grushenka (he took no stock in the Polish officer) or the three thousand roubles he needed to repay what he had embezzled from Katerina the moment she had encouraged him to do so. The two may perhaps have been unified in the fifteen hundred roubles he had *not* spent of the three thousand, which he kept as a kind of bad amulet under his shirt against his breast. At any rate virtue and shame, honor and lust, love and murder, all seem to come together—as for simultaneous interconversion—in that amulet of fifteen brightly colored hundred rouble notes, which even we the readers do not yet know exists, but which Dmitri knew as a sultry burn upon his honor. (One is reminded of the fire of roubles in *The Idiot,* set by that admirable female counterpart of Dmitri, Nastasya.) They remind him that however he may thirst for virtue he can have none until he returns the full sum. In his despair he tries to borrow from Samsonov, Grushenka's protector, who only sends him on the false errand to the drunken peasant at Tchermashnya. Then, just as he has resolved he must murder and rob, he tries Mme. Hohlakov, the woman of little faith, who gives him an idea worth millions and a tiny ikon on a silver cord.

Meantime he has taken Grushenka—the thought of whom was like a sharp knife—to Samsonov's where she promises to wait for him and his raging jealousy. But she has deceived him and is gone. At Grushenka's house, the maid Fenya denies knowing where she has gone. As he rushes off—everything is a rushing on this day for him—Dmitri picks up a six-inch brass pestle and runs with it to his father's house. There he shinnies up the fence and spies on his father, all dogged out, through the window. Spying like this may be an intimacy like a caress or like a rape. When answering Dmitri's knocks the old man opens the window, peers out into the dark, and wheedles the Grushenka who is not there, Dmitri is seized with full personal loathing, and pulls the pestle from his pocket. It is then that we get the gap, in our knowledge and on the page, into which our action pours.

And out of that gap, so to speak, further action pours upon Dmitri; his fate pours; and the stigmata show to everyone—old Grigory with his head bashed in by the pestle, the bloody handkerchief, the sudden wealth of hundred rouble notes, the feast sent on ahead to Grushenka at Mockroe: which to everyone else showed Dmitri guilty of murder, and to himself showed another, more engorging guilt, the guilt of his personal life. To see how deep all this action was, consider how nobody during its course could have given Dmitri any practicable advice. For himself he had taken the resolve to step aside. He will in his new drunkenness of spirit give a party for Grushenka and her Polish officer—her first and rightful lover—and then put a bullet in his brain. (This is why as soon as he discovers where Grushenka is, he redeems his pawned pistols from his amulet of roubles: one virtue overcomes another.) He has his own definitions for stepping aside: to make way for a dear creature and one I hate; and on a piece of paper, which he unfolds and shows to Perhotin as he prepares to go to the feast at Mockroe, he has written, "in a large, distinct hand": "I punish myself for my whole life, my whole life I punish!" There was, as he said, no order in him, no higher order. He was rather all action, the action of unmitigated and unmediated love. "I love life. I've loved life too much, shamefully much . . . I bless the creation. I'm ready to bless God and His creation directly, but . . . I must kill one noxious insect for fear it should crawl and spoil life for others." He has succeeded where his brothers have failed, that is to say, in the direct action of heart and body where things are their own meaning, that meaning we are wonderfully skillful in until we question or tarry when the cost overwhelms us. Until then our actions are a kind of thought whose current we follow. That is why, I think, Dmitri grasps us so warmly by the hand and pulls us after him into his guilt. There are heroic moments in us when actions such as his flood our dearest thoughts.

THE BROTHERS KARAMAZOV:

II. The Grand Inquisitor and the Wine of Gladness

Alyosha is indeed our future hero, as Dostoevsky calls him, but he is not our hero now, in the book Dostoevsky published. I do not know what the historians and biographers think or whether there is any consensus among them, but there is certainly a stupendous possibility that Dostoevsky meant to compose a trilogy about the three brothers, with the existing volume celebrating Dmitri or the Pride of Flesh, the second volume celebrating Ivan or the Pride of Intellect, and the final volume celebrating Alyosha or the Pride of Humility—each with his appropriate exacerbations and creative hysterias—and each, perhaps, compelled to a private Siberia as the last home we know for him, as it is with Dmitri at the end of the account we have. It is tempting to meditate, to see ahead, what might happen along the way with the remaining brothers as each in turn became the emphasis of the random hope and psychogenic suffering which here fastens on Dmitri.

In one of his *Soliloquies in England,* Santayana calls this mixture of hope and suffering the folly of the cross as compared to the wisdom of the cross, and it is the folly Dostoevsky's creatures mainly suffer from, with a chance for those like Alyosha to gain the wisdom. Alyosha remembers his mother, frenzied but beautiful, sobbing and crying in high hysteria, lifting his two-year-old self before the image of the Mother of God. Alyosha is like this, too, without the hysteria, with a wild modesty, accepting *and* grieving, an early lover of life, "more a realist than any one." Alyosha is like his mother, like his whole family, without caprice and with only the stirrings of hysteria. His actions spring neither from random hope nor anguished caprice but from deep momentum and clear possibility. His actions spring from love. It is so given.

Alyosha is indeed "our future hero," but it is perhaps as well that he remains always in the future, for he is created ahead of himself as well as ahead of the world for which he has an erotic love. It is hard to see Alyosha, moving from what we know of him, in the life of the great sinner. Theoretically in the mind, yes: for in the discursive intellect all things are possible, since they do not require creation; but in the theoretic form of life we call the novel, where everything must be created, no. What we might have got, had Dostoevsky lived and gone on with the life of Alyosha, could at best have been dramatized beyond the point reached in the existing book. The unity of apperception required for that dramatization does not seem to belong to the genius of the arts but to that of religion. Yet we ought not to say what can or cannot be done. Dostoevsky is so far the only writer of the first class who has attempted to dramatize the religious experience in this world and within the frame of the human psyche. Who knows what terrible rebellion against his own power, peace, and happiness might not rightly be in store for Alyosha? Surely there is an appropriate line of caprice through which the saint can break out of the shell of his sanctity, when it is oppressive, into a new tempest of behavior which should rage like reason itself. We can see the possibility, though not the enactment, when we remember how in *The Idiot* Myshkin was swept off in a rage of goodness. The evil good does is the tragedy of the saint.

Some such speculation as this, at any rate, permits us a way of looking at both Ivan and Alyosha as they come together in the tavern: we see them as if they were going on forever talking and living. All Ivan says, both in conversation and in his prose poem about the Grand Inquisitor, presents the conditions of his life—those which he accepts, those which he regrets, and those which he insists on—and makes a preface for what must come to him. All Alyosha's response to Ivan in the tavern and his further response, alone, hours of anguish afterwards, to the Grand Inquisitor, likewise make a preface for his further life. Each seems to look at the other as a saint: Ivan is the saint of the active mind, Alyosha of the steadfast spirit; at least such would be their rôles could they but play them. As it is, they are two young men who in their green youth must settle the eternal questions of God and society. Both have the "unseemly thirst for life" which is in their Karamazov blood, and both love life, as Ivan says, "with one's inside, with one's stomach. One loves the first strength of one's youth." Both love life more than the meaning of it. The difference between the two young men is that Alyosha in his monastic dress accepts both God and his world whereas Ivan accepts God but cannot accept his world. Ivan's words are crucial and point to what excruciates him. Naturally, the words are repeated many times and in many forms and are repeated by Alyosha in a form of his own.

It is what man does to his neighbor that compels Ivan to reject the world. "For anyone to love a man," says Ivan, "he must be hidden, for as soon as he shows his face, love is gone"—which may be put beside another of Ivan's notions: that man created or conceived of God because he loved life, but man also invented the devil because he misused life. Most of the chapter called "Rebellion" exhibits anecdotes of man's cruel misuse of life: the hunting of children with dogs, the beating of children to the point of orgasm, the lashing of a horse on "his meek eyes." All Ivan knows is that there is suffering and none are guilty, but also that one has not the right to forgive the tortures others suffer, only one's own. He does not want, he said, harmony or forgiveness or vengeance. "I would rather remain with my unavenged suffering and unsatisfied indignation *even if I were wrong.*" And it is in justification of that sentiment of rebellion from which he tries to escape (since one cannot live in rebellion) that he tells Alyosha his prose poem which he had made up about a year ago but which he remembered. To "tell" a poem is to reach way inside.

It is on this preface—the anecdotes of cruelty to horses and children—that half the strength of Ivan's fable rests; the other half is the series of lacerations through which Alyosha the listener has just passed. After the anecdotes and the lacerations—and *because* of them—we must have the abstractions: the dread account of what was not anywhere but nevertheless is immanently or virtually present everywhere. One way of expressing the central notion is to say that man, having in his necessity either conceived of God or endured and interpreted his revelation, cannot tolerate God's further interference, unless it be on behalf of man's own developing interest or changing circumstance. (Remember that Ivan—or Dostoevsky—was writing at the time of the Syllabus of Errors and when the Russian Church was an Erastian creature of the state.) Could we, today, tolerate the idea of any *second* conversion on a major scale? Could we bear, for instance, could we bear without horror even the shadow of the idea of a psychoanalyst a *second time* convulsing his patient's soul? In such matters once is the end of enough, and thinking of that, could we bear it once? The first time seems suddenly not necessary to have occurred. This sentiment leads to another way of putting the central notion of Ivan's poem. When man once possesses his religion (instead of being possessed by it, or caught in it), that is, when he has transformed his religion into a human institution, he will both persecute those who are still possessed by it and will find evil in the renewal of the original experience of it even in himself. He does not wish again to glimpse the early chaos of the heart. This situation arises when the exercise of power comes to seem the only bearable exercise of love, when indeed the assertion of omnipotence seems the only form of omnibenevolence. Power may indeed be said to love its object, as in private life we have all observed the tyranny of private love—whether of the parent, the lover, the spouse, or the friend. Think of the fanatic judgments of love which are called jealousy. But Ivan's poem speaks of the whole society; and of what, there, could those who hold power be more justly jealous than the second coming of Christ? Only Christ knows that the gift must be given again; only man sets a narrow limit of human reason on God and thinks the gift was given once and for all. It is our great arrogance to believe that any revelation is complete; but it is our worst humility to think that revelation is always at hand; in both cases we regard it as our possession.

Perhaps, since memory is weak, Ivan's poem had better be briefly rehearsed. Some time in the sixteenth century, Christ appears in Seville, where the people recognize Him and are drawn to Him, by Himself and by the miracles He performs. When the cardinal sees this, he darkens, and has his guards seize and imprison Christ, because He "hinders" and is a danger to the peace and safety of society. He tells Christ that he will burn Him tomorrow and that the people who kissed His feet today will heap embers tomorrow. The rest of the poem is the old Inquisitor's rejection of Christ for refusing the three temptations in the wilderness as they are presented in Matthew but which the cardinal represents as the three necessary powers capable of conquering rebellion and making happiness, and which he calls miracle, mystery, and authority. Christ chose rather what was beyond the power of man, and the church has been compelled to correct His work. It is like Ivan's account of man's cruelty to the children but at the universal level. Lastly, the Inquisitor accuses Christ of the pride of love and freedom in rejecting the temptations; for had He accepted them, man would have had all he "seeks on earth—that is, some one to worship, some one to keep his conscience, and some means of uniting all in one unanimous and harmonious antheap, for the craving for universal unity is the third and last anguish of men." Yet when for only answer Christ kisses the old man "on his bloodless aged lips," the old man released Him, telling Him to go "and come no more. . . . Come not at all, never, never!" So Alyosha kisses Ivan, for Ivan is, after all, the individual choosing to wrestle with God. Looking after him as they parted, Alyosha noted that Ivan swayed as he walked and that his right shoulder looked lower than his left, and then he himself ran off to Pater

Seraphicus—as Ivan called the Elder Zossima—to be saved. It is a tale, is it not, of saint and countersaint.

Ivan was right to set his fable at the time of the counterreformation which was the time of war between the two arrogances of church and state. The odor of bloody innocence is everywhere about; and he was right to choose Spain for his scene and the Grand Inquisitor as his instrument. But he was even more precisely right to retire to that early nonhistoric time in the gospel of Matthew for the seed-form of the temptations in the wilderness: the time when God interfered directly with human justice without regard to human institutions yet somehow with the consent of the institutions; that time which never was but always must be when equity was always superior to law.

Ivan knows—his anecdotes of the children tell him—that the power which is the creator and guard of love has as deep a lodgment in the heart that abides in society, as the lodgment that love which is the creator of power has in the heart that is free of society. Ivan is between the Grand Inquisitor and the Prisoner Christ. He is in society and free of it. Were it not for the Ivan in us, we could not accept a society which is given like a theme and taken for granted as intolerable to all our desires; we could not accept and deal with and run such a society. As Ivan sees it, the people will reject the temptation of the Second Coming until it is accompanied by the end of the world. Though it is what they might desire, they are not strong enough to accept it at the loss of miracle, mystery, and authority—bread, worship, absolute authority—for with that loss the world *would* become immitigably intolerable. If Ivan makes this the judgment of his poem, it is not so much out of his incurable love of life and disbelief in God's world as out of the baseness of the Karamazovs, their strength to endure. This is what Alyosha sees in Ivan's swaying walk and stooped right shoulder—sees and fears.

Can we not say that this is the actual pitch of things in their commotion—or, rather, that this is the actual state of the world, seen truncated and seen partially—when it is raised to the Dostoevsky pitch. Never mind Rome, Caesar-papism, and the Freemasons which were Dostoevsky's nineteenth-century bugbears: consider our own. Consider the mechanism which *makes* law and the vitalism which insists it is superior to law; consider the reign of law and the disorders of enlightenment. In literature, consider the artist who makes himself the hero; in politics, the State or Policy; in morals, Freud or instinct; in tempo, anxiety; in criticism, the neurosis. Consider any or all man's current claims to omnicompetence, but especially the kinds that go with the rebellious weakness in the individual. Is it not in terms of these that Ivan the rebel conceives in the Grand Inquisitor an answer he cannot himself accept? It is these, in the magnificent phrase Henry James once made for Flaubert, that made of Ivan a man deeply corrupted but uncorrupting. No wonder his body swayed when he walked.

Dostoevsky made of Ivan's poem a symbol; a real symbol in the drama of a parricide—his right shoulder is lower than the other because his father is about to be murdered by one of his brothers. But real symbols are inexhaustible and outlast the drama which produced them though they can never be detached from it; and we have the right to use this symbol like another (as we use Hamlet) in terms not alone of what Dostoevsky brought and found in it but also what we bring and find. It is the life of literature that we can do this. As the symbol got ahead of Dostoevsky in the process of making it, so it is likely to get ahead of us, too. Its very excess is its truth. Among the things it makes lawful is the question whether or not the position of Zossima—of any deliverer—is not also in excess. Does not that position come from turning an omnicompetence of love into power just as the Grand Inquisitor—who had eaten *his* roots in the desert—turns his omnicompetent power into love?

If this is not so, what are all those Brothers Karamazov doing here? Do they not show that the Elder and the Inquisitor each tell a noble lie, and do not the brothers tell lies too, so that we may live? Does the truth rest in reversibility? In the baseness of the Karamazov strength? Or in the collapsing cellar of the bastard Smerdyakov's baseness? If the world is not ready for atheism, it is not ready for total faith either. We only know that we endure but do not know what it is in us that endures.

Dostoevsky found Ivan's poem coming out of his mouth not from the convictions but from the behavior of his mind, from that astonishing behavior of word and thought and image which assault and assoil our convictions, and can do so the more irresistibly because they are a secret cause of our convictions. All is lawful in the circle of Circe and Medusa, of Lilith and the White Goddess. I believe in God—if you like—and because of that belief cannot accept the created world. Nobody is guilty, all are guilty. Nobody is guilty except the leader, which is the price he pays for miracle, mystery, and authority. But if you do not follow the leader you will become especially guilty, and the more so the guiltier the leader is whom you will not follow. If these things are contradictory, it is because behavior, not conviction, says and experiences them at the same time. It is the predicament of the soul conscious of these things together in private, social, and religious life—and most, as in this novel, the private—that leads to the choice of the nearest absolutism, then, that failing, the choice of the reverse absolutism, which was also all along equally the nearest. There was for Dostoevsky that absolutism of power which arrogates to itself the intention of love but which in no way absorbs what is loved *except* in the guise of power. This he hated because he felt it, and what he desired was the love that absorbs its object so completely that love becomes absolute power. The behavior of his mind encompassed both, and the one lurked in the other. Thus we have two poems, Ivan's and Alyosha's, the one preparing for, the other responding to the same desperation.

That the desperation, the predicament, in which Dostoevsky wrote, is in the conditions of life only because warranted by prior beliefs need not at present concern us, but we should keep it in mind because we must turn to it in any judgment of what Dostoevsky is. Prior beliefs often constitute our tragic faults.

Is there not a little illumination of Dostoevsky's own predicament and desperation if we consider how we should have to alter Dante's *En la sua voluntade é nostra pace,* which comes at the consummation of his vision of human behavior, to make it read well in Ivan's poem, which comes dead center in Dostoevsky's vision. It is unlawful to entertain such a conviction, but in this book, as Ivan says, and Dante could not have said, nothing is unlawful. We speak over Ivan's right and drooping shoulder. What shall we say?—In the Inquisitor's will—in the assent to his power—is our destruction. That is a kind of peace, a forced peace, only lasting as long as the force—the kind of peace which only a statesman or a senator would accept. To the rest of us, it only becomes acceptable with a further transposition: In the Inquisitor's will is our obligation: we owe it to him for his guilt, for our bread, for our determinedness and common fate, for the cord of unity that binds us. Perhaps here we have it, what the Inquisitor was up to all along, as if he were an anthropologist not a cardinal. This is a peace—this peace of obligation—appropriate to what we like to think is far behind us but is only deep within us. It is the peace of the Karamazovs not of Christian theology. It is so deep within us as to be inexhaustible, the peace of primitive man—that utterly sincere fellow, old true penny in the cellar, who howls our most precious convictions down—that first member of the underground fellowship of the Holy Ghost. Dante and Shakespeare knew most about him; Dostoevsky and Joyce come next. *Nostra pace* indeed!

Dostoevsky—or Ivan's poem—differs from these others in taking this fellow as extreme, as somehow treasonable—as if our origins could confound our future—as if they made it impossible to live in an intolerable world. Although he gives Ivan's poem full sway while it lasts, he took it as an extreme example of the ignoble lie, and at once opposed to it an extreme example of the noble lie: that lie which he never quite found out how to tell, so extreme it was—and so like, in its heartbeat, in its *opposed* heartbeat—to the lie of the Grand Inquisitor. I mean, of course, Book VI of the novel, called "The Russian Monk," of which the beginning and end constitute Zossima's exhortations to Alyosha to find, as a monk in the world, happiness in misfortune, to bless life and make others bless it, to see hell as the suffering of being unable to love, and to know that "Love can never be an offence to

Christ"; and of which the greater part is a short life of Zossima as a great sinner, followed by a series of short homilies on the Russian monk: how he redeems the time; how he is on the side of the people, and especially on the side of the peasant, for the peasant has God in his heart; how equality is only in the spiritual dignity of man; how attempts at justice without faith in Christ bring bloodshed; how prayer is an education and how by love you perceive the divine mystery in things; how the Eternal Judge asks of you what you can comprehend, not what you cannot; and lastly, how you cannot be a judge of anyone unless you realize the guilt of that man in yourself. After his last exhortation—"Love can never be an offence to Christ"—the Elder Zossima dies joyfully.

As you see, the two poems beat in each other's hearts—systole and diastole, if you like. Pride and Humility, Power and Love, and the temptations to arrogance in each, the dread temptations to assert omnicompetence and (and therefore to the fatal assertion of omnipotence)—all these are very close to each other. The difference is in nobility. Honesty about human life lies between, clutching both.

If they were not so close, the single nature of Dostoevsky could not have conceived both poems, nor could we as readers understand them, however they invaded us. We could not understand *both,* unless either we could compound them from a third point of view or we had access to the life that lies between, which it is certain we do have—access to all that knowledge we do not know that we know, the knowledge of what we are. It is that knowledge which Dostoevsky dramatizes in this novel of the gloomy death of old Karamazov at the hands of his sons: the brothers in baseness, in energy, in buoyant forward vitality, in love of life—which is our baseness, energy, vitality, love of life, which makes them our brothers. That is what they are there for; and that is what novels are for, to show them there, and that showing is what we here examine.

Let us look at the Elder Zossima. He is the vision of Alyosha, the vision of that young man who has just been through so many lacerations, the last the worst—Ivan's poem. How little would Zossima mean if he were not caught up, for us, in the momentum of the murder—if he were not, so to speak, packed to bursting in the interstices of the Karamazovs' doings;—if he were not given *among* their affairs so that he takes on (by attraction, by repulsion, by membership) their pitch or level of operation? How little he would mean, too, if he were not a tale, and a familiar tale of his own, and did not have an even more familiar tale behind him, that of his brother Markel—a saint dead at seventeen in that paradise which is the glory of creation seen—and with the most familiar tale of all behind that, the Gospels and the Epistles of Paul. Lastly, how insufferably little he would mean if he did not stink in death. We see it is not the man Zossima but his institution (his function) which succumbs to the temptation of love to become power. It is the triple institution of the Russian peasant, the Russian monk, and of revelation by conversion—by turning—which is to say the institution of second birth.

Thus we learn that Zossima has for long silently blessed Alyosha's face because it is a renewal of his brother Markel's face, whose death at seventeen had been the early seed-form of his own conversion. Alyosha is to go on where Zossima began. This is the dream of handing down or on: as if by handing on our rôles we could also hand on ourselves, and the privations of ourselves. Thus, too, Zossima requires of Alyosha that he seek out Dmitri (to turn him *from,* not *to,* what might be in store for him) as he himself had been turned, finally, by his brother Markel, not from the deed of murder, but after the deed, from the deed to himself, from denial to faith. And so on. In our ends are our beginnings. Except a corn of wheat fall into the ground and die it abideth alone; but if it die it bringeth forth much fruit. Well . . . are we not prepared to conceive this as applying to Dmitri, and as an honorable thing as well as a fatal thing? Has not Dmitri already stamped on his father's face?—Is it not right—as right as rain—that Zossima should see in Alyosha and Dmitri the drama of his own life reenacted? That Alyosha must go through with it, must endure it: an example of how harsh and dreadful a thing is love in action? It is also the temptation of love to power: to which Dostoevsky adverts only by saying that Zossima's death left Alyosha with too much faith—more than he had the experience to cope with. It seems implicit that Zossima charges Alyosha that he must endure more—more suffering, sin, guilt—than he himself had been able to; as much as Markel would have been able to endure had he lived. That was the story Dostoevsky did not live to write for Alyosha: the story of a mystery anticipated. Perhaps the story Zossima tells of the mysterious visitor can take the place of the unwritten story of Alyosha. It can be done in little—in anecdote or parable, which represent sincerity and insight short of mastery —when it cannot be done in great. The man had murdered and made another a scapegoat. Zossima imposed on him the dreadful harshness of love in two texts, the one from *John* about the grain of wheat and the other from *Hebrews:* "It is a fearful thing to fall into the hands of the living God." But the man's true confession was not believed and he dies suffering. We will let Alyosha meditate that.

Again—to emphasize the novel and the novelistic: this bursting of the novel if you don't like it, this stretching if you do—consider how the burden of Zossima's poem about man's fate, like Ivan's poem, rests upon the people, the peasants—those who lack bread and crave authority and unity. Dostoevsky—as novelist, as dramatist, as artist—even as critic who is also artist—cannot help showing it so; for in these rôles he is tied to the actual and cannot escape it so long as he is honest. Only when he is polemicist or politician or speechmaker can he choose and exploit his own bias and come out pan-Slav, Czarist, and theocrat. Here, in the novel, he has to do with the experience of the bias, the *materials* of his decision, and so far as his mastery of his art permits him, he is compelled to show the actual nature of the experience. Of course, art comes short of such purity, but not so short as the man of action thinks or the man of ideals feels. Art comes short: it does not tell you what to do but what you have to do *with.* Art in the long run is as good a measure of honesty as we have; moving in the actual, it plays on truth.

Consider once again the dialectic of parallels which Dostoevsky's novel affords us. Both the Elder and his monks and the Inquisitor and his church—both regard the lot of man as miserable, both put his redemption in an impossible future (as who should say, Yes, you will be well off then, but it will not be *you* who will be well off!), both see the path to redemption through a tyranny which is an affront to his nature: the one through the tyranny of total irresponsibility, the other through the tyranny of total guilt. (Oh yes, in the meantime it will be the inescapable *you,* all right!) To say that no man is guilty and all things are lawful is not much different from saying that all men are guilty of every man and all things are law. In either case the individual disappears—whether into absolute regulation or absolute absorption. It is no better to say that obedience is an act of love than to say that true freedom is an act of obedience. To believe either is an assault on one's nature—if the belief is carried beyond the providential and the provisional, where both, as they say, are in the nature of things. It is curious that Zossima should make his own claim to freedom by the purgation of desire and by trust in the misery and suffering of the peasant in terms so close to those of the Inquisitor's claim. Both believe man incapable of sustaining his own notions of freedom. For *both,* miracle, mystery, and authority are the primary needs of man. One would impose them by human reason, the other in terms of the peasant's miserable suffering. That the reasonable man and the peasant tend to rebel is nothing. Zossima believes that man's own notion of freedom produces "in the rich, isolation and spiritual suicide, and in the poor, envy and murder," which is much the same consequence the Inquisitor saw in the example of Christ. What else is black reaction?

Until the impulse is exhausted, in each sweep every pendulum swings nearly the same distance either side of its plumbline, whether you think of a clock and the escapement of seconds or of a novel and the clash of insights. Equilibrium stops time or obliterates insight, unless you wind the clock or take another look. After the Grand Inquisitor and the death of Zossima, Dostoevsky escaped the equilibrium of death by creating, not as a man but as an author, a second look. When, faced with such an equilibrium (essentially, the sudden weightlessness of our contrary beliefs), we are not driven to create, we tend to conceive necessity as the relapse into barbarism: as our history since 1914 in almost every public mode gives us a self-perpetuating series of examples: as if in this world we needed, not fresh blood, but fresh bloodshed. But Dostoevsky *was* driven to create. At the end of the portrait of Zossima, we find him seeing Zossima as almost repudiating the temptation of love to assume power. In effect he takes himself out of all institutions whatever. His secret heart is superior to the Church precisely because of the depth at which he accepts God and life. He stinks in death.

That stink, that "breath of corruption," is what Alyosha draws into his nostrils throughout the four chapters of the short book of this novel which bears his name, and it is that stink that sets the pendulum sweeping again. Before coming sharp on the stink itself, it is worth observing again that this little "Book of Alyosha" was possible because of the large plan of the "future hero." The book and the stink in it make room and incentive for what was to come; and I think the poetic or novelistic conception is a greater source of its strength than any "merely" religious consideration, and further it is the novelistic force which gives poetic justice to the religious. I am glad that I do not know any logic suitable to argue the matter, but remember comfortably how for a long time in his life Dante thought poetry set fictions to music, which remained true no matter how much else at a later time he also thought. Poetry and religion rise through us from a deeper and earlier source than any theology or any church—any prosody or any rule of genre. They do not burst their bonds of being but the bonds other people—those whom we are taught to call our masters—set upon them. At any rate, let us think of the "Book of Alyosha" as set to the music of the novel we do not have as well as to that of the novel we do have. It would have been one of those images of experience to which deep return can be made—both for renewal of impulse and for refreshment of understanding. Thinking of this we know better why, in these chapters, everybody—not Alyosha alone—is on the edge of new life or a fresh start. The patterns are about to cross, the patterns of the fictions we tell which make life intolerable and the patterns of the fictions we tell in which we find life tolerable. Alyosha is at the critical moment of his early experience when the kind of fictions he will make will be determined. It is good to think of a man's psyche as the music to which he sets himself, whether he—or we—know his fictions or not. Alyosha draws his first breath of corruption: the deep injustice to his Elder in death; he rebels against not God but His creation—and holds out impossible help (here called an onion —the whole brittle lily of the plant, not the bulb of tears and flavor) to Grushenka only to find that he has impossibly helped himself; and over the stench of his Elder's body he hears the music of the miracle of the water turned to the wine of the new gladness. These are the conditions of the marriage at Cana: how the best wine may by miracle come last.

But this immediate image of Alyosha in inebriation is also in proportional relation—in analogy—to the brothers and all their affairs, and the matters most deeply in analogy are the murder—what happens in the blank white space on the page in the chapter of Mitya's Book called "In the Dark"—and that other clash of spirit which lies between Alyosha's image of Zossima and Ivan's poem of the Grand Inquisitor. Alyosha somehow includes in himself murder and spirit; that is, in his response reducing everything to a "new" strain of the Kamarazov breed—to a new strain of the all-inclusive Karamazov baseness. It is, so to speak, Alyosha's entry into his first full engagement in the murderous warfare of the spirit—which begins with the recognition of diverse and disconcerted expectations and reaches crisis in the unseemliness with which the self confronts the other self. It is when the looking-glass looks at you, when the mirror holds you up to nature: when the expectation of the one self breaches the expectation of the other, and there is no glass left between the two. Then neither belief nor unbelief is possible; or at most, the one is seen as the result of the agony of the other. It is then, in such a state, as Dostoevsky says, that both believers and unbelievers rejoice at the downfall of the righteous. In the rejoicing is the vitality. This is the fable of the death of Zossima, as it brought Alyosha through one stage of rejoicing to the other, each in violent trespass on the other.

Forget the fable if you like and say, as the novel does, that everything is in the stinking body of Zossima, in the open coffin, with the black gauze over his face, and his gown slit and folded as a cross. He must have looked very small, with his death so big. It is a premature corruption, a stink rising in twelve hours instead of twenty-four, a stink that came too soon, in excess of humanity, precisely because so much, and so much false, expectation had been forced upon the death out of the places of secret motives. Father Païssy and Alyosha, no less than Rakitin and the monk from Obdorsk, had expectations too great. Thus fact closes in on fable again. Old Zossima was still an elder in his death; the corruption was in him when he died—was perhaps all there was left of him, as it must be for those who die at the right time; and as an elder, he took into himself the wills both of the believers and the unbelievers; he would not, even if he could, act on faith by miracle; but he would act—he could not prevent it—by his stink. Is his corruption not saying to both that the scandal of great humanity is its greater stink?—both to those for whom beauty is found in Sodom and in the dread spirit of destruction and to those others who have not yet learned *how* harsh and dreadful a thing is active love. If we understand this, we see why none even of the believing monks could reproach the delight of those whose secret motives shone in their malignant eyes, and we see why the stink of corruption was a crumpling shock to Alyosha. What was inside his intellect crumpled up and his intellect collapsed.

Father Ferapont's great uproar—his clanking irons—his casting out of the devils that were not there—is thus a necessary exorcism. For some, the devils were there; and perhaps most for Alyosha, who had believed too much in the *exampl*e of Zossima, too little in his own task, who had in short not earned more than a fragment of the faith he thought possessed him in entirety. He had yet to learn the harshness of active love confronted with the beauty of Sodom; he had yet to learn to accept the degradation of God's creation, to accept the injustice and imperfection and the dread spirit of destruction; he had yet to put down the rebellion within himself. He has to pass through the stage of Ivan; to rebel against God's world; and with the help or prompting of Rakitin, with his sausage and vodka, and by the active agency of Grushenka on his knee with her tragic need, so he does pass through it. It is no more than sketched in, but it is a dramatic sketch, with physical presence and action and voice. It could be filled out; it is credible as possibility that he becomes Grushenka's conscience and as it were the aggravation of Rakitin's need of conscience. But who knows at what level of his being he makes his passage?—or, rather, who knows at how many levels of being and through how many modes of conduct and mind he makes his passage? It is at this point that we remember Mme. Hohlakov's letter to Rakitin calling the stink of Zossima's body a kind of conduct—"such conduct," she writes; she understood better than she knew and everything that Rakitin denied in his spite; she understood, but Alyosha breathed the corruption into his soul.

Rakitin had found Alyosha face downward on the ground at dusk between the two agonies of belief and unbelief: in Shakespeare's endless jar of right and wrong in which justice resides. We leave him, at the end of his book, assenting to, or transcending, what lies under the endless jar, kissing and blessing and loving the earth of it, and rising, with that idea sovereign in his mind, changed from a weak boy to a resolute champion. The earth, God's world, the Karamazov baseness had gained new meaning and in doing so had transposed the idea of universal guilt to universal forgiveness. This transposition is here perhaps putative, an initial aspiration, a prefiguring in vision of things to come, and it seems to have had its inception in the image of Grushenka and her tragic phrase about taking the knife with her to Mockroe. Listening to Father Païssy read the gospel of the wedding at Cana, he reminds himself of that phrase. "Tragic phrases should be forgiven, they must be. Tragic phrases comfort the heart. . . . Without them, sorrow would be too heavy for men to bear." In a sense, the action of this whole novel is such a tragic phrase; and in another sense, this moment of conversion in Alyosha's life is such a phrase present *and* transcended.

It is worth while noticing—if this is true—how Dostoevsky handles the moment of conversion. There is the reading of the Gospel of the miracle of water into wine at the marriage feast in Cana of Galilee, there is the apparition of Zossima with the wine of new gladness as justice, there is Grushenka and her onion, her crisis of decision, and there is Alyosha Karamazov asleep on his knees, praying in his creative sleep, with Father Païssy reading over the dead and stinking body of Zossima. When that action is over, Alyosha goes outside under the stars among the gorgeous autumn flowers and, weeping in ecstasy—beside himself and himself beside himself—kisses the earth under the stars: "in contact with other worlds." I suggest that this is something like an instinctive resurrection of the medieval four-fold structure for the creation or interpretation of meaning. Here the sense would be Alyosha himself and the scene; the morals would be Grushenka; the allegory, Zossima; and the anagoge, the Gospel of Cana—which is truly miraculous only if understood with the other three. Other arrangements are possible, as is also the application of the Inquisitor's "Miracle, Mystery, and Authority." I only suggest—I do not assert—and I suggest because it brings to mind how it is we may believe—if we do believe—in the reality of Alyosha's conversion: we believe because it happens in so many ways at once; and in ways which, taken together, imply the active presence of other ways for which we do not have names but of which we possess skills and the remnants of skills—skills available to a posture of the mind or a rôle of the spirit—like that of Alyosha slumbering on his knees. This is Alyosha's poem.

THE BROTHERS KARAMAZOV:

III. The Peasants Stand Firm and the Tragedy of the Saint

With the arrest and examination of Dmitri for the murder of his father, Dostoevsky changes the phase of his story from something predominantly outside society and erupting into society, to something within society, acted upon by society, and reacting to society. At the center is Dmitri passing through ordeal after ordeal. In each ordeal he attempts to contribute himself *to* society, and in each he is rejected. Society will have none of what he is, in any sense that he can give himself. As Alyosha, at the death of his Elder, wanted justice, and got only the image of justice in his dream of the miracle at Cana, so here, Dmitri wanted justice at the hands of his inquisitors but received from them only the deformity of law; as if in the higher order which he knew he lacked, society could only express in the individual the injustice wreaked by institutions. It does him no good that he wishes to be punished for *his* guilt, *his* baseness, *his* disgrace; and he is in furious rebellion—burning indignation, but not like Swift—against the notion of general guilt or the worse notion of averaged guilt. It is that fury, that burning, which compel his confessions to be so insistently individual. This is why, when the preliminary examination is over, the officials cannot shake his hand, and this why the young Kalganov does shake his hand, believing him almost certainly guilty, and sits weeping when Dmitri is taken away, with no desire to live, asking, Is it worth it? For the officials, Dmitri has not made himself one of them. For the youth Kalganov, he has made it plain that there is a point in the foulest crime where there is no guilt in the criminal, the point where crime is the natural responsive act against the evil of God's creation. In the officials and in the youth there is an irretrievable kind of innocence, which keeps them from direct life. For Dmitri himself, as for Alyosha, there is the dream in which life is green again. Dmitri's dream of the peasants and the weeping babe is a lower version—perhaps a more fundamental version—of Alyosha's dream of his Elder. It will perhaps turn out to be about as far as he can go: the dream of the babe and the embrace of Grushenka. Dmitri is one of those for whom rebirth is not permanent, but only a deeper form of a New Year's resolution; and it would be only to contemn the gods to expect it to last or be complete. It is the straw to catch at, an onion for the moment. It is what men are like. His own words "I have had a good dream, gentlemen," are as much as can be said for it, and it is a great deal, for such dreams happen again. The dreams of Alyosha and the Elder, and of Ivan, are fierce theoretic creations of the ideal which the flesh abuses and which abuse the flesh. In the abuse is the very *plot* of man's created agony.

If Dmitri's ordeals and his dream have a further meaning, it may be that the dream suggests how he may come on himself and rid himself of the institutionalized society which the officials represent. To Dostoevsky, this is no society at all—these forms for judgment and toleration and indifference. True society, for him, is Christian society, full of compassion and intolerance and the sense of identification; based on the lives of those who know, and who are themselves, insult, injury, and humiliation: those who sin like children: elders and peasants and children themselves.

It should be observed that there is a great deal of comedy in the ordeals and examination of Dmitri. This is partly Dostoevsky's way of criticizing the operation of society. More important, it is his recognition that there is always comedy when an individual is confronted without perspective by institutions which wish to take him over; but it is a comedy which constantly edges into the unseemly, at least in Dostoevsky: into the unseemly, the shabby, the scream of degradation. Man is funniest seen against the immediate backdrop of his institutions, always most unseemly when he acts as if he were himself his institutions. If we think of Dmitri naked with his feet sticking out under his quilt, we see it is the three officials, not Dmitri, who have become unseemly. It is they who soil, sully, and rummage in Dmitri's heart. But it is the comedy and unseemliness of real forces: forces to which, for example, Dmitri speaks the truth, because of which he wishes to die honest, with which he must deal: forces which are in the conditions of life. What Dmitri stands for here is the plea that conditions are not ends, nor beginnings, nor meanings. A man does not need positive aspirations or ideals to be revolted at the conditions in which he finds himself; he will respond by tragic gestures and comfort himself by crying out in the most revolting conditions of all. Perhaps the young Kalganov in his own tears sees Dmitri, carried away in his cart, as such a tragic gesture both for Dmitri and for the life he himself has not yet lived. It is at such points that the comic passes through the tragic into the lyric.

It is as if Dostoevsky had some notion of enforcing such a pattern when he places at the beginning of Part IV and between the book of "The Preliminary Investigation" and the book of "Ivan," the comic, tragic, and lyric book of "The Boys," which has very little directly to do with the story of the murder and indeed provides Alyosha (and Dostoevsky) the opportunity to escape from that murder in the close of the novel. The story of the boys is of course woven into the story of the murder, and once we have read it we are tempted to see deeper parallels than the intention of the author could have commanded merely because it was going on at the same time—namely, the two autumn months between the murder and the trial. If we see different things at the same time it gives us a different vision, while if we see only one thing at a time we sometines see nothing. In the novel the episode of the boys is what is happening to Alyosha at the same time; it is Alyosha among the nestlings: the other half of his entry into the world at his Elder's command. With the affair and the arrangements and the amenities of the murder as one form of initiation, he must combine the affair of Kolya Krassotkin the mastermind of possibility at thirteen, and Ilusha Snegiryov, master of nothing but his furious anger—that furious indignation which, in the early teens and even before, is our earliest and first lesson as to what life might and cannot be if only there were no need for arrangements and no deceit in amenities beyond the need and the deceit of transforming the shaggy dog Perezvon—the peal of bells—into the even shaggier dog Zhutchka, whose presence comforts death—a chime of bells to come. Alyosha is the young Scout Master or the Camp Counsellor or the social service worker among the underprivileged or the potentially delinquent boys: Kolya Krassotkin's gang; but he is so in the Russian or Dostoevsky style and to the comedy of Kolya and the tragedy of Ilusha supplies the lyric at the end.

It is good in itself, this narrative of the *enfant terrible* Kolya and his dog Perezvon, good like something from a more ferocious Dickens or a more "possessed" Cervantes; but let us think what it turns out to be doing here. It is an example of the straight look transforming itself into a deep mimesis. It is the naïve rather than the innocent view of the whole affair of the Karamazovs: baseness, vitality, recklessness, pride, humiliation, humility and all. The naïve is the direct and unimpeded, the innocent is the ignorant and untainted. It ends not with a dream but with Kolya's declaration of love for Alyosha: a declaration not at all innocent. Dostoevsky's babes are innocent but not his young boys. Here we have the special naïvety of the precocious, which with regard to experience and maturity means what is forced and not earned. It is the *jump* to kingdom come, and it is a wrenching, distorting jump: what gets there is not all that ought to have got there. The precocious is like the *cliché* with too little of the original experience animating it. There is the language without its underpinning; like eunuchs on Love. Kolya in his precocity is obedient to the attraction of two forces, one the vanity and ridiculousness of intellectual man which he thinks he is, and second the spiritual goodness of Alyosha to which he gradually submits. In a way—the precocious, naïve way—he responds to everything that confronts him; and he suffers everywhere from the anguish of not being more than he is. He suffers what he has not yet become. He has the great advantage of precocity and naïvety of not knowing how to *accommodate* himself to the quarrel of the forces that infect him. He has no incentive either to action or to the compromise of action except the incentives of possibility and recklessness as these represent the conditions, not of life, but of his own nature—though his own nature is a parody of life—life in general and his own specific life to come. Dostoevsky exposes his secret almost immediately: he is nowhere equal to his role, is always either excessive or minimal, when he looks either for words or for actions to correspond to his feelings. Not that he lacks a full life of feeling; but that life is not organized, and its parts compete: which must happen in the precocious mind. Its real life is disorganized and its superficial life is mechanical, and the mechanics work wonderfully on the organic, wonderfully right and wonderfully wrong. Thus he has an ascendancy over the other boys that is a parody of the ascendancy of Alyosha or Zossima. He is a "desperate character" because it is only by assuming that role that he can express his feelings. He is not so very different from Ivan, and his pranks represent the same sort of imagination as that which produced the Grand Inquisitor: he is a primitive and ferocious form of Ivan—and he feels the same need for Alyosha as Ivan does.

If we think of Kolya in this way, we see why Alyosha's words on buffoonery are rightly addressed to him. In his precocity and naïvety the boy is himself a kind of buffoon *manqué*. His pranks and vanity and recklessness, his fear of ridicule, his very ascendancy itself, come out in expression a very near thing to buffoonery:—"a form of resentful irony against those to whom [he] daren't speak the truth." A near thing but not the same thing.

What is different is why Alyosha could speak these words to him, and the quality of the difference is plain in what Kolya says to Ilusha in his effort to prove that the new dog Perezvon is "really" the little boy's old dog Zhutchka. " 'You see, old man, he couldn't have swallowed what you gave him [a pin in a piece of bread on Smerdyakov's suggestion]. If he had, he must have died, he must have! So he must have spat it out, since he is still alive. You did not see him do it. But the pin pricked his tongue, that is why he squealed. He ran away squealing and you thought he'd swallowed it. He might well squeal, because the skin of dogs' mouths is so tender . . . tenderer than in men, much tenderer!' Kolya cried impetuously, his face glowing and radiant with delight." Kolya Krassotkin has a power of understanding by mimesis—by dramatic imitiation—extraordinarily superior to any mere mechanical precocity. He is brother in precocity to the Karamazovs, especially to Ivan.

The book of "Ivan," like that of "The Boys," covers the two months between the murder and the trial, and the two months reach as far back or forward as you will. It is another mirror held up to the mighty effort of the novel to show how the stress of life is between the harsh and dreadful thing of active love and that beauty which for the immense mass of mankind is found in Sodom. This time the stress is shown in a single soul and is in the end neither resolved nor transcended but is rather tautened to the breaking point of pride. We leave Ivan unconscious, incapable of bearing the burden which he has yet taken up; which he may come to deny or come to affirm: the final version of his tragic gesture that all things are lawful. It is that lawfulness which has reduced him.

But the book is not simply Ivan's, nor his fate simply his own fate. It is the book in which the guilt for the murder is factualized in Smerdyakov, specialized in Ivan, and, so to speak, generalized all round, but not yet realized. But Ivan is only reached after he has been "grown on" a little in the general muddle of guilt and awareness and the consequent atmosphere of mutual self-distrust and plain conspiratorial mistrust that spreads among them all. He is at first only an embittered and half-withdrawn comment upon the others—on Grushenka and Katerina in their raging jealousy of each other; on Mme. Hohlakov, that woman of little faith, with her swollen foot; on Lise who would eat a pineapple compôte at a crucifixion and who smashes her finger in the door after having said so; on Dmitri, turbulent and wayward in prison, bursting with new life and despairing of God: he will both sing a hymn from underground and will escape to America. It is Alyosha who is the agent of all this as he goes from one to the other, and it is Alyosha who precipitates us into the marmalade of illness in which Ivan struggles for the identity of his own mind as that mind splits: in which dreams become reality and reality evaporates like a dream, and in which the coming of the man who makes himself God is prophesied. Ivan struggles with a devil who does not exist as a means of wrestling with the God in whom he does not believe. He is like Jacob at the stream's edge, but without the treasure of blessings to support him. He would wrestle like a Karamazov, who would give rather than receive blessings. He has lived little, he has hardly begun to love; his mind thus falls apart, reptiles devouring each other. It is the gift of Alyosha to see this: that God was mastering Ivan's unbelieving heart: "He will either rise up in the light of truth, or . . . he'll perish in hate, revenging on himself and on everyone his having served the cause he does not believe in." It is at the end of Ivan's book that Alyosha sees this. We are at the beginning.

Let us see again how the approaches to that end are made. Each is an approach through emotion, the emotion which is at large and quite beyond grasping, and also the emotion which we look to create, though we know it will be inadequate, for the circumstances at hand. At the beginning, Ivan is in the air; something is working him up and he is at the edge of working something up. Dmitri has a secret he cannot fathom. His relations with Katerina are imperfect, as Katerina's with Dmitri are mutilated. Yet all three are clearly bound together, after a fashion which will be the end of Grushenka, as it is at present the source of her jealousy; and out of this relation there is engendered a vast unusable, unchannelable emotion which can vent itself only in quarrels and jealousy and new profundities of distrust. That other proud man, Rakitin the intellectual, sees no less than Grushenka that the emotion is there; a buffoon of pride, he eggs the emotion on by gossip and spite, by the undifferentiated caprice of the underground intellect, until love itself is an early form of jealousy and jealousy the only certain form of love.

Mme. Hohlakov, on the other hand, is looking for emotion. Her foot swells when Rakitin presses her hand, and she throws him out because to do so makes such a fine scene. For her, aberration is the explanation of everything, and from the point of view of little faith she is right: she says that Dmitri and Katerina and Ivan will all go to Siberia "and they will all torment each other." In her daughter Lise, we find put together both unusable emotion and looked-for emotion worked up together into the great theme of pride as destruction and crime. Ivan is right when, after tearing up unread her letter to him, he says of her that this girl of sixteen offers herself for sale. Lise is parallel to the boy Kolya in precocity, but she is a true phase; she speaks not distortions as Kolya did but base and basic truths. She has a longing to revile God aloud, which is awful fun and takes the breath away. Kalganov, the boy of twenty who shook Dmitri's hand and wept, has made love to her. Lise says of him that he spins like a top and wants to be lashed. Lashed, lashed with a whip. She loves disorder and wants to set fire to the house, to do evil of all sorts so that everything may be destroyed. And so on. The moments when everyone loves crime are every moment; everybody secretly loves Dmitri's killing his father. To all this Alyosha assents; it is part of his lesson. But it was Ivan whom she had sent for; and no wonder—she was the pure expressive form of that of which Ivan was only the critical form. She *imagines* the crime and the sweetness of the crime of which she has read: the Jews who crucify the four-year-old boy who dies "soon" in four hours: it was like eating a pineapple compôte. She rejoices in what Ivan found intolerable. She believes where Ivan cannot believe. She has learned the harshness of love and the beauty of Sodom in exactly the sense represented when after she crushes her finger in the door she cries "Wretch wretch wretch," and watches the finger end blacken.

She has learned in little and for the moment what Dmitri has learned in big and uncertainly. Dmitri in prison is in full rebellion against society. Papa was a pig, he quotes Ivan, but his ideas were right enough. His rebellion has three clear forms, and for each there is a corresponding assent and image. There is Rakitin, who has the power of creating the blackguard in you by his bite. Rakitin has a dry, flat soul like a bedbug or a tick which has not eaten for a long time: he is one of those full of rhetoric and pus. He is man the reformer without the idea of God, one of those who make a "social justification for every nasty thing they do." Again, Dmitri rebels at losing God: "One cannot exist in prison without God; it's even more impossible than out of prison. And then we men underground will sing from the bowels of the earth a glorious hymn to God." And third, there is Grushenka's love, which is a kind of conscience he abuses as he abuses his own, by asking forgiveness for an offense which is repeated in the asking: "They are ready to flay you alive, I tell you, all these angels without whom we cannot live." But of Grushenka he also says, "I love such fierce hearts." By that love, by that suffering, he *uses* the unusable emotion. Yet he is tempted between singing the hymn from underground and the idea of escape to America. He wants his guilt and also to be free of it in the world because he was not guilty in the world. In prison he can be the guiltless new man—but outside, who knows? That is why he has to wrench unwilling out of Alyosha a declaration of faith in his innocence.

It is fresh from that declaration, and the accompanying perception of unsuspected depths of hopeless grief in imprisoned innocence, that Alyosha charges Ivan with his general guilt by absolving him, in God's name, of particular guilt. *It was not you.* He spoke by irresistible command; and it leads Ivan at once to assume into himself the nature, if not the mystery, of things: as they have been imaged out by God's spies, Alyosha, Smerdyakov, and his own other self.

This is the preparation for Ivan's three visits to Smerdyakov and his crushing self-communion. The three visits are in parallel to the lacerations of Alyosha and to the ordeals of Dmitri. Each ends in a dream—Alyosha's of his Elder, Dmitri's of the Babe, Ivan's of the Devil. Ivan's dream is the most human of the three from—for us, at any rate—the pressure into it of the dream of humility in miracle and the dream of innocence in mystery. It is the dream of pride in authority, the last of the Inquisitor's three terms for the temptations of Christ. Unlike the others, which were additions in stature of soul, this third dream is an exorcism or purgation. Perhaps the three dreams represent the vision of the whole novel and suggest that the culmination is in this dream of lacerated, exacerbated pride; but it may be that the three dreams represent only parallel intimations of another structure: which will emerge in the trial.

But let us look at the three visits. We see at once that the intimacy and cruelty of Ivan's relations to Smerdyakov come about from Ivan's overwhelming knowledge that Smerdyakov is his own other self. This at first he denies, though he wears its burden in the image of himself the night before the murder listening in the dark at the top of the stairs to his father's movements below. That was the crossing point between the two selves, and to remember it now, after Smerdyakov has said, "Forgive me, I thought you were like me," is the laceration of self-suspicion, the awakening of the self to suspecting the self.

When in the second visit, Smerdyakov supplies him with a motive good for both his selves, he finds that he must kill his other self. Then the image of the stairs becomes not the crossing point but the merging point of the two selves. He had not only helped the murder along by awareness, he had partly created it and shared the guilt of Smerdyakov by being a murderer at heart. That—that recognition—was why he and Katerina had become like two enemies in love. This is the laceration of created motive, when the creation has been done without conscience.

The third visit completes this part of the movement of Ivan's soul. It begins with the peasant, drunk and freezing in the snow by Ivan's doing as it ends with Ivan reviving him, sobering him for the judgment to come. This is Ivan's wretched rejoicing—the sweet excitement of the pineapple compôte; he is approaching a mature form of the precocity of Lise and, in his own way, the fierce hearts of Dmitri and Grushenka. On this visit the night before the trial Ivan falters when he says "I knew it was not I"—as if he knew he could never save himself from the real by retreat upon the mere actual. But he learns most by understanding that Smerdyakov was not a fool, that he had enacted "All things are lawful," and that he, too, had dreamed of a new life. How wonderful it is, that as Ivan is about to go, leaving Smerdyakov to hang himself among the crackling cockroaches, Smerdyakov cries "Stay a moment. . . . Show me those notes again," and looks at the money for ten seconds. Perhaps the money burned Ivan, too. When he goes, though he helps the freezing peasant who on the morrow will come to judgment upon them all, he is not himself ready to act on his own resolution. The irritating monster of his other self is still within him, the monster of the truth refused; which is the worst laceration of all, and altogether the right last preparation for his dream of the devil—that poor relation of the best class who lives within us. The dream needs no comment. It is with the poor relations within us we see where we ourselves are shabby.

One has an odd feeling in the book of "Ivan" that the guilt of Ivan, or Smerdyakov, or of the others, is not adult guilt but childish guilt. Think of any of them and you think of Lise and her smashed finger. Perhaps Dostoevsky thought that for guilt, as for redemption, at the crisis the thing is to become a child. Just the same, Dostoevsky does not show us so much the relapse to the child as the breakdown of the mature. It is the mature that is precarious—with one moment of ripeness—not the childish that is safe. Maturity, if ever we had had it, would haunt us like the Muse. The old innocence cannot be recovered—though a new one may be achieved, whether along Alyosha's exemplary path or Ivan's wrestling fling, if it does not kill him. One wonders whether Alyosha was old enough to follow. There is a curse on us about children, which is the baggage we carry and which we think they do not. But *we* know that the children know, and so does Dostoevsky's novel. That is why the trial of Dmitri is "A Judicial Error"

—any child would know that!—and why it is essentially, as any trial may seem to the individual tried, trial by ordeal and laceration and calumny: by injury, insult, humiliation: fire, water, whips. That is why, in defense, the prisoner tries—as any child would—tantrums, hysterias, stigmata. Perhaps it is in the nature of guilt to be childish; perhaps guilt does not mature well; perhaps that is why so many of us don't want to grow up: we cling to our guilt as the only thing that is ours.

Before going into the trial of Dmitri, it is worth considering once again how after Dmitri's arrest everything takes a different direction, which is the direction of society—the very society *within which* the Elder and the Karamazovs had been operating all along. What we get is a series of smudges from the dirty thumb of society without loss of the sense of what is smudged. When Dmitri breaks down, it is into society—both in his confession about the three thousand roubles and in his dream of the babe. He is at once sent into Coventry by "official" society and is ever afterwards left there without being "understood" and without the possibility of being understood. Official society is not meant to understand; it absorbs or expels; and leaves the job of understanding to the individual to whom society happens. All along, here, the author is working on those instincts which prophesy society and make it necessary, but which differ sharply in object from any society which has ever existed. That is why when we see Dmitri on the verge of going to trial, he is torn by the motive of escape to America and also by the motive of the hymn from underground or submission. This is not just a contrivance of the novelist, not motive (or the conflict of motives) at the level of plot; it is the created motive which is the positive achievement of literary art; it rises from way under the social routines in which it is engaged. One way of defining the "form" of the novel is as the sum of stresses upon character by which such motive is elicited—is elucidated—is created. It was *in order* to create such a motive that in the beginning the Karamazovs were given as without motives but as with conflicts; that there was a murder posited; that the figures of Zossima and the Grand Inquisitor were furnished *outside* the brothers and the murder, though tied to them; and—still *in order* to create motive—that Dmitri is precipitated by his act, and by his dream, into "society" both official and other. Only in society could the motive show as moving anything worth moving, for it is only in society that all of us partly live.

But Dmitri alone would not have been enough. We need all the brothers and all their women. They must all break down into society—and so they do in the fellowship of jealousy and suspicion and devils. We need also Smerdyakov and the death of Smerdyakov: to provide the foil of a full breakdown of the man without a motive—but with possibilities of only the routine sort of nastiness (the epileptic half of the saint). We need also the Boys, the affair of Kolya and Ilusha, to provide another foil of plain unseemliness, of original evil, where those who are not yet ready or ripe for motive are broken down into a society stripped of routine to a bare piety which has no place to lodge. We need all this—at this point in this novel—as provision and bedding for Dmitri's motive and Dmitri's innocent guilt or guilty innocence. It seems thus in the natural order to introduce Dmitri's motive with Lise slamming the door on her finger after her epiphany, not of guilt but of crime or positive evil; and equally natural to follow it with the affair of Ivan and the freezing peasant. What are peasants for—even to Dostoevsky—but to strike down and, after an indecent interval in hell, to raise up? It is the peasant in us who can stand both the act of murder and the act of creation; he is the fellow who can take up the slack of both kinds of unseemliness, both kinds of faith, both kinds of motive: the social and the rebellious; and he gets back at us, when the line is taut, by collectively standing firm. The peasant is under society, or used to be, and is ready to receive it when it is played out; yet he needs society to fulfill his rôle—in that respect only resembling the proletariat, his political successor, for otherwise he is the proletariat's deadly enemy. Neither the peasant nor the proletarian needs to understand himself; the function of either is to judge those who presume to understand him. Should one say that the proletariat—those who are in but not of the society—is what an urban society does to the peasantry? Can the imagination turn for succor to the proletariat as it has so long turned (when its apparent foundations were shaken) to the peasantry? Does the proletariat represent the extreme of that "mighty movement against nature" (Bergson's phrase) which we call democracy? Dostoevsky would have refused these questions. We cannot.

Dostoevsky had the earlier question. At the trial the paradigm of Society and the Peasants is at once set up and never dropped till the verdict is brought in. Society is the audience, the jury without a vote, and divides by sex in its sympathies. The presiding judge is interested in crime as a product of society. The prosecutor is interested in the security of society. The defending attorney is interested in psychology in the "scientific" or explanatory sense (rather than in the penetrating, identifying sense). In short, we have society in an hysterico-official form. The prisoner wears a new frock coat, black kid gloves, fine linen: a dandy; and pleads guilty to dissipation and debauchery, innocent to the crime as charged. Beyond the prisoner is the jury, composed of two stolid and silent merchants, four petty officials almost peasants who never read books, the rest artisans and peasants. The whole jury was thus potentially peasant and half of it actually so. Could such a jury try such a case? Dostoevsky says of them: "Their faces made a strangely imposing, almost menacing, impression; they were stern and frowning." This jury would try the case it saw—which is what juries commonly do when provoked or cheated or implicated.

What Dostoevsky is showing is that in law—in society—Dmitri is guilty and ought to be acquitted, and that in fact—in the peasants—Dmitri is innocent and must be convicted. It does not matter in the least that to secure either of these imperatives the reading of the facts must be mistaken. A false reading may be nearer the creative heart, and to Dostoevsky it is Dmitri's new-created motive that must be judged and judged through the medium of judicial error. We see the error happen.

The prosecution with cross-examination takes three forms. The Dangerous Witnesses establish motive and opportunity with much sound circumstantial evidence. But the witnesses themselves are also on trial and are subjected to the ordeal of humiliation. Old Grigory was drunk enough to have seen the gates of heaven, let alone a garden gate. Rakitin is making money and prestige out of the trial and is smirched by his relations with Grushenka—the twenty-five roubles received for bringing Alyosha to her in his monk's clothes. Trifon Borissovitch, the innkeeper, has evidently mulcted Dmitri. The Poles had cheated at cards. The evidence is sound but the witnesses are shown unsound. The Medical Experts, who make the next stage of the prosecution, no doubt fuddled the jury as much as they annoyed Dostoevsky and outraged the prisoner. In the third stage, called "Fortune Smiles on Mitya," we have the unsupported goodness of Alyosha stating his conviction of Dmitri's innocence and remembering how Dmitri had struck his breast meaning he had the money before the murder. He is followed by Katerina, all in black. She says she had given Dmitri the three thousand roubles not only to post but to use if he wanted. He had a right. She tells her story how Dmitri had saved her father from arrest for embezzlement with his own five thousand roubles and how he had bowed down to her. When she has done humiliating herself, everybody thinks she has helped Dmitri. The prisoner knows better and cries out that she has ruined him and that now he is condemned; and he was right. Grushenka, also all in black and shawled, adds nothing not harmful: how she had played with the father and the son and Katerina. She accuses Katerina of general guilt and Smerdyakov of particular guilt. All this stirs up fresh emotion and hysteria and leaves her in contempt.

It is now Ivan's turn to present the Sudden Catastrophe: his assumption of guilt and Katerina's consequent reversal of her first testimony. Ivan enters, irreproachable, but with an earthy look, like a dying man's look. He struggles within himself, hesitates—like the peasant girl, as he says, who will stand up if she likes and won't if she doesn't. He then produces the three thousand roubles for the sake of which "our father was murdered." He then states that Smerdyakov did it but that he incited him. Here, from an upward urge, is the visible conversion downwards. In some sense he does not believe the cause which he is serving and therefore revenges it on himself and everyone else. Even so, within the intention, he is honest. Perhaps it is the honesty of the sick soul: of the soul which discovers itself to be sick; a universal possibility.

"Who doesn't desire his father's death?" he cries and looks at the "ugly faces" in the courtroom. "They all desire the death of their fathers. One reptile devours another. . . . If there hadn't been a murder, they'd have been angry and gone home ill-humored." Here is the fruition of Lise who, when she hears the story of a murdered child, thinks of a pineapple compôte. Here is Ivan, like Lise, slamming his finger in the door. It is a whole school of insight: whether or not there is guilt, and especially if there is no guilt, there must be a crime. One would not doubt that Ivan is speaking for the official society which the court—all but the jury—represents. Thus he goes on that the devil who does not exist is his only witness—that bad half of himself—and urges that *that* monster, Dmitri, singing a hymn, should be released . . . But society is never sure enough of itself to accept any one hysteria except in the form of another hysteria, only superficially more healthy, such as crime or love. Katerina is good in both cases. When she is confronted by Ivan's vision of "that monster," she gives in evidence his letter of desperation and murderous intent and tells the "other" truth (for doubtless both accounts were true enough) about the three thousand roubles. She had given them to tempt and humiliate Dmitri: to dishonor him. They had hated each other in their love, which had risen on a point of honor, and each strove to dishonor the other, since neither trusted the other's love and each was injured by his own. At the height of her hysteria, Katerina turns to Ivan and sees "how Ivan had been driven nearly out of his mind during the last two months trying to save 'the monster and murderer,' his brother." What then was the true nature of Katerina's love, or Ivan's love, or Dmitri's: pride, revenge, honor, the ignominy which is attached to all these, at any rate a laceration? Like the money—and whichever three thousand roubles you like—the love, any of these loves, was convertible. —At any rate, the evidence ends in the coil and recoil of contentious hysterias. It is at least true that everybody has been stripped of his finery, whether of simple crime or active love.

Forthwith, in the two speeches for the Prosecution and for the Defense, Dostoevsky puts the finery right back but with the thing stripped naked more than ever there: the beauty and the horror of seeing people naked under their clothes. The Prosecution, the Defense, and the Jury all look at the Karamazovs as characteristic, as representative Russian criminals, Russian heroes, Russian Christs. We have a triptych on an altar, with the Jury of Peasants in the center. We have also a trial at law.

The prosecutor argues for the security of society and he uses the language of a liberal sociology. The criminal must be socially punished to alleviate the sting of his conscience and as part of an effort to halt the furious course of the Galloping Troika which was Russia on her wild and irrational way. To this Dmitri listened and looked on, and at one time, when Rakitin's opinion of Grushenka is mentioned, he murmured: "The Bernards!"—as if the evils of this sort of thinking were children of Claude Bernard, of the new physiology and the new medicine.

The speech for the defense must have been nearly as unwelcome to Dmitri as the prosecutor's. The first part merely upset the chain of evidence; and the second part, though technically claiming innocence, assumed factual guilt but so reconstructed the crime that mercy was the only possible punishment for it. It was again liberal sociology, but this time on the psychological side. The very reasons the prosecution had advanced to give Dmitri motive for the murder, now become palliatives and even justification for his having done it. The argument in short is that Dmitri is guilty but his father was not a father, the money did not exist, and so on. It is not Dmitri who is guilty in any justiciable sense, but society. To the Elder Zossima's belief that all are guilty of all sin; to the Grand Inquisitor's or Ivan's belief that none are guilty, all is lawful; —to either of these, counsel for defense argues: Society is guilty of my sin.

Zossima's peasants—the "krest'yánye," as the word goes in Russian—those who were there first, will have neither the sociology nor the psychology nor any facts not pertinent to their own rôle.

The peasants stand firm and find Dmitri guilty of a crime he did not commit: which they might even know ever so well and still find irrelevant. From their point of view, and I think from ours, as the old Karamazov was the proper man for murder, so Dmitri was the proper man for guilt. If it is thought about at all, it ought surely to be held that the jury, in its own way, was possessed of our superior knowledge. But it is better not to think about it that way at all. The peasants may or may not have seen a crime; they certainly saw guilt: hysteria, upset, hubbub, the creature of the dark; and in their verdict they only said what they saw. Granted the story, granted the characters, and granted the pitch or level at which the characters take over the story, no less a mystery—and no more of a mystification—would have been possible. The blank space had to be left in the darkness: to be filled partly by the momentum of the novel, partly by the needs of the brothers Karamazov, and partly by the needs of the readers. The one thing certain is that society had to convict the wrong man; and the one prophecy certain is that the wrong man of society should be—no matter who he was—the right man for the peasants.

There is always a deeper justice done to the whole of society in the conviction of a wrong man than there can ever be in the conviction of the right man. The wrong man is guilty regardless; the right man only incidentally. The wrong man is guilty of ourselves, if not of ourselves individually, then of our ideals or of our institutions. The right man is guilty only of—some paltry crime like another. . . . This would be seemingly true with or without Dostoevsky's anterior convictions, for it has to do with an incontrovertible actuality: that the determination of guilt is a very human process forced upon us equally by our ideals and the failure of our ideals in action. That is why we have scapegoats, and why we have so often conceived scapegoats as innocent. The innocence of the scapegoat is sometimes a terrible enlargement of our individual experience of guilt. Naturally we are tempted to let him off, to let him escape, if we could. After all we are not peasants; we only resort to them; we know all along that they are an impossible ideal of which our best knowledge, like our other knowledge, is what is seen in the mirror of the possible.

We resort to the impossible and enact it dramatically or symbolically in art or religion, as Dostoevsky does, because we have no satisfying measure of the possible. Yet it is our grace to revert to the possible when we are not fanatic.

So, in the "Epilogue," when the sense of the possible returns to her, Katerina is desperate because of her treachery at the trial. So, too, Alyosha can tell Dmitri that *because he is innocent* he cannot take up the cross of Siberia: "Such heavy burdens are not for all men. For some they are impossible." And so again, between Dmitri and Katerina, each will always be a sore place in the other's heart because each had tried to make a scapegoat of the other. But Dostoevsky cannot let it go at that; he must reverse the insight and give it pristine form. Just before Ilusha's funeral, Kolya the teen-ager, hearing from Alyosha that Dmitri is innocent, Smerdyakov guilty, of the murder, cries out: "So he will perish an innocent victim! though he is ruined he is happy! I could envy him!" When asked why, he answers: "Oh, if I, too, could sacrifice myself someday for truth!" As if this were not enough, we have the funeral, the crumbling of the bread on the grave so the sparrows will come, and the breakdown of the "wisp of tow," the dead boy's father. Sorrow and then pancakes, says Kolya. But before the pancakes Alyosha makes it plain at the stone that Ilusha "at whom we threw stones," is a scapegoat willy-nilly and must be remembered come evil or come good. They go in to eat pancakes, and the boys cry to Alyosha, "Hurrah for Karamazov!"

Before we repeat that cheer, let us go back once again to the trial. Those who longed for acquittal were convinced of guilt: the guilt of their own humanity, sentiments, and new ideas. Many of those who testified against Dmitri—Grigory a servant, Rakitin a sneak, Snegiryov a drunkard, Trifon Borissovitch a thief, the Poles who were cheats—are all discredited forms of truth. The two doctors are impertinent forms of truth. Alyosha shows the goodness of truth incredibly. Katerina shows first incredible immolation, then incredible hysterias of truth. Grushenka in the flaring revenge she takes at the contempt shown to her belittles the truth. Only Ivan tries to tell the truth straight and is compelled to act like a buffoon; he, like Katerina, is taken as hysterical. He is right when he says he is not mad, only a murderer. He remembers his last night in his father's house.

The speeches of counsel reach the same conclusion by a different route; each is after a scapegoat, one to stop the Troika, the other to find a means in mercy to ignore—or accept—it: one masculine, the other feminine. The prosecutor insists on the credible truth—the creditable "social" truth—all but the "truth" itself. The defense discredits all the credible truth, any version of it, insisting that no one is up to his own actions; he too wants a creditable "social" truth: that you can punish only by mercy. In either case, Dmitri is not a murderer but mad: mad by the pressure of society. When the peasants stand firm, it seems to me they stand opposed to all the forms and versions of the facts to which they have been exposed. They take what is there and react. Like the underground man, when given an instant of power, they react by caprice, by a goatish act of their own inner natures—an act, that is, both goatish and the result of contemplation, long digested in long silence. I do not say Dostoevsky would have admitted this; but the underground was nearer the steady surface of him than he thought, a part of every balance, however brief, however recurring, that his nature struck. The idea of the scapegoat and the idea of caprice are as close as the words.

There is a trick of the mind, a caprice of our own, to which we can here resort in looking at this tale of parricide. Is there not something capricious—however recurring, no less capricious—about the notions of both guilt and innocence whenever we see them stripped of their conventions and their sanctions in institutions? This is one of the possibilities to which Dostoevsky's extraordinary powers of mimesis led him. This is what is intermittently envisaged in the baseness of the Karamazovs; and it makes a magnificent example of the inevitable irresponsibility—that is, the absolute responsiveness—of the aesthetic imagination to any *instance* of life once seen and felt as possible. The imagination itself, what apprehends the instance, and what survives it, is something else again; perhaps inevitably responsible, perhaps at some point, by a great act of will, capable of uniting in a single responsive act the two forms of responsibility—to the possibilities and to the everlasting necessities of life. Some believe that such acts took place at certain moments of history when tradition united with experience: Sophocles, Dante, and the later Shakespeare. (Thus we speak of *The Tempest* as the prophetic image of the modern mind; a prophecy unfulfilled.) This is a convenient belief. I wonder if it is not the better part of tradition to believe that on the evidence such imaginative acts are so rare as to escape particular instants of history; they yield rather to the rigors and simplicities of aesthetic form by some even rarer contingency of miracle, mystery, and authority and not always—certainly not in *The Brothers Karamazov*—in the conclusion of the work. I think Dostoevsky knew that, and the title to his next to last chapter—"For a Moment the Lie Becomes the Truth"—is his acknowledgement. There the lacerated love of the two elder brothers and the two women becomes, in the midst of vindictiveness and inadequacy, at once a mutual sore spot and something like a full motivation, not only for them all together but for each in his or her independence.

Again, lastly, the final chapter is by way of a sermon, a prayer, and an invocation. The last thing Dostoevsky can find to say is about the good memory of a dead boy: of a great evil and a greater good without innocence without guilt without sin, but under the images of all these: about what happened before life had begun to be fully lived and what, so to speak, could not happen in full life at all. It is almost as if Dostoevsky was compelled to say that as a regular thing the truth will at most for a moment become a lie. I suggest that in the last words of the novel—"Hurrah for Karamazov!"—Dostoevsky is making for his whole novel one of those tragic phrases which comfort the heart beyond possibility and denying necessity, and which must be forgiven, for "without them, sorrow would be too heavy for men to bear." The whole novel? Let us say that "Hurrah for Karamazov!" covers and includes the tragic phrases of the three dreams: the wine of new gladness, the babe, and the devil of the other self, and does so under the triple aegis of Zossima's harsh and dreadful thing which is active love, of Dmitri's beauty of Sodom, and of Ivan's wise and

dread spirit of destruction. This is how it is that in *The Brothers Karamazov,* the plain and overwhelming story of a murder is lifted into the condition of miracle, mystery, and authority. Hurrah for all the Karamazovs! for here is the condition where all are guilty and none are guilty. To live in that condition, and to love life, is to endure the tragedy of the saint. In this novel the saint is migratory among the three brothers, nowhere at home.